lonely

EGYPT

Jessica Buxbaum, Mary Fitzpatrick, Paula Hardy, Anthon Jackson,
Lauren Keith, Lama Obeid, Sanad Tabbaa, Dr Jenny Walker

Meet our writers

Jessica Buxbaum
@jess_buxbaum

Jessica is a political journalist covering the Middle East. Holidays are usually jam-packed for her, but in Dahab, she felt the push to slow down and recharge. This whimsical wonderland of colourful cafes, bold murals and eccentric wanderers leaves her in a daze.

Mary Fitzpatrick
@MaryFitzTravel

Mary loves everything about the Southern Nile Valley, especially sunset felucca sails, dawn at Abu Simbel and exploring Nubian culture.

Paula Hardy
@paulahardy

Paula is fascinated by the exchange of cultures across the Mediterranean, and Alexandria is the archetypal Mediterranean city. Digging into its past and hearing the city's stories told by today's Alexandrians is one of the great pleasures of travel.

Anthon Jackson
@anthonjackson_

Under the Nile Valley's spell for about twice the lifespan of the heretical city of Akhetaten, Anthon still finds the same deep allure in exploring here as on his first, fateful visit (ages ago), equally drawn to its Downtown Corniches and pulsing souqs (markets) as to its quiet, hidden reaches.

Lauren Keith
@noplacelike_it

Lauren's favourite experience is spending hours in Cairo's museums. The finally-maybe-really-this-time soon-to-fully-open Grand Egyptian Museum, announced in 2002 and slated to unveil its final galleries in late 2025, is another incredible addition to Egypt's culture-filled capital.

Previous spread Bedouin desert tour (p162)
GIVAGA/GETTY IMAGES

ALEXANTON/SHUTTERSTOCK

■■■■ Experience the weight of the ages through the ruins of the Pharaonic era. Dive unspoiled coral reefs. Let the mouth-watering scents of *molokhiyya*, *kushari* and stuffed duck guide you. Hop between the oases of the breathtaking Western Desert. Laze on sandy beaches. Behold the brilliance of the past in its Islamic monuments. Stroll through museums that illuminate its enduring mysteries. Hike the hidden canyons of Sinai. Understand the Coptic people, and in doing so understand the country.

This is Egypt.

TURN THE PAGE AND START PLANNING YOUR NEXT BEST TRIP →

Mosque & Madrasa of Sultan Hassan (p74), Cairo

Lama Obeid
@ *@Lama_writes4u*

Lama is a Palestinian writer on gastronomy, travel, culture and politics. Her favourite experience in Hurghada is the Halaka Fish Market, tying the story of the city together – fisherfolk supply the market with daily catch for visitors craving fresh seafood.

Sanad Tabbaa
sanadtab.net

Sanad's favourite experience is going for a reef dive in Sharm El Sheikh. At the end, he really enjoys surfacing suddenly next to some unsuspecting swimmers and putting the fear of God in them.

Dr Jenny Walker
@ *@jennywalkertravel*

Drawn to the desert, Dr Jenny Walker is often found camping in what she describes as 'velvet blackness, unknown magic'. Suspecting sand now runs in her veins, she often returns to the Middle East – formerly her home of two decades.

Contents

SUN_SHINE/SHUTTERSTOCK

Above White Desert National Park (p164)

About 10% of Egypt's population is estimated to be Christian, totalling around 11 million people. The vast majority of those are Coptic.

Egypt only became majority Muslim around the 12th century. Technically, it's been majority Christian longer than Muslim.

COPTIC
CULTURE

Egypt is home to the largest Christian community in the Middle East, and possibly the oldest. Coptic Christians, whose still-spoken language was the key to deciphering the Rosetta Stone and, through that, the Pharaonic language, maintain a rich cultural heritage all over the country. Seek out and discover the uniquely Egyptian heritage of the Copts, from monasteries to festivals, foods and more.

Left Monastery of St Anthony (p207)
Right Monastery of St Paul (p207)
Below St Katherine's Monastery (p230)

→ **COPTIC CHURCH**

The Coptic Church traces its theological ancestry back to Mark the Evangelist, making it over 1900 years old!

COPTIC LANGUAGE

The Coptic language is our only link to the ancient Pharaonic language. Its alphabet is a mix of Greek and ancient Egyptian Demotic script.

Best Coptic Experiences

▶ **See the alleged original burning bush at St Katherine's Monastery.** (p230)

▶ **Join Discover Esna's Coptic Experience tour for a deeper dive.** (p137)

▶ **Stroll around Coptic Cairo, with a stop in the Coptic Museum.** (p61)

▶ **Hike up to the fantastical church at Gebel At Teir (Bird Mountain).** (p88)

▶ **Meditate at the monasteries of St Paul and St Anthony, hidden among desert cliffs.** (p207)

↑ **RELIGIOUS ATTIRE**

Make sure you dress modestly and conservatively when visiting religious sites. Shorts and flip-flops aren't usually considered acceptable religious attire.

ISLAMIC
MONUMENTS

Egypt has been a centre of Islamic learning, art, architecture and culture since pretty much the inception of the religion. Additionally, varied foreign influences – from Fatimids to Mamluks – have contributed to giving Egyptian Islamic monuments a distinct sense of style not seen anywhere else. If you're at all curious about the religion, or simply enjoy seeing well-preserved, deeply interesting monuments, check out a few of these spots.

CITY FOUNDERS

Cairo's precursor, Fustat, was founded by Amr Ibn Al As, who conquered Egypt for the Rashidun Caliphate. Cairo itself was founded by the Fatimids.

Left Muhammad Ali Mosque (p74), Cairo **Right** Citadel (p75), Cairo **Below** Woman in Alexandria (p174)

OLD CAIRO

A jaunt through the narrow streets of Old Cairo will expose you to an abundance of historical Islamic sites.

↑ ETIQUETTE TIP

Women should bring a scarf to cover their hair if visiting these spots. Many sites have clothes to borrow, but bringing your own is best.

Best Islamic Experiences

▶ **Behold the dazzling domes of Cairo's Muhammad Ali Mosque.** (p74)

▶ **Gaze across the Mediterranean from Fort Qaitbey in Alexandria.** (p179)

▶ **Check out the seat of power for centuries at the Cairo Citadel.** (p75)

▶ **Visit Hurghada's striking Grand Mosque, set along the seaside.** (p205)

Pharaonic culture flourished from around 5000 BCE until 30 BCE, ending with the death of Cleopatra.

Such a long period of time separates some temples from others that religious currents and chosen gods for worship can shift before your eyes.

PHARAONIC
WONDERS

Today, the Pyramids and other wonders of Egypt's ancient past are staples of human civilisation, as they were yesterday and as they will be tomorrow. Throw yourself head-first into that world of yesteryear, which continues to influence Egyptian traditions, values and even language, and emerge with a far more robust understanding of what it means to be Egyptian.

Left Sphinx and Pyramids of Giza (p48) **Right** Mummy, Egyptian Museum (p54) **Below** Ramesses II statue, British Museum

→ MUMMIES AS FOOD

There are relatively few mummies in Egypt today since a gruesome fad from the turn of the 19th century had Europeans consume them for health benefits.

PHARAONIC WORDS

Many Pharaonic words remain in use in Egypt and broadly in Arabic, including *shib-shib* (slipper), *tannesh* (ignore) and *fouta* (towel).

↑ LOOTED ARTEFACTS

Egyptian artefacts are all over the world today as a result of colonialism. While the government has been pushing for repatriation, the process is slow.

Best Pharaonic Experiences

▶ Go see the Pyramids of Giza, one of the wonders of the ancient world. Seriously. (p48)

▶ Behold the towering statues at the Valley of the Kings, the site of royal tombs. (p116)

▶ Sail across Lake Nasser to the relocated temple ruins at Abu Simbel. (p142)

▶ Check out the bas-reliefs of the Temple of Hathor at Dendara in the desert. (p98)

Many oases don't have the cartoon-like image of a pool of water surrounded by sand dunes, but some actually do!

Keep in mind that travel into the Western Desert requires a permit and sometimes a police escort.

OASIS-HOPPING IN
THE DESERT

Breaking up the huge, unforgiving expanses of desert that covers Egypt are pockets of life, stunning and stark against a backdrop of barrenness. It's difficult to describe the sensation of seeing a sudden burst of green surrounded by nothing but sand dunes, except that it's a simple, if sharp, reminder that life always finds a way. The oases of Sinai and the Western Desert are certainly worth a visit.

CHANTRAMILK/SHUTTERSTOCK

Left Siwa Oasis (p158) **Right** Farafra Oasis, White Desert National Park (p164) **Below** Ain Khudra Oasis (p221)

→ TRAVEL PERMITS

Permits for visiting parts of the Western Desert must be acquired through an Egyptian travel agency at least 21 days before entry. Be prepared!

OASIS ETYMOLOGY

The word 'oasis' is a direct borrowing from the Demotic Egyptian *ouahe*, though with the corruption from millennia of retransmission.

FROM LEFT: MARINADA/SHUTTERSTOCK, STEFAN_SUTKA/SHUTTERSTOCK

↑ TREAD LIGHTLY

Oases are extremely rare and fragile ecosystems, constantly under threat from both climate change and human activity. Be careful with them – they break.

Best Oases Experiences

▶ **Explore the Graeco-Roman ruins surrounding the Dakhla Oasis.** (p169)

▶ **Set out for a desert adventure from the Farafra Oasis.** (p164)

▶ **Take a refreshing dip in Cleopatra's Spring in the Siwa Oasis.** (p159)

▶ **Hike through Ain Khudra Oasis for a peaceful Sinai experience.** (p221)

▶ **Stroll between Pharaonic artefacts and Christian cemeteries at Al Kharga Oasis.** (p168)

Egyptian food is regional, with a wide variety of preferred flavours and ingredients unique to each area.

Many seafood restaurants have you choose the fish and charge by weight.

TASTE OF
EGYPT

From *kushari* (pictured above; mix of noodles, rice, black lentils, fried onions and tomato sauce) to stuffed pigeons, plus eels, ducks, camels and so much more, Egyptian cuisine is as complex as it is varied. This should come as no surprise – after all, Egypt has had millennia of experimentation and getting comfortable with local and international ingredients, even as different civilisations have come and gone.

Best Food Experiences

▶ **Dine with a view of the pyramids at Khufu's in Giza.** (p68)

▶ **Sample Nubian-style seafood at Al Modhish near Abu Simbel.** (p143)

▶ **Taste camel meat at OLA Restaurant in the Siwa Oasis.** (p173)

▶ **Explore Alexandria's local spots and hidden holes-in-the-wall on a food tour.** (p185)

▶ **Check out Hurghada's Halaka Fish Market for the freshest seafood possible.** (p205)

You need a guide to hike in Egypt, both for reasons of legality and, more importantly, safety.

The desert can be unforgiving to the unprepared.

Much of the hiking in Egypt is technical, though some routes are friendlier than others.

RICHARDERNESTYAP/SHUTTERSTOCK

Best Hiking Experiences

▶ **Summit Mt Sinai (pictured; Gebel Musa) and behold an unparalleled view of the peninsula.** (p226)

▶ **Hike through Closed Canyon, exploring its hidden cracks and crevices.** (p221)

▶ **View the magnificence of El Arag Oasis at the end of a longer hike.** (p160)

▶ **Stroll alongside burial sites near the Tombs of the Nobles in Luxor.** (p117)

STEP BY
STEP

Although the multiday hikes of the Red Sea Mountain Trail and its sister project, the Sinai Trail, have ceased, options for exploring the country on foot are plentiful, particularly in the Sinai Peninsula. From the canyons surrounding Nuweiba, with their hidden oases and fertile valleys, to summiting Mt Sinai, to pleasant countryside walks around monasteries, there's no shortage of opportunities for adventure.

LOUNGING IN
THE SUN

Visitors are drawn to Egypt's sandy shores along the Red Sea and the Mediterranean year-round, and for good reason. These spots offer great opportunities for a dip in the sea alongside optimal conditions for some serious relaxation above water. Find yourself an umbrella, a lounge chair and a fresh mango smoothie.

Best Seaside Experiences

▶ **Dive off Sharm El Sheikh's beaches for an up-close view of the underwater world.** (p222)

▶ **Have an ice-cold Sakara beer after some windsurfing in Dahab.** (p228)

▶ **Relax with the locals along Sidi Abdel Rahman's Mediterranean coast.** (p193)

▶ **Meander across the paved walkways of Hurghada Marina at sunset.** (p205)

FROM TOP: SOLODOVA EVA/SHUTTERSTOCK, DIY13/SHUTTERSTOCK

★ PICK A CITY BASE

If you're exploring Sinai, fly to Sharm El Sheikh; for the continental Red Sea coastline, fly to Hurghada. Alexandria is your go-to for Mediterranean exploration.

BEACHWEAR

It's good practice to dress a bit more conservatively depending on your choice of beach. Some are more bikini-friendly than others.

Above Dahab (p228)
Left Sharm El Sheikh (p222)

MARVELLOUS
MUSEUMS

A truly amazing thing about Egypt is that despite centuries of looting, the sheer quantity of history that unravelled here means the country has plenty of world-class museums. From modern history to Ottoman trinkets, there's a museum for pretty much anything imaginable somewhere in Egypt.

FROM TOP:TAMER A SOLIMAN/SHUTTERSTOCK, ORHAN CAMN/SHUTTERSTOCK

★ TREASURE TROVE

The Egyptian Museum has struggled with overcrowding of artefacts since its inception. It's been moved four times to accommodate the size of its collection.

Best Museum Experiences

▶ **Get overstimulated by the weight of history in Cairo's Egyptian Museum.** (p54)

▶ **Visit the recently (partially) opened Grand Egyptian Museum right beside the pyramids.** (p53)

▶ **Roam around the Hermopolis open-air museum near Minya.** (p89)

▶ **Peek at a collection of precious pieces in Alexandria's Royal Jewellery Museum.** (p191)

SPECIAL DISCOUNT

An interesting holdover from Nasserist-era Pan-Arabism is that Arabs enjoy a discounted rate at every museum and historical site in the country.

Above Grand Egyptian Museum (p53), Cairo
Left Egyptian Museum (p54), Cairo

DIVE THE
DEPTHS

Egypt is one of the world's premier destinations for scuba diving (and snorkelling for those who prefer their air uncanned). There's a huge variety of sites, from historical wreck dives to reefs bursting with colour. Even better, these spots are populated by sea turtles, whale sharks and other marine life, all accentuated by unparalleled visibility and warm waters.

Left Diver, Ras Mohammed National Park (p223) **Right** Ras Za'atar (p224), Ras Muhammed National Park **Below** Giftun Islands (p203)

→ DON'T FEED THE FISH

Around the more popular diving destinations, fish have become accustomed to humans. However, playing with them and giving them food is not advised.

LIVEABOARDS

For serious scuba enthusiasts, liveaboards usually sail from Hurghada. The currents further asea can be strong; only attempt these dives if you're a confident swimmer.

↑ SHORE DIVES

You don't need a boat to enjoy diving the Red Sea. The marine life is so abundant that even shore dives can result in rarities.

Best Diving Experiences

▶ **Peer at some WWII-era sunken motorcycles in the Thistlegorm wreck dive.** (p224)

▶ **Test your luck with some hammerhead sharks in Ras Mohammed National Park.** (p223)

▶ **Dive as deep as you dare in the waters around Giftun Islands.** (p203)

▶ **Weave through the illuminated caverns and reefs of Ras Za'atar.** (p224)

The average daytime temperatures don't tell the whole story. Days that reach 40°C can be common, especially in Upper Egypt.

The humidity makes outdoor exploring a sweaty venture. Most indoor locations will have the air-con on full blast, so consider a shawl to avoid getting sick.

This is peak season for regional and domestic travellers. Prices can skyrocket along the coast, especially the Mediterranean Sahel.

← Scuba Season

The summer is ideal for snorkelling, scuba diving and anything that involves a dip to escape the heat.

JUNE

Average daytime max: 35°C
Days of rainfall: 1 (Cairo)

JULY

Egypt in
SUMMER

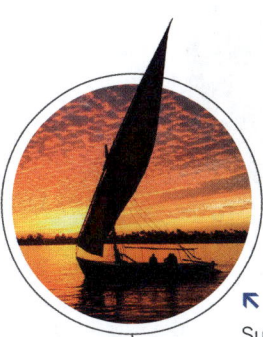

↙ Beachside Beats

Summer is the peak season for concerts and raves in Egypt, especially in Dahab along the Red Sea coast.

📍 Dahab p228

↖ Evening Exploration

Summer's hot nights present unique opportunities for comfortable night dives and swims, as well as nighttime discovery in general.

The hours between noon and 4pm are too hot to reasonably go out – consider taking a siesta and a late lunch.

AUGUST

Average daytime max: 35°C
Days of rainfall: 1 (Cairo)

Average daytime max: 35°C
Days of rainfall: 1 (Cairo)

Packing Notes

Pack a hat, sunscreen and light clothes with longer sleeves and trousers to avoid sunburn.

Demand for accommodation peaks from mid-October through November. View tours and overnight adventures in advance at lonelyplanet.com.

The softer light during this season makes it perfect for photography, and the deserts are visitable.

↑ Harvest in Siwa Oasis

During the first full moon in October, the annual harvest festival takes place in Siwa.
📍 Siwa Oasis p152

↑ Solar Alignment Festival

This biannual festival has people flocking to Abu Simbel on 22 October (Ramses II's birth) to witness the sun strike the gods' statues in the temple's inner sanctuary.
📍 Abu Simbel p142

SEPTEMBER

Average daytime max: 33°C
Days of rainfall: 1 (Cairo)

OCTOBER

Egypt in
AUTUMN

↓ El Gouna Film Festival

The 10-day El Gouna Film Festival, a haven for cinema buffs, takes place every October on the Red Sea coast.

📍El Gouna

▶ elgounafilmfestival.com

↖ Downtown Contemporary Arts Festival

Cairo's Downtown Contemporary Arts Festival (D-Caf) goes on for a full three weeks in October, chock-full of theatre, dance and arts exhibitions.

📍Cairo p42

▶ d-caf.org

↑ Coptic New Year

Nayrouz, the Coptic celebration of the new year, takes place on 11 September with low-key festivities.

NOVEMBER

Average daytime max: 30°C
Days of rainfall: 0 (Cairo)

Average daytime max: 25°C
Days of rainfall: 1 (Cairo)

Packing Notes

It's still quite hot in autumn but a light jacket for cooler nights is recommended.

Scuba-Less Season

Rougher seas along both coastlines make diving less pleasant during these months and impossible for boat dives.

Alexandria and the Mediterranean coast can be rainy during these months, especially in December. Consider bringing a rain jacket.

📍 Alexandria p174

→ Winter Solstice at Qasr Qarun

The light strikes inside the sanctuary of the Qasr Qarun temple for an unforgettable experience only during sunrise on 21 December.

📍 Al Fayoum p82

Solar Alignment Festival

This biannual festival also takes place on 22 February (the anniversary of Ramses II's ascension), for another opportunity to see the gods illuminated.

📍 Abu Simbel p142

DECEMBER

Average daytime max: 21°C
Days of rainfall: 1 (Cairo)

JANUARY

Egypt in
WINTER

Coptic Christmas

The largest Christian community in the Middle East celebrates Christmas on 7 January (according to the Orthodox calendar) with a feast.

→ Ramadan

The holy month for Muslims moves annually due to the Islamic lunar calendar. It's predicted to start in February in 2026 and 2027, and January in 2028.

↑ New Year's Eve

There are always interesting events all over the country for New Year's Eve, though tickets can be costly.

Average daytime max: 19°C
Days of rainfall: 1 (Cairo)

FEBRUARY

Average daytime max: 21°C
Days of rainfall: 2 (Cairo)

🧳 Packing Notes

Nights can be quite cold with whipping desert winds, so bring some layers.

Plankton Blooms

In April and May, visibility underwater around the Red Sea coast can be reduced almost to zero.

Khamsin (hot desert wind) blows in from the south, causing sandstorms, which can make sightseeing impossible and breathing unpleasant.

Due to the erratic weather, this is the low season, especially along the Red Sea coast.

↖ Eid Al Fitr

Eid Al Fitr (Festival of Breaking the Fast), which celebrates the end of Ramadan, is projected to be in March in 2026 and 2027, and in February in 2028.

MARCH

Average daytime max: 24°C
Days of rainfall: 1 (Cairo)

APRIL

Egypt in
SPRING

FROM LEFT: TAMER A SOLIMAN/SHUTTERSTOCK, ANADOLU/GETTY IMAGES, ANADOLU/GETTY IMAGES, BOTTOM:TAMER A SOLIMAN/SHUTTERSTOCK

Coptic Easter

The second holiest day in the Coptic Christian faith is celebrated with banquets. It falls in April or May according to the Orthodox calendar.

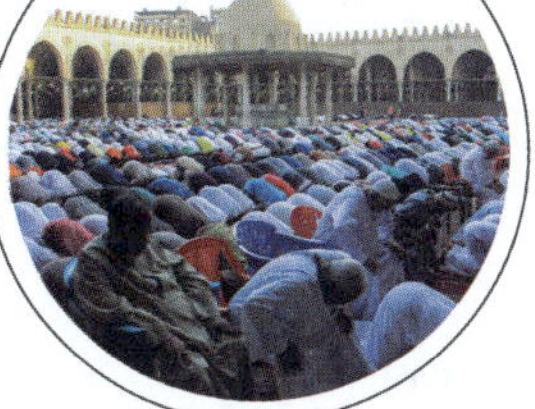

↘ Sham An Nessim

The Sham An Nessim festival is celebrated by Egyptians of all creeds, and heralds the start of spring the day after Coptic Easter.

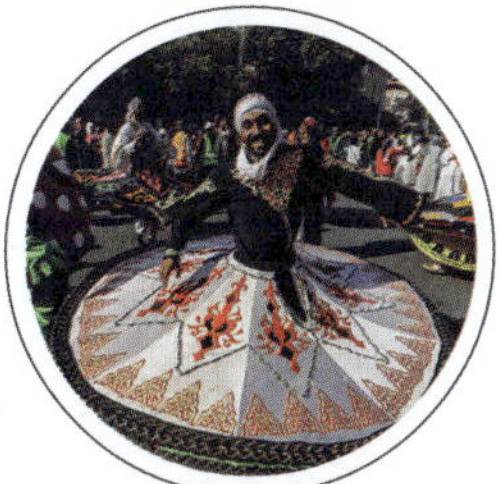

← Eid Al Adha

Cairo empties out significantly during Eid Al Adha (Feast of Sacrifice), making it a great time to explore in (relative) silence. It's projected to be in May in 2026, 2027 and 2028.

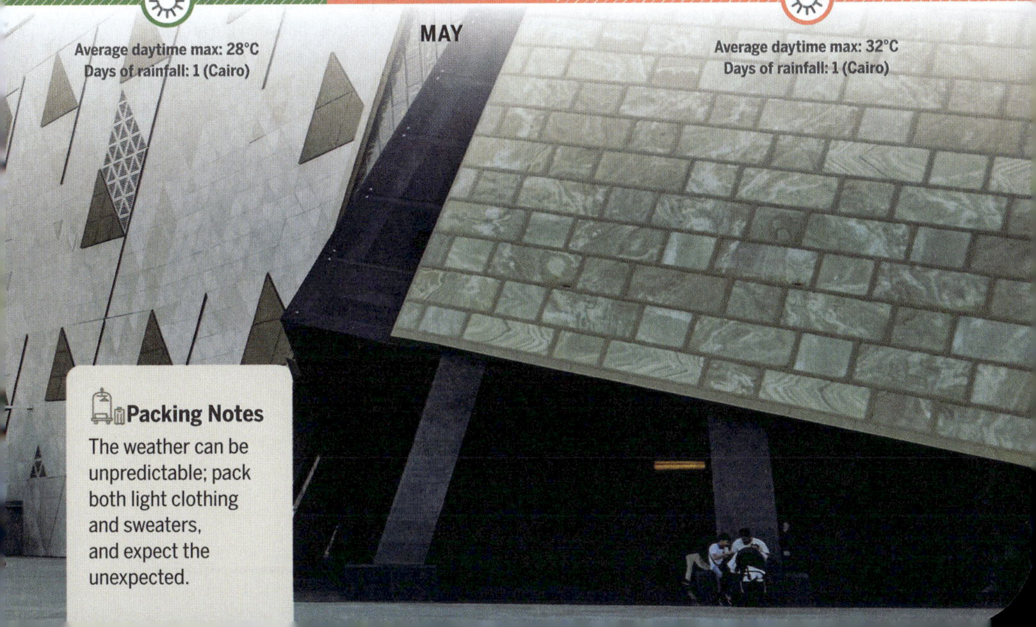

Average daytime max: 28°C
Days of rainfall: 1 (Cairo)

MAY

Average daytime max: 32°C
Days of rainfall: 1 (Cairo)

Packing Notes

The weather can be unpredictable; pack both light clothing and sweaters, and expect the unexpected.

SIWA & THE MEDITERRANEAN COAST
Trip Builder

TAKE YOUR PICK OF MUST-SEES AND HIDDEN GEMS

▬▬▬ Go for leisurely strolls along the Mediterranean coast, whether on Alexandria's Corniche with its 19th-century class, or through Sidi Abdel Rahman's chilled-out beaches. End with a dip in the solitary Siwa Oasis, bursting with life in the middle of the harsh desert.

🗺️ Trip Notes

Hub towns Alexandria, Siwa

How long Allow 10 days

Getting around While you can rely on taxis and public transport, renting a car or hiring a driver will allow you to explore more flexibly and at your own pace.

Tips The Mediterranean coast is packed with locals in the summer and foreigners in the winter. If you're looking for solitude, go in the early autumn or late spring.

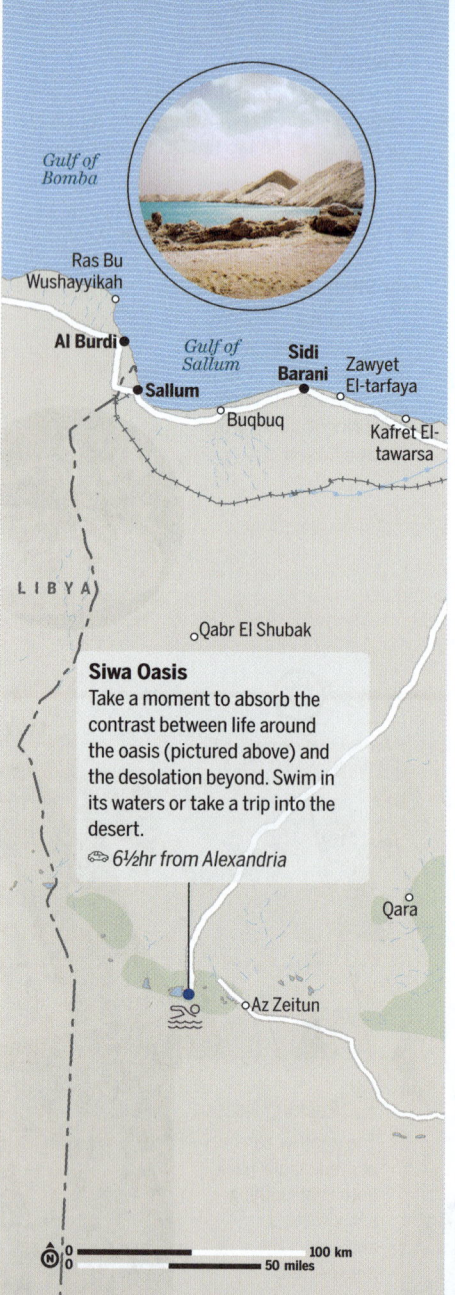

Gulf of Bomba

Ras Bu Wushayyikah

Al Burdi

Gulf of Sallum

Sidi Barani Zawyet El-tarfaya

● **Sallum**

Buqbuq

Kafret El-tawarsa

L I B Y A

○ Qabr El Shubak

Siwa Oasis
Take a moment to absorb the contrast between life around the oasis (pictured above) and the desolation beyond. Swim in its waters or take a trip into the desert.
🚗 6½hr from Alexandria

○ Qara

○ Az Zeitun

0 ___ 100 km
0 ___ 50 miles

Sidi Abdel Rahman

Scuba dive or snorkel the Mediterranean Sea (pictured below) from here. The beaches are a bit more bikini-friendly and the amenities more prevalent.

🚗 *30min from El Alamein*

El Alamein

Visit this town's WWII monuments (pictured right), or walk around enjoying the views. Locals favour this area during the summer; the weather is temperate and the water bright.

🚗 *1½hr from Alexandria*

Mediterranean Sea

Kafret Saber

Marsa Matruh

Qaryet El Qibashi

Ras Al Hikma

Kafret Eilet El-taflal

Abu Haggag

Galal

El Dab A

Arab's Gulf

El-hamman

Al Burg

Burg Migheizil

Lake Burullus

Aboukir

Mutubis

Sidi

Disuq

Damanhur

Kafr Al Sheikh

Hosh'Isa

Tanta

Tala

Minuf

Alexandria

Explore the gem of decaying grandeur and old culture that is Alexandria – your best entry point to the dazzling beaches of the Mediterranean coast and the Siwa Oasis.

🚆 *3hr from Cairo*

Western (Libyan) Desert

Pyramids of Giza

Qaran Protected Area

Tamiya

Tunis

Shakshouk

Medinat Al Fayoum

Itsa

Wadi Rayyan

Al Lahun

Qattara Depression

E G Y P T

Biba

Maghagha

Sandafa El-far

Bawiti

Gebel Az Zuqaq

El-harra

Gebel Gala Siwa

Samalut

Gebel At Teir

GUIDED BY THE NILE
Trip Builder

TAKE YOUR PICK OF MUST-SEES AND HIDDEN GEMS

Get under Egypt's skin by using the Nile as your guide. Starting from Cairo, make your way down to Aswan where you can sail the river, with reeds, ruins and winds your only companions. Explore Luxor, then head to Al Fayoum's desert for sandy hills hiding whale skeletons.

🗺 Trip Notes

Hub towns Cairo, Luxor, Aswan

How long Allow two weeks

Getting around Take public transport from Cairo to the south, then make your way back with the sailing vessel of your choice. Sleeper trains are your best bet for this trip.

Tips The stops on this route regularly reach 40°C during summer and much of this itinerary is outdoors. Avoid mid-May to mid-September, or you'll risk heatstroke.

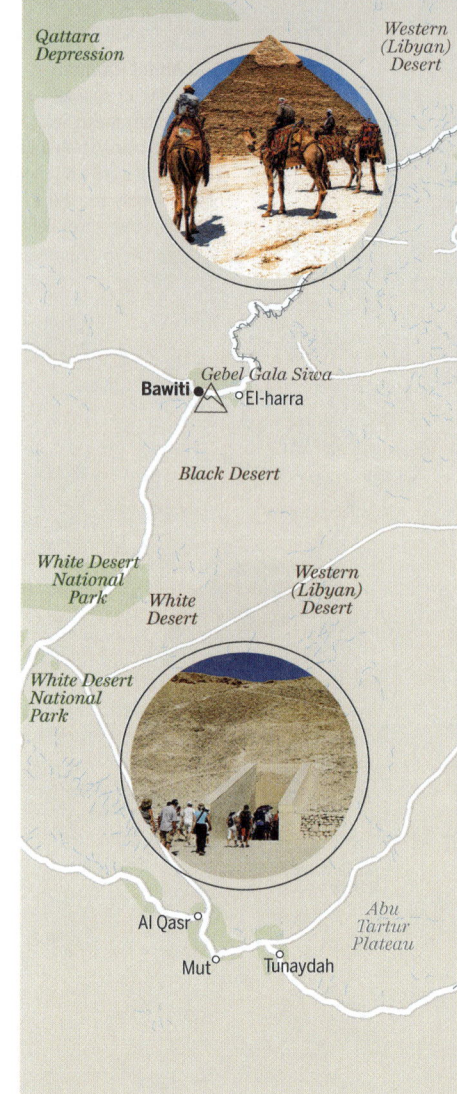

Qattara Depression

Western (Libyan) Desert

Gebel Gala Siwa
Bawiti ● △ ○ El-harra

Black Desert

White Desert National Park

White Desert

Western (Libyan) Desert

White Desert National Park

Al Qasr ○

Mut ○   Tunaydah

Abu Tartur Plateau

0 ——— 100 km
0 ——— 50 miles

Sadat City ○ Tukh Fayid ○ *Great*
Birqash ○ *Bitter* *Lake* *Giddi Pass*

Cairo
Check out the Grand Egyptian
Museum and the Pyramids of Giza
(pictured left), then explore Cairo.
This hyper-stimulating city has
tons of options for food, drink,
culture and everything else.
� *3hr from Alexandria*

Giza ○ *Gulf* **Suez** ○
Harrāniyya ○ *of Suez*
Ain Sukhna ○ Ras Sudr

Ma'an ○
En Naab ○
El Quweira ○
Aqaba ○ **JORDAN**
Ad Durra ○

Qaran
Protected
Area Shakshouk ○
○ Al Maharraqa

Tunis ○
Qalamshah ○
○ El-maimun
Beni
Biba ○ **Suef**
Sandafa ○
El-far ○
○ El-sheikh Fadl
Samalut ○

Al Fayoum
Hire a 4WD and disappear
into the desert for a few days.
Consider visiting Wadi Al Hitan
(pictured below) to see the fossilised remains of whales from
when the desert was sea.
� *8hr from Luxor*

Gebel Barga △ ○ Nuweiba
△ *Gebel Foga* Bir El Oghda ○
Feiran ○ *Sinai*
Abu ○ *Wadi Nasb Pass* **SAUDI**
Durba Al Milga ○ △ **ARABIA**
○ Dahab
Mt Sinai (Gebel Musa) ○ Al Bad

Gebel At Teir △
Minya ○
○ Abu Qirqus

Eastern
(Arabian)
Desert
Ras Shu Kheir ○
○ Al Tor
Nabq ○ Nabq
Straits *Protectorate*
of Gubal
Sharm El Sheikh ○

Al Khuraybah ○
Al Muwaylih ○
Duba ○

Dashlut ○
○ Dairut
Jemsa ○
Shedwan
Island

Asyut ○
Beni'Adi el El-
Bahariya badari
& Beni'Adi el Qibli
Nile
Tahta ○

Hurghada ○
Safaga ○
△ *Gebel Ash*
Shayib

Red Sea Mountains
Brothers
Islands

Sohag ○
○ Girga
○ Al Balyana
Nag Hammadi ○

Qena ○
El-
barahma ○
○ Khuzam
Armant ○
El Hamarawein ○
Red Sea

Luxor
Walk along Luxor's Corniche and
watch the vivid colours bloom as
the sun sets over the Nile. The
Valley of the Kings (pictured far
left), Karnak Temple Complex and
more beckon.
⛵ *3–4 days from Aswan*

EGYPT

○ El-maariq
Al Kharga ○
○ Ginah

Esna ○
Esna
Barrage
El-
saayda ○
○ Nagel-gesira El-gedida
○ Silwa Bahari

Elphinstone
Reef
Marsa Alam ○

Gurmashin ○
○ Port
Said
Ezbet
Maks
El-qibli ○

Aswan
Sail across Lake Nasser and
see Abu Simbel from the water,
explore Al Qīsāriyya Market, or
take a ferry to Elephantine Island
for a taste of Nubian culture.
� *13hr from Cairo*

Gebel
Hamata
△
Shams Alam ○
Wadi
Gimal
Island

Kom Ombo ○
Philae ○ *Lake Nasser*
Hamata ○

DEEP DESERT ADVENTURE
Trip Builder

TAKE YOUR PICK OF MUST-SEES AND HIDDEN GEMS

For those who prefer the whisper of the winds to the clamour of the cities, this journey into the White Desert National Park can't be beaten. Begin in Middle Egypt and roam its quaint villages, then hire a 4WD and escape into the oases of the Western Desert.

🗺 Trip Notes

Hub towns Minya, Qasr Al Farafra

How long Allow eight days

Getting around Hire a 4WD vehicle and a driver.

Tips Entering the Western Desert requires a permit, which must be submitted by an Egyptian travel agency to the government at least 21 days in advance of your entry. Some roads require police escorts. Plan accordingly, but don't be discouraged. Once the bureaucracy is done, the journey begins.

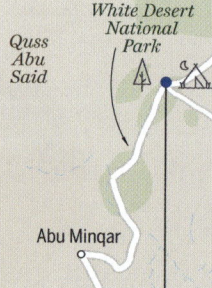

White Desert National Park

Quss Abu Said

Abu Minqar

Qasr Al Farafra
Admire the simple splendour of the Farafra Oasis. This is the perfect base to begin your trek through the White Desert National Park (pictured above), replete with options for desert camping.
🚗 *3hr from Minya*

Great Sand Sea

N 0 — 80 km
0 — 40 miles

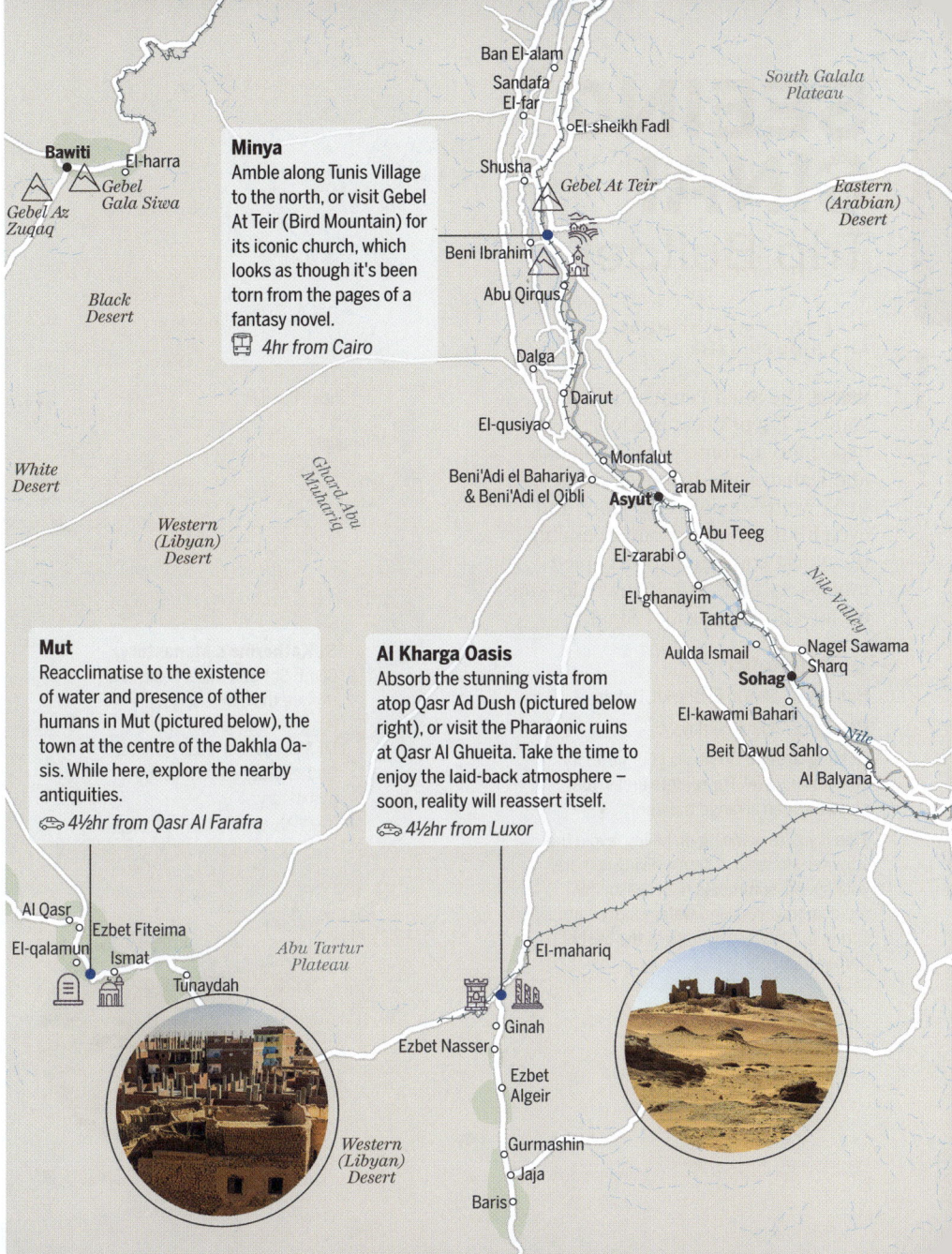

Minya
Amble along Tunis Village to the north, or visit Gebel At Teir (Bird Mountain) for its iconic church, which looks as though it's been torn from the pages of a fantasy novel.
🚌 4hr from Cairo

Mut
Reacclimatise to the existence of water and presence of other humans in Mut (pictured below), the town at the centre of the Dakhla Oasis. While here, explore the nearby antiquities.
🚗 4½hr from Qasr Al Farafra

Al Kharga Oasis
Absorb the stunning vista from atop Qasr Ad Dush (pictured below right), or visit the Pharaonic ruins at Qasr Al Ghueita. Take the time to enjoy the laid-back atmosphere – soon, reality will reassert itself.
🚗 4½hr from Luxor

Bawiti
El-harra
Gebel Gala Siwa
Gebel Az Zuqaq

Ban El-alam
Sandafa El-far
El-sheikh Fadl
South Galala Plateau
Eastern (Arabian) Desert

Shusha
Gebel At Teir
Beni Ibrahim
Abu Qirqus

Black Desert

Dalga
Dairut
El-qusiya

White Desert

Western (Libyan) Desert

Ghard Abu Muharriq

Monfalut
Beni'Adi el Bahariya & Beni'Adi el Qibli
arab Miteir
Asyut
Abu Teeg
El-zarabi
El-ghanayim
Tahta
Nile Valley

Aulda Ismail
Nagel Sawama Sharq
Sohag
El-kawami Bahari
Beit Dawud Sahl
Al Balyana
Nile

Al Qasr
Ezbet Fiteima
El-qalamun
Ismat
Tunaydah

Abu Tartur Plateau

El-mahariq
Ginah
Ezbet Nasser
Ezbet Algeir
Gurmashin
Jaja
Baris

Western (Libyan) Desert

SEEING SINAI
Trip Builder

TAKE YOUR PICK OF MUST-SEES AND HIDDEN GEMS

The Sinai Peninsula offers some of Egypt's best outdoor experiences, from Sharm El Sheikh and Dahab's awe-inspiring dives, to Nuweiba's canyoning spots, and even hiking in and around possibly the oldest continuously occupied monastery on Earth. If you're looking for adventure, consider Sinai.

🗺️ Trip Notes

Hub towns Sharm El Sheikh, Dahab

How long Allow nine days

Getting around Go Bus is your go-to for inter-town travel. For remote areas, tour operators can arrange transport.

Tips If you're planning on hiking, avoid the summer. However, if scuba diving is more your speed, summer is high season for regional travellers and water clarity. Late spring to early summer gives the best of both worlds.

Wadi Al Homur

Gebel Foga ⛰️

○ Sheikh Barakat

○ Abu Rudeis

Wadi Mukattab

Wadi Feiran

Feiran ○ *Wadi Feiran*

Gebel Serbal ⛰️

St Katherine's Monastery
Climb St Katherine's peaks and explore the monastery. This is a great connection point to Mt Sinai (Gebel Musa) and the Protectorate surrounding the monastery.
🚗 *3½hr from Sharm El Sheikh*

Gulf of Suez

○ Gebeil

Ras Shu Kheir

Eastern Desert

Jemsa ○   Gemsa ○

Qeisum Island

Gubal Island

Eilat

Taba

Pharaoh's Island

● **Aqaba**

J O R D A N

Ad Durra

○ Taba Heights

○ Al Humaydah

Nuweiba

Hike through the canyons of
Sinai from Nuweiba, or start with
Wishwashi Valley (pictured left)
and into the stunning oasis at
Malha Valley.

🚐 *1½hr from St Katherine's
Monastery*

○ Ras Shaitan

Gebel Barga

E G Y P T

Sinai

*Gebel El
Gunna*

Gulf of Aqaba

Dahab

Party, dive or simply lounge
in the sun in Dahab (pic-
tured below). This town has
recently become a hub for
digital nomads, brimming
with youthful energy.

🚗 *1hr from Nuweiba*

Bir El Oghda ○

Bir Sugheir ○

*Ras Abu
Gallum
Protectorate*

Wadi Nasb Pass

Al
Milga ●

△ *Mt Sinai (Gebel Musa)*

Al Bad ○

△
*Gebel
Katarina*

*Gebel
Feiran*

Sharira Pass

*Straits
of Tiran*

*St Katherine
Protectorate*

*Nabq
Protectorate*

Nabq ○

Al Khuraybah ○

S A U D I
A R A B I A

Ash
Sharmah ○

Ras
Nasrany ○

*Tiran
Island*

Sharm El Sheikh

Take a boat (pictured left) to
the Ras Mohammed National
Park or Tiran Island for some
truly fantastic dives and
snorkelling experiences.
Alternatively, chill out on the
beach.

✈ *1hr from Cairo*

Na'ama Bay ○

Sharm El Sheikh ○

*Sanafir
Island*

*Ras Mohammed
National Park*

Al Muwaylih ○

Red Sea

N

0   30 km
0   15 miles

RED SEA RELAXING
Trip Builder

TAKE YOUR PICK OF MUST-SEES AND HIDDEN GEMS

While often dismissed as tourist-resort land, Egypt's continental Red Sea coast has far more to offer than all-inclusive packages. Ample opportunities exist for desert exploration, deep-sea diving and hermetic haunts just off the beaten path for travellers willing to take that extra step.

🗺 Trip Notes

Hub towns Luxor, Hurghada, Marsa Alam

How long Allow eight days

Getting around Fly to Luxor or, for a purely coastal experience, straight to Hurghada. From there, Go Bus can take you all the way to Marsa Alam with ample stops on the way.

Tips The summer heat in these areas can be oppressive, potentially even making a beach trip unpleasant – all the more so considering the distances involved.

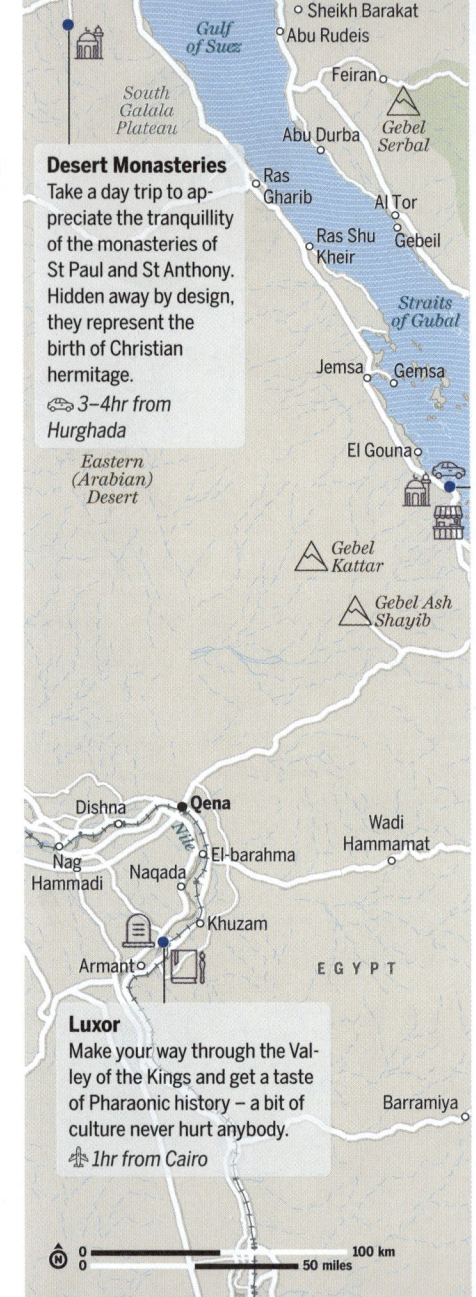

Desert Monasteries
Take a day trip to appreciate the tranquillity of the monasteries of St Paul and St Anthony. Hidden away by design, they represent the birth of Christian hermitage.
🚐 *3–4hr from Hurghada*

Luxor
Make your way through the Valley of the Kings and get a taste of Pharaonic history – a bit of culture never hurt anybody.
🏛 *1hr from Cairo*

Gulf of Suez
Sheikh Barakat
Abu Rudeis
Feiran
South Galala Plateau
Abu Durba
Gebel Serbal
Ras Gharib
Al Tor
Ras Shu Kheir
Gebeil
Straits of Gubal
Eastern (Arabian) Desert
Jemsa
Gemsa
El Gouna
Gebel Kattar
Gebel Ash Shayib
Dishna
Qena
Wadi Hammamat
Nag Hammadi
Naqada
El-barahma
Khuzam
Armant
EGYPT
Barramiya
Nile
0   100 km
0   50 miles

Sinai

Bir El Oghda
Bir Sugheir
Al Milga
Mt Sinai
(Gebel Musa)
St Katherine
Protectorate

Dahab
Al Bad
Straits
of Tiran

Nabq
Al Khuraybah
Na'ama Bay
Shark's Bay
Sharm El Sheikh
Ash
Sharmah

Al Bir

Tabuk

SAUDI
ARABIA

Al Muwaylih

Hurghada
Taste the delectable chaos of the Halaka Fish Market, or dive the Giftun Islands. At night, check out the brightly lit Grand Mosque (pictured above).
🚌 *4hr from Luxor*

Duba

Shaghab

Ras
Nasrany

Safaga

Red Sea

Al Quseir
Experience a true off-the-beaten-path Egyptian town going about its daily business, dominated by a 16th-century citadel – a must for independent travellers.
🚌 *2hr from Hurghada*

El Hamarawein

Red Sea Mountains

Zurayb
Al Wajh

Marsa Alam
Dive the unspoiled reefs of Marsa Alam (pictured above), out of the way enough to only be of interest for the most hardcore of travellers, and with the requisite charm.
🚌 *1½hr from Al Quseir*

Elphinstone
Reef
Marsa Shagra

Masra Nakari

Wadi El Gemal
National Park
Explore the desert wilderness of Wadi El Gemal (pictured above) with Bedouin guides, learning their ways and experiencing the desert in its truest form – harsh and beautiful.
🚗 *2–3hr from Al Quseir*

Al Fuqayyir
Umm Lajj

Gebel Hamata
Shams Alam
Wadi Gimal Island

7 Things to Know About
EGYPT

INSIDER TIPS TO HIT THE GROUND RUNNING

1 Navigating Numbers

Some unsavoury actors depend on tourists not being able to read the Indian numerals often used in Arab countries. If you can't understand the numbers, or the price of something isn't clearly indicated, it's best not to buy it. It's likely that the actual price and the verbally quoted price bear little relation to one another.

2 Personal Space?

Among Egyptians, the concept of personal space is somewhat varied, with affectionate touches, hand-holding and the occasional hug quite common. If you are uncomfortable, some resistance and a polite but firm 'no, thank you' will usually suffice. No offense is intended by these actions.

3 Lounge Like a Local

The social hub of virtually every Egyptian city is the *ahwa*, literally meaning 'coffee'. These coffeehouses often sprawl into the street and serve juices, strong unfiltered coffee, tea and shisha (water pipe).

4 Street Food Smarts

Egyptian street food can be delicious and unique, but exercise caution as hygiene standards can vary between stalls. Trust your nose!

5 Local Lingo

Egyptian Arabic contains very particular words for referring to others based on age, social status and gender. Tourists get a pass, but correctly using these terms can help you blend in better and show respect to the people you are addressing.

m'allem A term often used for male service workers in menial positions. It can be extremely offensive if misused, but good to know regardless.

basha The catch-all respectful term for men whose names you don't know. Virtually anyone can be a *basha* without offense.

effendim Used for a man you intend to show extreme respect, such as a police officer. Using it to refer to regular people may cause embarrassment.

doktora A secular term for referring to an older or professional woman. Think 'madam', but classier.

Haj/Hajjeh (m/f) A specifically Islamic term for respectfully referring to an older person. Use sparingly.

6 The Ubiquity of the Tip

Tipping culture is heavily entrenched in Egypt and a tip is often expected. There's an art to it, but you can be certain that the quality of future service is correlated to the tip provided; however, overtipping can result in being taken advantage of. Between US$2 and US$5 usually goes a long way.

7 Need a Ride?

Uber and Careem are the ridesharing apps of choice in Egypt. They're cheap, convenient and well worth the small additional price. They also have a scooter option for the brave of heart. Taxis are also easy to come by, but come with the risk of having to haggle.

Read, Listen, Watch & Follow

 READ

Children of Gebelawi (Naguib Mahfouz; 1959) Existentialist tale set in a 19th-century Cairene alley.

The Days (Taha Hussein; 1967) Hussein's autobiography serialised over 40 years tackles a changing Egypt.

The Yacoubian Building (Alaa Al Aswani; 2002) Class-based allegory set in a decaying former palace turned apartment complex.

God Dies by the Nile and Other Novels (Nawal El Saadawi; 2024) Classic novellas by Egypt's preeminent feminist author.

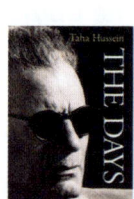

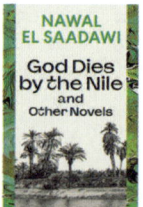

 LISTEN

Ahwak (Abdel Halim Hafez; 1957) Lilting set of love ballads sung by the Dark Skinned Nightingale.

Inta Omri (Umm Kulthum; 1965) Quintessential song from the woman hailed 'The Planet of the East'.

Nour El Ain (Amr Diab; 1991) Defining album of the best-selling Middle Eastern artist of all time.

Mahatet Masr (Donia Massoud; 2009) Painstakingly collected folk songs unearthed and sung with passion.

MOHAMED EL-SHAHED/GETTY IMAGES

El Album (Massar Egbari; 2018) Oriental-style blues mixed with progressive rock (pictured above).

▷ | **WATCH**

Ismail Yassin in the Navy (Fatin Abdel Wahab; 1957) Egyptian family comedy featuring the slapstick star of the era.

Madraset El Moshaghbeen (pictured top right; Galal al Sharkawy; 1971) Comedy about continually failing high-school seniors in their twenties.

The Sparrow (pictured right; Youssef Chahine; 1972) Enduring work of Egyptian cinema about the 1967 war.

The Treasure: Truth and Imagination (Sherif Arafa; 2017) Modern historical epic about Pharaonic Egypt.

Fe Koul Osbua Youm Gomaa (2020) Contemporary TV drama about vigilante justice.

PUBLIC DOMAIN/WIKIMEDIA

PHOTO 12/ALAMY

◎ | **FOLLOW**

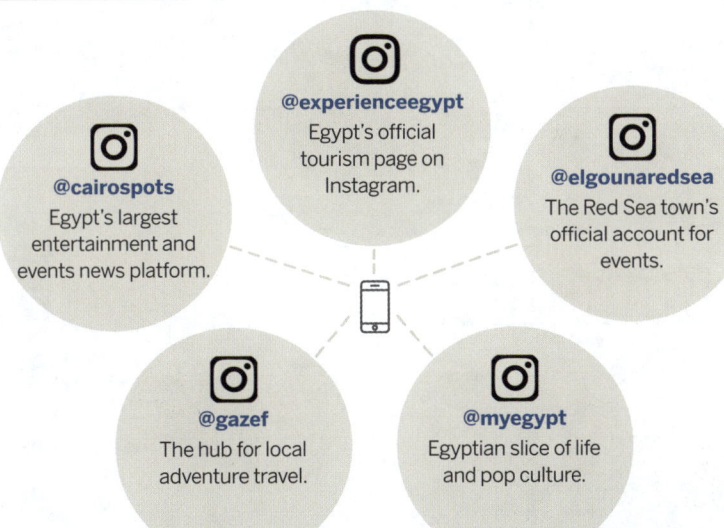

@experienceegypt
Egypt's official tourism page on Instagram.

@cairospots
Egypt's largest entertainment and events news platform.

@elgounaredsea
The Red Sea town's official account for events.

@gazef
The hub for local adventure travel.

@myegypt
Egyptian slice of life and pop culture.

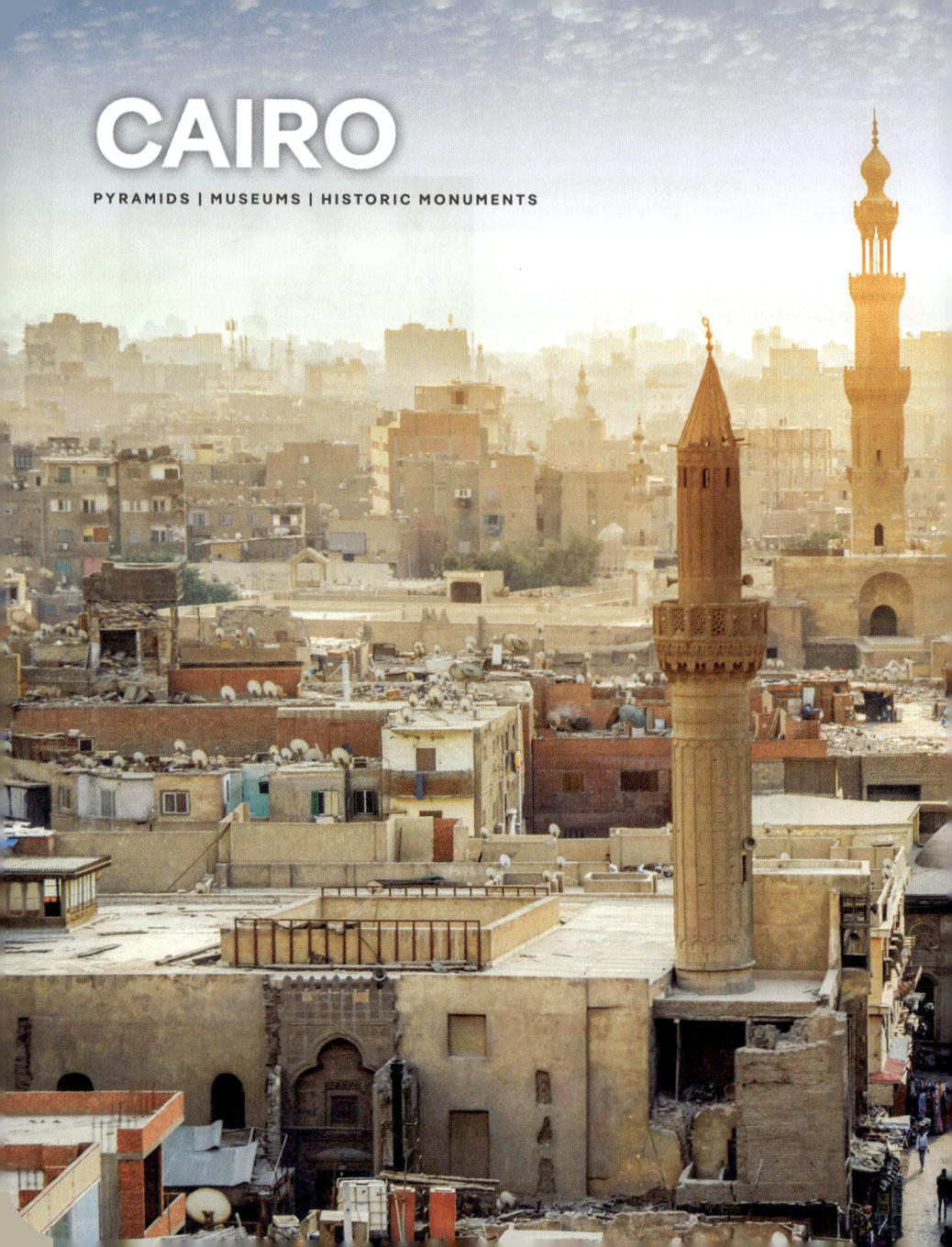

CAIRO

PYRAMIDS | MUSEUMS | HISTORIC MONUMENTS

CAIRO
Trip Builder

Cairo's dazzling chaos is an assault on your senses. Many travellers are overwhelmed on their first encounter, but this city rewards as much as it befuddles. Spend time here and you'll understand why Egyptians call their country – especially its capital – *umm al dunya*, the mother of the world.

Admire artefacts at the **Grand Egyptian Museum**, the country's newest cultural institution (p53)
🚌 *30min from Tahrir Square*

Kom Birah

July 26 Road · Ahmed Orabi Road

King Faisal Street
Al Haram St
Tersa Street
El Lebeny St

Dahshur Link Road

El Wahat Rd

Dreamland

Nazlet El-Semman Cemeteries

Kafrat al Jabal

Sphinx Tourist St

Dolphina Park

Al Tariq Al Daeri (Ring Road)

El Wahat Rd

Al Fardous

Come face to face with the **Pyramids of Giza** (pictured left), the last remaining wonder of the ancient world (p48)
🚌 *30min from Tahrir Square*

Zewail Street

October Gardens

Degla Gardens

As-Salam St

Cairo-Fayoum Desert Road

Beta Gardens

Southern Dahshur Link Road

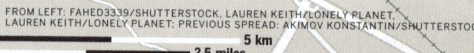

N
0 — 5 km
0 — 2.5 miles

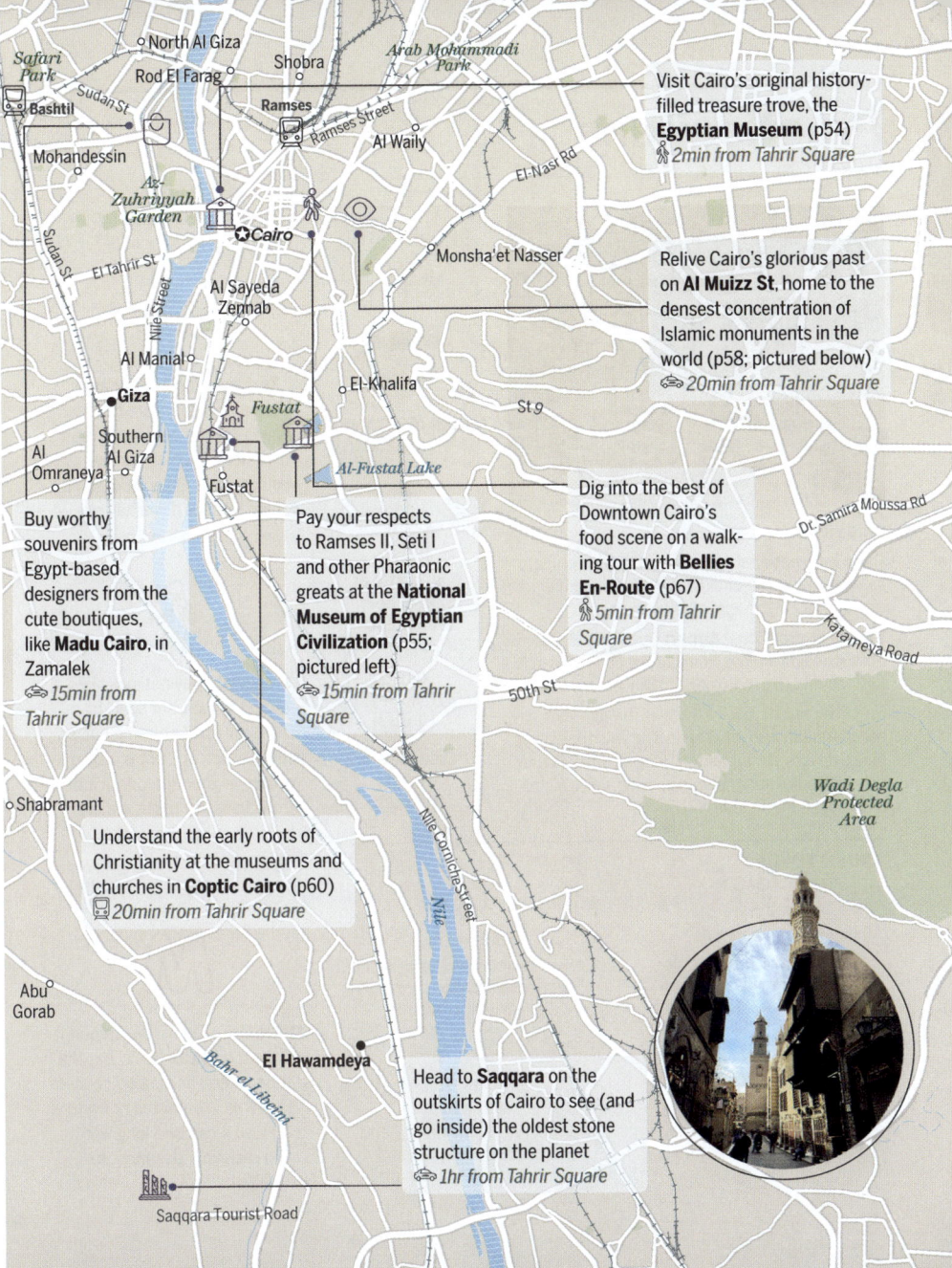

Visit Cairo's original history-filled treasure trove, the **Egyptian Museum** (p54)
🚶 *2min from Tahrir Square*

Relive Cairo's glorious past on **Al Muizz St**, home to the densest concentration of Islamic monuments in the world (p58; pictured below)
🚕 *20min from Tahrir Square*

Buy worthy souvenirs from Egypt-based designers from the cute boutiques, like **Madu Cairo**, in Zamalek
🚕 *15min from Tahrir Square*

Pay your respects to Ramses II, Seti I and other Pharaonic greats at the **National Museum of Egyptian Civilization** (p55; pictured left)
🚕 *15min from Tahrir Square*

Dig into the best of Downtown Cairo's food scene on a walking tour with **Bellies En-Route** (p67)
🚶 *5min from Tahrir Square*

Understand the early roots of Christianity at the museums and churches in **Coptic Cairo** (p60)
🚆 *20min from Tahrir Square*

Head to **Saqqara** on the outskirts of Cairo to see (and go inside) the oldest stone structure on the planet
🚕 *1hr from Tahrir Square*

Safari Park
Bashtil
Sudan St
North Al Giza
Rod El Farag
Shobra
Arab Mohammadi Park
Ramses
Ramses Street
Al Waily
El-Nasr Rd
Mohandessin
Az-Zuhriyyah Garden
✪Cairo
Monsha'et Nasser
Sudan St
El Tahrir St
Nile Street
Al Sayeda Zennab
Al Manial
Giza
El-Khalifa
St 9
Southern Al Giza
Fustat
Al Omraneya
Fustat
Al-Fustat Lake
Dr. Samira Moussa Rd
Katameya Road
Shabramant
50th St
Nile Corniche Street
Nile
Wadi Degla Protected Area
Abu Gorab
Bahr el Libeini
El Hawamdeya
Saqqara Tourist Road

Practicalities

TRI WI FARMA/SHUTTERSTOCK

ARRIVING

Cairo International Airport The capital's primary gateway, where major airlines from around the world arrive; about 20km east of Downtown.

Sphinx International Airport Opened in 2022. Serves budget airlines from Europe and the Middle East; about 50km northwest of Downtown.

For either airport, book a transfer through your accommodation instead of dealing with the scrum of taxi drivers. Do not rely on Uber, as drivers often demand more money before arriving. Cairo Metro does not go to either airport.

HOW MUCH FOR A

Bowl of kushari from LE30

0.5L bottle of Sakara beer from LE60

Cairo Metro ticket from LE5

GETTING AROUND

Taxi and ride-hailing apps Uber and Careem are the best way to cover medium or longer distances, and you can pay by card or cash. Do not expect to get local prices if you hail one on the street.

Walking It may not look like it at first glance, but apart from the problem of crossing busier streets, much of Cairo is walkable. Within neighbourhoods, it's the quickest way to get around.

WHEN TO GO

DEC–FEB
Best time to visit; cooler weather means you can sightsee without sweating

MAR–MAY
Crowds dwindle as the weather warms; watch for spring sandstorms

JUN–AUG
Avoid visiting in summer when the temperatures are boiling

SEP–NOV
Warm days, balmy nights, and lower accommodation prices

Metro Cairo Metro runs frequent services on clean trains, but the stations aren't as densely concentrated as in other major world cities, so it can be a long walk to reach your destination.

EATING & DRINKING

In Cairo, you can spend LE30 or LE3000 on dinner. At the budget end of the spectrum are the street carts (pictured top right) and *kushari* canteens, where the majority of Cairenes feed themselves. One step up are Egyptian fast-food joints – forget KFC and Pizza Hut – that serve some of the most delicious and cheapest meals around. At the upper end, Cairo's dining scene turns cosmopolitan, with chefs coming straight from the relevant country, along with all the ingredients.

Best street-food tour Bellies En-Route (pictured bottom right; p67)

Must-try home-style cooking Fasahet Somaya (p76)

CONNECT & FIND YOUR WAY

Wi-fi Available in most hotels and some cafes and restaurants, but the signal is often spotty and slow. It's worth buying an inexpensive local SIM card when you arrive at the airport.

Navigation Addresses and street signs are scarce in many neighbourhoods, but navigation apps generally have accurate locations for museums, restaurants and hotels.

WHERE TO STAY

Cairo has tons of places to stay all over town. Downtown has the densest concentration and is the best base for most travellers. Luxury hotels lie along the banks of the Nile.

Neighbourhood	Pro/Con
Downtown Cairo	At the heart of the action, which means street noise at all hours. Good choices for budget travellers.
Giza	Close to the Pyramids; far from everything else.
Islamic Cairo	Atmospheric monument-filled area, but few accommodation options.
Zamalek	Leafy Nile island with hip cafes and boutiques. Often heavy traffic on the bridges.
Garden City	High-end hotels in a quieter neighbourhood; nowhere to stay if you're on a budget.

POUNDS OR DOLLARS?

It's helpful to have US dollars in cash for when you can't use a card, such as tipping tour guides. Some taxi drivers also ask for USD.

MONEY

Cash is king for street food and small purchases, but many midrange and top-end restaurants and hotels accept cards. Students under 30 can get 50% off entry fees to all historic sites with an International Student Identity Card (ISIC).

01

Gawk at the
PYRAMIDS OF GIZA

WORLD WONDER | PHARAONIC HISTORY | ICONIC MONUMENTS

Standing for more than 4500 years, the Pyramids of Giza are among the most recognisable landmarks on the planet, but nothing quite prepares you for the sheer scale of the world's last remaining ancient wonder up close.

🗺 How To

Getting here/around Most people visit on a guided tour. Every hotel, guesthouse and hostel can arrange one (quality varies), but for a guaranteed good guide, book with **Magic Carpet Travel** (magic carpetegypt.com).

When to go The complex opens at 7am (usually closer to 7.15am). Starting around 8am is better, as stray dogs on the Giza Plateau tend to settle once more visitors arrive.

Tickets Buy tickets online (egymonuments.com) to save time at the often-crowded entrance.

Great Pyramid of Khufu & Painted Tombs

Built as a tomb for the 4th dynasty Pharaoh Khufu (reigned c 2589–2566 BCE), the **Great Pyramid** is the oldest on the Giza Plateau and the largest in Egypt, standing 146.5m high when it was completed around 2570 BCE. It was the tallest structure in the world for nearly four millennia, but after 46 windy centuries and the loss of its limestone casing, its height has been reduced by 9m.

It's possible to go inside the Great Pyramid, and although there's not much to see, for most visitors, just being able to explore such an ancient monument is an unforgettable experience despite the high ticket price (LE1500). However, if you suffer from claustrophobia or have mobility issues, give it a miss. Your reward

👁 Forever is Now

For three weeks in October and November, part of the Giza Plateau transforms into an open-air sculpture park. Set for its fifth season in 2025, 'Forever is Now' features large-scale, site-specific works before the desert returns to its natural state.

Top left Pyramids of Giza
Left Great Pyramid of Khufu
Above The Queens' Pyramids

at the end of the journey is the dark King's Chamber, where Khufu's empty sarcophagus stands at one end.

East of the Great Pyramid is the Eastern Cemetery. Members of the royal family and high-ranking nobles were buried here, and unlike the unadorned interior of the Great Pyramid, these tombs have beautiful decorations. The **Tomb of Meresankh III**, the granddaughter of Khufu, is generally open and has some of the best in situ wall paintings from this era. Visiting without a guide or being unable to speak Arabic can be tricky. The tombs are kept locked, so finding the entrance and the keeper of the keys is difficult on your own. Even though you pay for a ticket, the site guardians expect baksheesh (a tip).

Pyramid of Khafre

From certain angles, the Pyramid of Khafre, the only pyramid still capped with its original polished-limestone casing, looks taller than the Great Pyramid. But it's an illusion: it stands on higher ground.

◎ Must-Do Experiences

Eat at Khufu's Traditional Egyptian dishes get the fine-dining treatment with a view of the Pyramids. Reservations and a Giza Plateau entry ticket are required.

Take that camel photo Is there any place more iconic? Agree on a price with the handler and make sure the animal looks healthy.

Soak in the view from 9 Pyramids Lounge Cafe-restaurant with traditional cushioned ground seating, far from the bustle.

Paramotor over the Pyramids You and an instructor sit in a contraption like a tandem bicycle with a motor and parachute overhead.

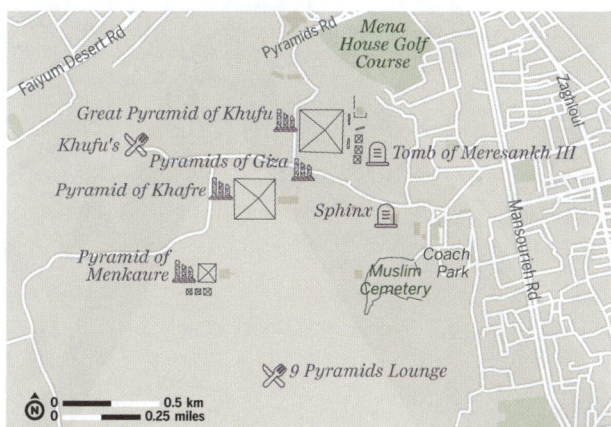

Left Pyramid of Khafre
Below Sphinx

Khafre (reigned c 2558–2532 BCE), son of Khufu, was the fourth pharaoh of the 4th dynasty. While the interior of the Great Pyramid is always open to visitors, access to the interiors of Khafre's and Menkaure's pyramids alternates every few years. (As of early 2025, Menkaure's pyramid was open.)

Pyramid of Menkaure

At 62m (originally 66.5m), the Pyramid of Menkaure is the smallest of the trio, only about one-tenth of the size of the Great Pyramid. If this pyramid is open, you'll descend into three distinct levels – the lowest surprisingly large – and you can peer into the main tomb.

Sphinx

The ancient Greeks dubbed this sculpture the Sphinx because it resembled their mythical winged monster that set riddles and killed anyone unable to answer them. In Arabic, it's known as Abu Al Hol (Father of Terror). Although no one knows which pharaoh it's supposed to portray, geological surveys have confirmed that it was most likely chiselled out from the bedrock during the reign of Khafre.

02 Cairo's Three
MEGA MUSEUMS

MUMMIES | KING TUT | HISTORY

▬ Cairo added another notch to its cultural belt with the opening of the Grand Egyptian Museum (set to be fully unveiled in late 2025). But now with three massive museums with similar names, which do you pick? All of them, if you can.

AHMED FAWZY EL ARABY/SHUTTERSTOCK

🗺 How To

Getting here It's easiest to get a taxi or Uber. The Egyptian Museum is the only one near the Cairo Metro (Sadat station, Line 1) and within walking distance of many Downtown hotels.

When to go Tour groups tend to visit first thing in the morning or right after lunch, so choose another time for fewer crowds.

Guides The labelling in the historic Egyptian Museum is limited, so it's worth hiring a guide.

AHMED ALATTAR/SHUTTERSTOCK

CREATIVITY LOVERY/SHUTTERSTOCK

Grand Egyptian Museum

The Grand Egyptian Museum (GEM) in Giza is the largest institution dedicated to a single civilisation. As this book went to print, the museum was set to fully open in late 2025. When we visited in early 2025, the Tutankhamun galleries, showcasing the boy king's famous golden grave goods, and the Solar Boat section, displaying Khufu's funerary vessel (Khufu being the builder of Giza's Great Pyramid), had yet to open. The grounds were under development, with a planned boardwalk linking the museum to the Pyramids of Giza, 2km away, still to come.

Fronted by an alabaster-and-glass pyramid inscribed with cartouches and hieroglyphs, the museum astonishes from the start. Visitors are greeted by a colossal 11m-tall statue of Ramses II and can ascend the **Grand**

👁 If You Must Pick One

Short on time Visit the Egyptian Museum (Downtown) or take the 90-minute GEM tour.

For mummies Head to NMEC.

See King Tut's death mask GEM if the Tutankhamun gallery opens in July; otherwise, the Egyptian Museum.

Don't want to hire a guide? GEM and NMEC both have clear labelling.

Top left Grand Egyptian Museum
Left National Museum of Egyptian Civilization (p55)
Above Egyptian Museum (p54)

Staircase (by foot or escalator), pausing at floor-to-ceiling windows with breathtaking pyramid views.

The galleries span four time periods, from 700,000 BCE to 394 CE, across three themes: society, kingship and beliefs. Displays of statues, tomb furniture, and painted reliefs are beautifully lit and labelled, but it's hard to fit centuries of stories into a single paragraph, so it's worth joining the 90-minute **guided tour** before exploring on your own.

Egyptian Museum

The oldest museum in the Middle East, the Egyptian Museum opened in 1902 and takes pride of place in Downtown Cairo. While many of its treasures have been crated up and sent to the Grand Egyptian Museum in Giza, this vast powder-pink building still houses one of the world's most important collections of ancient artefacts.

The ground-floor galleries are arranged so visitors can follow 700,000 years of ancient

⛫ Tahrir Square

Fronting the Egyptian Museum, Tahrir Square has been a focal point of Downtown Cairo for more than 150 years, long before it gained international recognition when hundreds of thousands of Egyptians converged here to oust then-President Hosni Mubarak during the 2011 Arab Spring. It was originally called Ismailia Square and was renamed *tahrir* (liberation) after the Revolution of 1952, which toppled the king and changed Egypt from a kingdom to a republic. The Ramses II obelisk crowning the traffic circle is from Tanis in the northeastern Nile Delta, and the surrounding ram-headed sphinxes come from Karnak in Luxor.

Left Ramses II obelisk, Tahrir Square
Below Ramses II mummy, National Museum of Egyptian Civilization

Egyptian history in chronological order by turning left from the entrance and moving clockwise. Upstairs, the galleries are organised by theme and by discoveries from specific tombs.

National Museum of Egyptian Civilization

The incredible collection of royal mummies at the National Museum of Egyptian Civilization (NMEC), transferred here in a regal procession in 2021, is not to be missed. But this museum is more than its prized collection of pharaohs; it's an attempt to encompass the entire sweep of Egyptian heritage under one roof.

In a subterranean space, the **Royal Mummies** Hall has a series of vault-like rooms that contain some of Egypt's most famous pharaohs and queens. Seti I's mummy, with his smooth black skin, is one of the most flawlessly preserved, and Ramses II, with his grey hair tinged with henna, is a close rival.

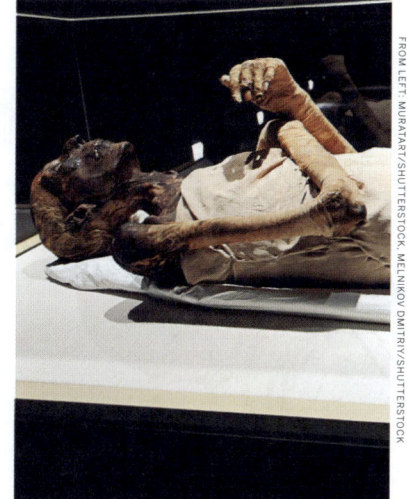

Most Iconic Artefacts in
CAIRO'S MUSEUMS

01 Death mask of Tutankhamun

An icon of ancient Egyptian opulence: made of solid gold and weighing 11kg. Set to move from the Egyptian Museum to the Grand Egyptian Museum (GEM) in July 2025.

02 Solar boat of Khufu

This 43m-long boat has never touched water but was meant to ferry the pharaoh to the afterlife. Gallery set to open in the GEM in late 2025.

03 Narmer Palette

Pharaoh Narmer wears the crowns of Upper Egypt and Lower Egypt, suggesting his reign was the first unification; Egyptian Museum.

04 Coffin of Akhenaten

Nearly all of the face of the 'heretic pharaoh' is missing, and his cartouche has been removed so that his soul can't find its way back to his body; Egyptian Museum.

05 Mummy of Ramses II

The body of Ramses II is so well-preserved that you can still see his grey hair, tinged with henna, more than 3200 years later; National Museum of Egyptian Civilization.

06 Statue of Khufu

The only surviving representation of the builder

of Giza's Great Pyramid stands just 7.5cm tall; Egyptian Museum.

07 Statue of Djoser
This limestone carving of the pharaoh behind the Step Pyramid is backed by a wall of blue faience tiles; Egyptian Museum.

08 Colossus of Ramses II
This 3200-year-old statue stands 11m high in the entry hall of the GEM. Its twin still lies in its original location in Memphis, the first capital of Egypt.

09 Statue of Kaaper
An astonishing sycamore wood statue of a chief priest with a protruding belly and lifelike eyes. A masterwork of the Old Kingdom; Egyptian Museum.

10 Papyrus of Yuya
Running for nearly 20m, the Papyrus of Yuya is the most complete ever found, containing the Book of the Dead written in cursive hieroglyphs; Egyptian Museum.

11 Silver coffin of Psusennes I
Silver was rarer than gold in ancient Egypt, making the gleaming, highly detailed silver coffin of Psusennes I (c 1047–996 BCE) even more remarkable; Egyptian Museum.

03 Medieval Monuments in
ISLAMIC CAIRO

ARCHITECTURE | ART | MOSQUES

Named after the Fatimid caliph who conquered Cairo in 969 CE, **Al Muizz Li Din Allah St** was once Cairo's grand thoroughfare reserved for the elites. Today, the street's great Mamluk complexes provide the most impressive assembly of medieval Islamic architecture in the world.

AKIMOV KONSTANTIN/SHUTTERSTOCK

ⓘ Top Tips

Beyond the ticketed monuments are plenty of mosques that are free to enter. Bring a headscarf, dress modestly and wear shoes that are easy to slip off.

Would-be guides may follow you and start giving you a tour, expecting baksheesh in return. If you're not interested, politely but firmly say no from the start.

🗺 Trip Notes

Getting here/around Most of Al Muizz St is pedestrianised, so if you're arriving by taxi, ask to be dropped off on Al Azhar St.

When to go Devote at least half a day to exploring this street and shopping in nearby Khan El Khalili (p65).

Tickets To visit all the ticketed monuments, you must pay for a multisite ticket online *(egymonuments.com)* or at the window across from the Mausoleum and Madrasa of Qalawun.

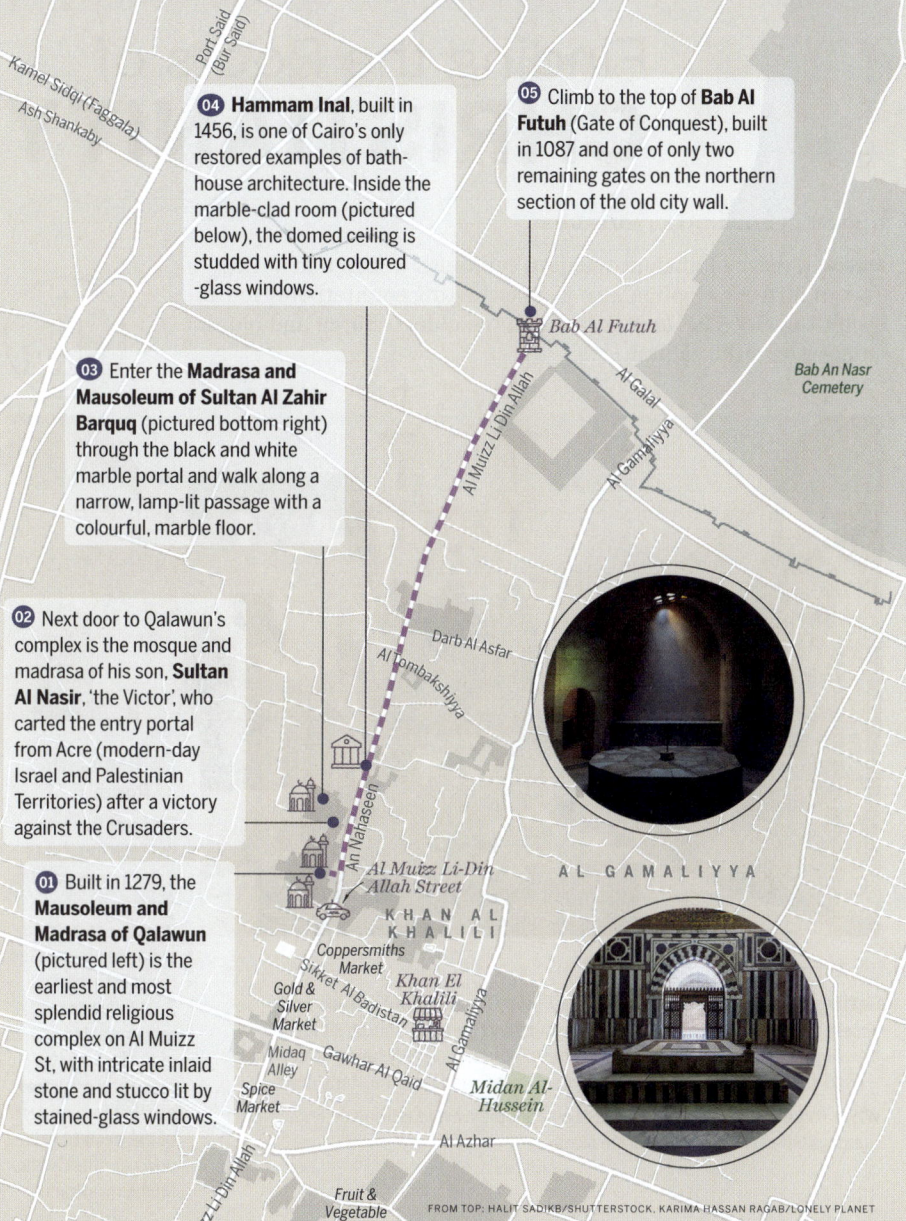

04 **Hammam Inal**, built in 1456, is one of Cairo's only restored examples of bathhouse architecture. Inside the marble-clad room (pictured below), the domed ceiling is studded with tiny coloured-glass windows.

05 Climb to the top of **Bab Al Futuh** (Gate of Conquest), built in 1087 and one of only two remaining gates on the northern section of the old city wall.

03 Enter the **Madrasa and Mausoleum of Sultan Al Zahir Barquq** (pictured bottom right) through the black and white marble portal and walk along a narrow, lamp-lit passage with a colourful, marble floor.

02 Next door to Qalawun's complex is the mosque and madrasa of his son, **Sultan Al Nasir**, 'the Victor', who carted the entry portal from Acre (modern-day Israel and Palestinian Territories) after a victory against the Crusaders.

01 Built in 1279, the **Mausoleum and Madrasa of Qalawun** (pictured left) is the earliest and most splendid religious complex on Al Muizz St, with intricate inlaid stone and stucco lit by stained-glass windows.

Kamel Sidqi (Faggala)

Ash Shankaby

Port Said (Bur Said)

Bab Al Futuh

Al Galal

Bab An Nasr Cemetery

Al Muizz Li Din Allah

Al Gamaliyya

Darb Al Asfar

Al Tombakshiyya

An Nahaseen

Al Muizz Li-Din Allah Street

AL GAMALIYYA

KHAN AL KHALILI

Coppersmiths Market

Sikket Al Badistan

Gold & Silver Market

Khan El Khalili

Al Gamaliyya

Midaq Alley

Gawhar Al Qaid

Spice Market

Midan Al-Hussein

Al Azhar

Fruit & Vegetable Market

FROM TOP: HALIT SADIKB/SHUTTERSTOCK, KARIMA HASSAN RAGAB/LONELY PLANET

Al Muizz Li-Din Allah

N

0   200 m
0   0.1 miles

04 Finding the Roots of
CHRISTIANITY

HISTORY | CHURCHES | MUSEUMS

A maze of ancient religious buildings within a historic Roman fortress, Coptic Cairo is a fascinating counterpoint to the rest of the city. This area is home to the oldest church and oldest synagogue in the capital.

ALEKSANDRA TOKARZ/SHUTTERSTOCK

🗺 Trip Notes

Getting here/around Cairo Metro Line 1 (Mar Girgis station) provides easy access from Downtown. The Coptic Museum and Hanging Church sit just off Mar Girgis St, but the rest of the Coptic compound is slightly below street level – head north to the Church of St George entrance and take the steps down.

When to go If you're here to sightsee and not pray, avoid visiting on Fridays or Sundays when churches celebrate Mass.

🏛 Remnants of Rome

Emperor Diocletian built the fortress of Babylon – not of the hanging gardens variety – to guard a canal that connected the Nile to the Red Sea. Today, the only recognisable features of the fort are two stone and brick **towers** that formed part of the western gate, now near the Coptic Museum entrance.

03 The **Church of St Sergius and Bacchus** (pictured right) is built over a cave where, according to Coptic tradition, the Holy Family sheltered during their flight into Egypt to escape King Herod.

04 The **Church of St Barbara** houses rare icons of its namesake saint, the Virgin Mary and Jesus Christ. St Barbara was a Christian convert who was beaten to death by her pagan father.

Hassan Al Anwar

Ain As Sirah

Athar An Nabi

Mohammed Al Sagheir

M Mar Girgis

Church of St Sergius & Bacchus

Coptic Museum

Church of St Barbara

Ben Ezra Synagogue

COPTIC CAIRO

Hanging Church

02 The **Hanging Church** (pictured left) is so old that its founding date is uncertain, likely dating back to the 9th century or possibly the 7th. Its name comes from being suspended over the Water Gate of Roman Babylon.

01 The **Coptic Museum** contains one of the most important collections of Coptic antiquities in the world, including colourful frescoed niches from the Monastery of St Jeremiah in Saqqara.

05 Visit the 9th-century **Ben Ezra Synagogue** (pictured above), built within a 4th-century church. Tradition holds that the Prophet Jeremiah gathered the Jews here after the destruction of the temple in Jerusalem.

Mar Girgis

N
0
0
200 m
0.1 miles

■ By Shoroq Galal
A storyteller from Egypt

Religious Festivities in Egypt

WHERE THE PARTY NEVER STOPS

Egyptians are renowned for their sense of humour and sense of joy – national traits that they love to share with others, again and again. After all, *eid,* the Arabic word for 'celebration', 'festival' and 'holiday', shares its root with the word 'repeat'.

NOVIE CHARLEEN MAGNEZ/SHUTTERSTOCK

Religion & Religious Holidays in Egypt

Approximately 90% of the population identifies as Sunni Muslim, while the remaining 10% belongs to the Coptic Orthodox Church. Other religious groups – various Christian denominations, Baha'is, a residual Jewish community and the occasional atheist – make up a small fraction of society. Questioning the existence of God is largely frowned upon by Egyptians, regardless of their personal beliefs. If you don't believe, have faith that most Egyptians do.

Egypt observes 18 national holidays each year, 11 of which are religious – two for Coptic Christian celebrations and nine for Muslim observances. As a majority Muslim country, Egypt gets especially busy around Eid Al Fitr, marking the end of Ramadan, and Eid Al Adha, following the hajj pilgrimage. Egyptians abroad often return home to celebrate, and locals take advantage of the time off to explore tourist attractions.

Religious festivals follow the Islamic (lunar) and Coptic calendars, rather than the Gregorian. During Ramadan, many restaurants close during the day, and government offices shut early. Opening hours, like meal times, become a movable feast. Regardless of religious affiliation, one burning question unites all Egyptians when Eid approaches…

'But What Shall We Eat?'

Festivities and food go together in Egypt like icing and cake. For Eid Al Fitr, biscuits take centre stage. It's informally known as the Lesser Eid, but there's nothing 'lesser' about the amount of food.

For 11 months of the year, Egypt is filled with vendors selling delectable syrupy pastries. These double during Ramadan – and you may notice the holy month's parting gift to your waistline.

Left *Iftar,* Khan El Khalili (p65)
Centre *Kahk* (sugar-dusted biscuits)
Right Ramadan night market

Traditionally, every household bakes 5kg of *kahk* (small, sugar-dusted biscuits served plain or filled with something sweet) and 1kg to 2kg of *ghorayeba* (shortbread cookies).

Two months after Ramadan comes Eid Al Adha, a four-day feast centred on the sacrifice of a cow, buffalo, goat or sheep.

Coptic Christmas (on 7 January) and multiple saints' days are also marked by *kahk* and ritual sacrifice. But whether Christian or Muslim, the key part of all festivities in Egypt is the *eidiyya* – the tradition of giving (and receiving) fresh wads of cash.

Keep Calm & Carry On (Eating)

During Ramadan, Muslims refrain from food, water, coffee and cigarettes during daylight hours. Days can feel long, and tempers short – especially among taxi drivers. In the coming years, Ramadan will fall during cooler months, ideal for absorbing the festive atmosphere on foot and taking in the glittering bunting while planning dinner.

> Questioning the existence of God is largely frowned upon by Egyptians

As sunset nears, Egyptians return home for *iftar* (the fast-breaking meal), though many stay out to hand out food and drink to waylaid travellers and anyone in need. In the small hours before dawn, restaurants fire up for *suhoor,* the pre-dawn meal. Staple dishes like *fuul* (fava bean paste) and *ta'amiyya* (fava bean falafel) fly from street carts to lively gatherings of people who likely haven't moved since sundown.

And bright and early the next day, Egyptians are up – stomachs and hearts already set on the next Eid. Rinse, repeat, rejoice!

It Can't Be a Celebration Without Sweets

Egyptians' enthusiasm manifests in their religious festivities, which – while rooted in the same traditions found across the region – take on a distinct character in Egypt. You might say the Egyptians gave to religion what the inventor of icing gave to cake: more flavour (and more sugar).

While the Islamic world celebrates the main occasions of Eid Al Fitr and Eid Al Adha by visiting relatives and giving to charity, Egyptians do all this and more. The year is marked by *mawlid* (birth celebrations) for Sufi saints and the Prophet Muhammad, each with its own special traditions and sweet treats.

05 Shopping Cairo's STREETS

BAZAARS | BOUTIQUES | LOCAL DESIGNS

Faced with the mountains of tacky souvenirs and over-eager hustlers trying to sell them to you over endless glasses of tea, it's tempting to keep your wallet firmly shut in Cairo. But then you'd be missing out on some of Egypt's most beautiful treasures, many ethically made by Egyptian women and Cairo-based designers using local materials. The trick is knowing where to look.

CAIRO EXPERIENCES

UNAI HUIZI PHOTOGRAPHY/SHUTTERSTOCK

📷 How To

Getting here/around Find traditional handicrafts in Islamic Cairo and modern boutiques in Zamalek. Taxis are the easiest way to get around.

When to go Some shops in Islamic Cairo are closed on Friday mornings and all day on Sunday.

Bargaining Expected in markets, but not in fixed-price shops. Bargaining may seem like an annoyance, but it helps to treat it as a game.

EMILY M. WILSON/GETTY IMAGES

Top left Khan El Khalili
Bottom left El Fishawy

Khan El Khalili & Islamic Cairo

Khan El Khalili, Cairo's medieval market, is a warren of skinny lanes where merchants have been plying their trades since the 14th century. You can buy pretty much anything, from hand-crafted copper crescent moon finials that top mosque domes to plastic pyramid keyrings. Rest your feet at **El Fishawy**, said to be the oldest *ahwa* (coffeehouse) in Cairo, opened in 1773.

Because of mechanisation, many artisan professions that Khan El Khalili was once famous for have disappeared, but some shops and schools are keeping this heritage alive. Wander into **Gamaleya** to watch artists working their magic in copper, silver filigree, inlaid wood and wool.

Boutiques in Zamalek & Beyond

Egypt is so well-known for its traditional handicrafts that it's easy to forget that this heritage has a contemporary side. The upscale neighbourhood of Zamalek has become a hub for designers to show off their wares. At **Fair Trade Egypt**, find crafts from across the country, including Bedouin rugs, Fayoum ceramics and beaded jewellery from Aswan. **Asfour El Nil** puts modern takes on traditions with colourful hand-bags, homewares and clothing. **Madu Cairo** stocks gorgeous Egyptian cotton bed linens, patterned textiles and more made by Malaika.

Head to **Cairopolitan** in Garden City to discover local work by Cairo's contemporary artists. Another branch, called **Gizapolitan**, is opening soon near the Sphinx.

Egyptian Brands to Look For

A growing number of local designers are crafting modern, ethically made goods using traditional materials and methods. Look for these brands in Zamalek and elsewhere:

Malaika (malaikalinens.com) 100% Egyptian cotton linens (bedsheets, tablecloths, accessories) hand embroidered or silk-screen printed by underprivileged women.

Up-Fuse (up-fuse.com) Employs Egyptian women to create trendy upcycled totes, wallets and accessories from discarded plastic bags and car tires.

Rasha Pasha (instagram.com/rashapashacairo) Boldly accented coats, cloaks, blazers and dresses that are sure to turn heads.

Ramla (ramlastore.com) Beautiful babouche-style slip-on shoes with Pharaonic and desert motifs.

06 Cairo's Favourite FOODS

STREET EATS | LOCAL DISHES | WALKING TOURS

▬▬▬ Cairo is the country's showcase of food, with Egyptian and international options for every budget. This country has unique foods not found elsewhere in the Middle East, such as *kushari* (mix of noodles, rice, black lentils, fried onions and tomato sauce), *ta'amiyya* (fava bean falafel) and *fuul* (fava bean paste), and the preparation of some foods can be traced all the way back to Pharaonic times.

BOAZ ROTTEM/ALAMY

🗺 How To

Getting there/around Downtown Cairo is the top spot for street food, reachable by taxi or public transport. Walking is the best way to get around.

When to go Egyptians usually dine late, particularly in summer when nights offer a reprieve from the heat. Roaming vendors and hole-in-the-wall food stops are open until the wee hours.

Paying the bill Cash is king at street food stalls, but cards are accepted at higher-end restaurants.

ALEXANDERSTOCK23/SHUTTERSTOCK

Top left *Fuul* (fava bean paste)
Bottom left Koshary Abou Tarek

Bellies En-Route

If you want the lowdown on Downtown Cairo's food scene, tours run by local foodie guides of **Bellies En-Route** (belliesenroute.com) are packed with insider know-how on the classic dishes and street-food favourites that keep the capital running. Better yet, local culture takes centre stage as you munch your way between family-run canteens, a famed old-school coffee roaster, a traditional patisserie, and hole-in-the-wall *ta'amiyya* and *fiteer* (sweet or savoury flaky pastry) stands.

Their Downtown Cairo Food Tour is the polar opposite of Egypt's many cookie-cutter tours: infused with local knowledge and providing first-timers and return visitors with deeper insights into modern Egypt and Downtown's heritage.

The 'King of Kushari'

The epitome of Egyptian street food is *kushari*, a carb-heavy mix of noodles, rice, black lentils and sometimes chickpeas, topped with crispy fried onions that you smother in tomato sauce, douse with garlicky vinegar and dab with hot sauce. Cheap, filling and tasty, *kushari* is the fuel that keeps Egypt going, and many Egyptians regard it as their national dish.

For your first experience, head to **Koshary Abou Tarek**. This temple of *kushari* in Downtown Cairo has been in business for 70 years and continues to hold onto Cairo's unofficial 'best *kushari*' title. The friendly staff are used to foreign visitors, and the menu has only two items anyway (*kushari* and lentil soup in a bread bowl).

Say Hello to Egyptian Food

We use food as a medium to showcase a different side of Egypt and act as a starting point to talk about Egypt and Egyptian culture. We want to show a different side of the country that gives visitors the opportunity to enter into a dialogue and helps them have a more meaningful experience.

As well as that, we've set out to create a tourism model that both protects and supports the local businesses we use, paying them fairly and making sure that our tour visits are a help to them rather than a hassle.

■ By **Laila Hassaballa**, co-founder of Bellies En-Route *@belliesenroute*

■ **By Nada El Sawy**
Nada is a Cairo-based freelance journalist who writes about travel, arts and culture, and human interest. @Nada_El_Sawy (X)

Elevating Egyptian Cuisine

FROM STREET FOOD TO FINE DINING

Egypt is known for the Pyramids, hieroglyphics and King Tut – but not especially for its food. Traditionally, Egyptian cuisine has been found in homes or on street carts rather than in upscale restaurants. But Khufu's restaurant and Executive Chef Mostafa Seif are changing that, sprinkling experimentation with a serving of national pride.

Left Diners at Khufu's
Centre *Kushari*, Khufu's
Right Pyramid-view tables, Khufu's

NADA EL SAWY/LONELY PLANET

It is a busy Friday afternoon at the Giza Pyramids. The entrance gate is crowded with vehicles, tourists capture selfies in horse-drawn carriages, and visitors throng the plateau. Stepping into Khufu's restaurant is like entering another world, away from the chaos, yet with a panoramic view of the three pyramids.

True to its setting, everything about Khufu's is Egyptian – from the interior and architectural design, to the tableware, to the cuisine crafted by Executive Chef Mostafa Seif.

For those expecting the usual *fuul*, *ta'amiyya*, *kushari* and *molokhiyya*, they are on the menu. But this is no standard fare. The *kushari* salad skips the pasta and rice, and adds quail eggs and small wheat dough pearls called *mefatela*. Other inventive creations include a savory *qatayef* filled with pulled beef and chili jam, a quail tajine infused with dates and ginger, and spiced fried vinegar-soaked potatoes.

Since opening in September 2022, Khufu's has been recognised as a 'Hidden Gem' by La Liste and ranked among the top five of MENA's 50 Best Restaurants for two consecutive years. Fine-dining restaurant Khufu's Bistro, opened upstairs in September 2024, is poised to achieve similar acclaim with cross-cultural dishes like okra risotto and confit duck leg with freekeh.

Seif takes pride in these accolades, but values his mission: showcasing the potential of Egyptian cuisine and the talent of Egyptian chefs.

'I feel like I'm representing Egyptian culture. I'm trying to show people what Egyptian food is,' Seif told us. 'We have our own rich food culture going back to Pharaonic times, so why cook food that is borrowed from other cultures?'

As a child, he helped make liver and sausage sandwiches for his grandfather's food cart. After two years cooking for the Egyptian army, he became a chef, winning Top Chef Arabia in 2017.

Since most of Egypt's fine dining is European, he ended up at Italian restaurant Pier88. Giovanni Bolandrini, CEO and owner of Pier88 Group, then offered him the chance to create an Egyptian menu for a new restaurant at the Pyramids.

'My vision was to make Egyptian food that both tourists and Egyptians would enjoy,' Seif said.

Others share Seif's mission to put Egyptian food on the global map. Suzanne Zeidy, author of the 2014 cookbook *Cairo Kitchen*, said increased nationalistic feelings after the 2011 revolution extended to gastronomy.

Zööba, a fresh take on traditional Egyptian street food, opened in 2012. Head chef Moustafa El Refaey's menu includes

> Stepping into Khufu's restaurant is like entering another world, away from the chaos

ta'amiyya with fried aubergine and beetroot-hibiscus tahini. Zööba has expanded across Cairo, including the Grand Egyptian Museum, debuted internationally in New York in 2019, and opened outlets in Bahrain, Kuwait and Saudi Arabia.

'Zööba kickstarted the shift in perception of Egyptian food. They branded it exceptionally, created a beautiful story, and exported it to the world,' said Cairo Food Week founder Hoda El Sherif. 'Now you have chefs like Mostafa Seif elevating the cuisine further by blending Egyptian recipes and ingredients with fine-dining techniques.'

⚔ Cairo Food Week

Hoda El Sherif and Sharif Tamim, co-founders of the food content studio Flavor Republic, started Cairo Food Week in 2023 to celebrate Egypt's gastronomic heritage. The first edition took place in June 2023, the second in May 2024, and the third is set for 25 September to 2 October 2025. The event will be held annually in September.

The week features over 40 culinary experiences, talks, exhibitions, film screenings and activities across the city. It brings together celebrated chefs from Egypt, the Middle East and North Africa region, and beyond, along with food enthusiasts, restaurateurs, entrepreneurs and artists.

Leap Back in Time
AT SAQQARA

TOMBS | PYRAMIDS | ANCIENT ART

A popular day trip from Cairo, Saqqara was the vast necropolis of Memphis, ancient Egypt's first capital. It was an active burial ground for pharaohs, their families and high-ranking officials for more than 3500 years and is Egypt's largest archaeological site.

🗺 How To

Getting there/around
Saqqara is a huge site
with no public trans-
port. Visit on a guided
tour from Cairo, which
often also includes the
pyramids at Dahshur
and a museum in
Memphis.

When to go Get an
early start to beat
traffic and squeeze
more into your day.

Get a guide Good
guides truly enhance
a visit. Contact a tour
operator like **Magic
Carpet Travel** (magic
carpetegypt.com) to
arrange one.

Step Pyramid of Djoser

Around 2650 BCE, Pharaoh Djoser (reigned
c 2667–2648 BCE) asked his chief architect
Imhotep to build him a Step Pyramid. It is
the world's earliest stone monument, and its
significance cannot be overstated. You can
go inside the pyramid through an entrance
on its southern side, where a wide, columned
and atmospherically lit corridor tunnelled out
during the 26th dynasty leads to a viewing
platform that looks down into Djoser's vaulted
granite burial chamber and onto the top of his
mammoth sarcophagus.

Pyramid of Unas

Stroll west from Djoser's funerary complex
to the Pyramid of Unas (who reigned c 2375–
2345 BCE), now a modest pile of stone blocks
once 43m tall. Its interior marks a significant

🏛 Dahshur & Memphis

Dahshur's **Bent Pyramid**
and **Red Pyramid** represent
the architectural trial and
error between the Step
Pyramid and the Pyramids
of Giza.

The only remaining
evidence of Memphis, ancient
Egypt's first capital, is a small,
open-air museum built around
a fallen statue of Ramses II.

Top left Step Pyramid of Djoser
Left Pyramid of Unas
Above Tomb of Ty (p73)

shift in funerary practices, as the first royal burial chamber to be decorated.

A short, easy descent deposits you in the antechamber and burial chamber, whose white, alabaster-lined walls are inscribed with blue hieroglyphs and the ceiling is adorned with stars. These hieroglyphs are among the earliest examples of the funerary inscriptions known as the Pyramid Texts (later compiled into the Book of the Dead), which were 'spells' to protect the soul of the deceased. Of the 283 separate phrases in Unas' tomb, most were prayers, hymns and lists of items, such as food and clothing, that the pharaoh would require in the afterlife.

Painted Tombs

More than 200 tombs have been excavated near the Pyramid of Unas. Those most often open to visits are the 5th- and 6th-dynasty **Tombs of Idut, Unasankh and Inerfert**, where you can spot finely detailed scenes of hunting, fishing and butchery on the walls. In

◎ How to Spend Your Time at Saqqara

Count on spending at least half a day at Saqqara, though it's most often sold as a full-day tour from Cairo and includes visits to Dahshur and Memphis.

If you're short on time Visit the Step Pyramid of Djoser and see the painted Tombs of Idut, Unasankh and Inerfert nearby.

Half a day Check out the Step Pyramid and the Tombs of Idut, Unasankh and Inerfert before driving to the Serapeum and Tomb of Ty.

Full day Squeeze in as many Saqqara sights as you're interested in, plus climb inside the pyramids at Dahshur and visit the museum in Memphis.

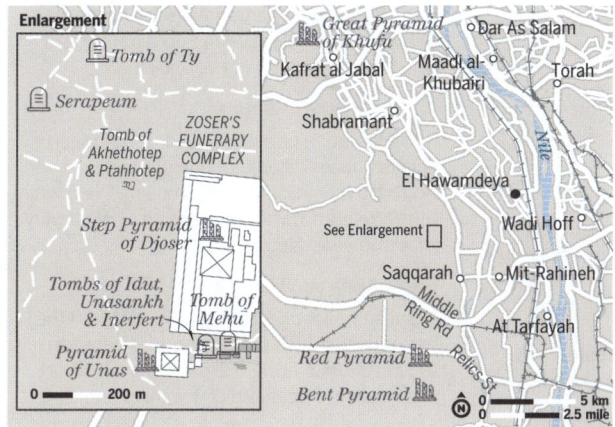

Enlargement

Tomb of Ty

Serapeum

Tomb of Akhethotep & Ptahhotep

ZOSER'S FUNERARY COMPLEX

Step Pyramid of Djoser

Tombs of Idut, Unasankh & Inerfert

Tomb of Mehu

Pyramid of Unas

0 — 200 m

Great Pyramid of Khufu

Kafrat al Jabal

Dar As Salam

Maadi al-Khubairi

Torah

Shabramant

El Hawamdeya

See Enlargement

Wadi Hoff

Saqqarah

Mit-Rahineh

Middle Ring Rd

At Tarfayah

Red Pyramid

Relics St

Bent Pyramid

Nile

0 — 5 km
0 — 2.5 mile

Left Serapeum entrance
Below Tomb of Idut

the **Tomb of Mehu**, a 6th-dynasty vizier, the walls are covered with depictions of daily life – from cooking geese to brewing beer.

Serapeum & the Tomb of Ty

A five-minute drive northwest of the Step Pyramid is the curious **Serapeum**. This subterranean warren of tombs was used for the burial of sacred animals, particularly bulls called Apis, which were worshipped in Memphis. Walking through the tunnels past the enormous stone coffins, which weigh up to 80 tonnes each, it's impossible not to be impressed by the sheer effort put into it. The first Apis burial took place during the reign of Amenhotep III (1390–1352 BCE), and the practice continued until 30 BCE, at the end of the Ptolemaic era.

The nearby **Tomb of Ty**, overseer of the Abu Sir pyramids and sun temple during the 5th dynasty, is not only the finest example of Old Kingdom art but also one of the main sources of knowledge about life in Old Kingdom Egypt. The detailed scenes of daily life covering the walls include peo-ple farming, fishing, building boats, dancing and avoiding crocodiles. Their images are accompa-nied by chattering hieroglyphic dialogue.

Listings

BEST OF THE REST

 Must-See Mosques

Mosque & Madrasa of Sultan Hassan

Massive yet elegant, this grand structure is regarded as the finest piece of early Mamluk architecture in Cairo.

Al Azhar Mosque

One of Cairo's oldest and most esteemed mosques. Its grand imam is considered the highest theological authority for Egyptian Muslims.

Muhammad Ali Mosque

A bold, brassy statement of Ottoman styling, with domes upon domes, twinkling chandeliers and striped stone, overlooking the city from the Citadel.

Mosque of Ibn Tulun

The city's oldest intact, functioning Islamic monument is easily identified by its high walls topped with neat crenellations. Its geometric simplicity is best appreciated from the top of the unique spiral minaret.

Mosque & Madrasa of Sultan Al Ghuri

The interior reveals gilt and painted wood panelling, panels of white and black marble, soaring ceilings, and intricate geometric paving.

 Eccentric Architecture & Museums

Manial Palace

Cairo's 20th-century one-percenters once lived it up amid these lavishly eclectic salons, whose interiors are a fascinating merging of Ottoman, Moorish, Persian and European rococo styles.

Baron Empain Palace

This brilliantly bonkers building is nicknamed the 'Hindu Palace' for its facade carved with elephants and serpents. It was the home of Belgian industrialist Baron Édouard Empain, who built the suburb of Heliopolis.

Abdeen Palace Museum

A small portion of the 500 salons in Abdeen Palace houses a hodgepodge of museums, including the unintentionally amusing Presidency Gifts Museum, packed with an array of sparkly gifts from world leaders.

Gayer-Anderson Museum

A British major and army doctor restored the two adjoining 16th-century houses between 1935 and 1942, filling them with furniture, art and souvenirs acquired on his travels.

Cairo Marriott Hotel

The former Gezira Palace is fronted by orange-gold columns and glittering chandeliers from triple-height ceilings. Dine in style at the Saraya Gallery, and hotel guests can join free tours led by the in-house historian.

 Cairo From on High

Cairo Tower

For 360-degree views across the central city with the Nile below, zoom up the 187m-high Cairo Tower, which was built in 1961 and resembles a stylised lotus plant with its latticework casing.

HALIT SADIK/SHUTTERSTOCK

Baron Empain Palace

Sheraton Cairo

Book an upgraded room or pay to access the 26th-floor Club Lounge with wraparound floor-to-ceiling windows for unforgettable views of the Pyramids of Giza in the distance and the Nile.

Bab Zuwayla

Built in 1092, Bab Zuwayla is the last surviving southern gate of the medieval city. From the roof, enjoy panoramic vistas of Islamic Cairo, or you can climb even higher up the minaret stairs.

Bab Zuwayla

Bab Al Futuh

Look for inscriptions left by Napoleon's troops, carved animals and Pharaonic figures as you climb this northern city gate – then peer into the gleaming white courtyard of Al Hakim Mosque.

Crimson Bar & Grill $$$

Enjoy elevated Nile views from the east-facing balcony over breakfast or late-night cocktails in Zamalek.

Citadel

Perched on a limestone spur, the Citadel, begun by Saladin in 1176, housed Egypt's rulers for 700 years. From its terrace, you can see why Cairo's nickname is the 'city of a thousand minarets'.

Immobilia

Grit meets glamour when you rent one of the four luxe private apartments in this Art Deco building, Cairo's first skyscraper, built in 1939 with spacious plant-filled balconies overlooking Downtown.

On the Nile

Mamsha Ahl Misr

The two-level 'Walkway of the Egyptian People' along the Nile is lined with restaurants, cafes and boat docks, making it a great spot for a stroll, especially for families, women and solo travellers.

Dok Dok Landing Stage

The most gentle and traditional way to get on the river is to hire a felucca (traditional sailing boat) for a golden hour or nighttime cruise.

M/Y Christina

For a stylish, no-hassle, private Nile cruise, book this yacht departing from its own dock in Dokki. Reserve online in advance for a comfortable way to soak up Cairo's riverine life.

Capital Art & Culture

Darb 1718

This cultural centre and creative space in Fustat hosts art exhibitions, craft workshops and evening concerts in the garden or on the roof, as well as film screenings.

Makan

Explore Egypt's musical traditions with a live show at Makan (Egyptian Centre for Culture and Art), a venue dedicated to preserving the country's musical heritage.

El Dammah Theatre

For a deep dive into traditional Egyptian music, catch a concert at El Dammah Theatre, home to El Mastaba Center's roster of nearly a dozen folk bands from across the country.

Maq'ad of Sultan Qaitbey

In Cairo's Northern Cemetery, this former royal hall is now Multicultural and Artistic Spaces at Qaitbey's, hosting market days, walking tours, live music and history talks.

El Sawy Culture Wheel

One of the best spots to dip your toe into Egypt's contemporary music scene, with concerts and performances from up-and-coming local rock bands to traditional folk ensembles.

Hyatt Centric Cairo West

Opened in late 2024, Egypt's first 'art hotel' features playful site-specific installations and a uniquely painted ancient Egyptian–style baboon in every room, hands raised to greet the morning sun.

Essential Egyptian Eats

Zööba $

Zööba in Zamalek gives classic cheap eats a contemporary twist: think pickled lemon and spicy pepper *ta'amiyya* sandwiches. There's also a branch in the Grand Egyptian Museum.

Fasahet Somaya $$

A highly recommended taste of Egyptian home cooking from the small daily-changing menu. Opens for just a few hours at dinner in Downtown Cairo.

Fish & Chips $$

Egyptian-style seafood dishes served in a cute, colourful Downtown restaurant.

Zeeyara Restaurant $$$

Drool over contemporary takes on Egyptian cooking at this restaurant on the rooftop of Le Riad Hotel de Charme in Islamic Cairo.

Felfela $$

A Downtown Cairo institution since 1959, this restaurant serves Egyptian classics below colourful glass ceiling panels.

Abdel Rahim Koueider $

The jury is out on who serves the best mango ice cream, but this spot Downtown is known for its mastic and pistachio flavours.

El Abd $

Cairo's most famous bakery is always packed with customers jostling for cookies, cakes and ice cream every hour it's open in Downtown Cairo.

Fuul Mahrous $

Perhaps Cairo's best *fuul*, served from a tiny stand on a residential block in Garden City.

International Restaurants

CaiRoma $$

A little slice of Italy in Downtown Cairo with excellent pizza, vegetarian options and off-street courtyard seating.

Almería $$$

The best flavours from all around the Med (pomegranate, yoghurt, honey, aubergine) in a mod-retro space Downtown.

Sachi $$$

This intimate sushi spot, with its low-lit interior and cocktail-bar vibes, is cementing Heliopolis' reputation as the most vibrant upmarket dining destination in Cairo.

DAVID SUTHERLAND/ALAMY

Felfela

Barranco $$$

Romantic, elegant restaurant at the Hyatt
Regency in New Giza, dishing up phenomenal
Japanese-Peruvian fusion plates that you
won't find anywhere else in the city.

8 Restaurant $$$

Find the country's best Cantonese food at
the Four Seasons at Nile Plaza in Garden City.
Don't miss the Friday dim sum feast or the
Peking duck.

 Breakfast & Brunch

Eish + Malh $$

This high-ceilinged Downtown cafe, with
arched windows and floor-to-ceiling city
scenes, is a favourite hang-out for hip, young
Cairenes. Great flat whites, brunch and Italian
dishes.

Oldish $$

Cute Downtown courtyard cafe with Middle
Eastern and European breakfast options, plus
flavoured lattes.

Granita $$

A contemporary take on Cairo's old European-
style cafes, inside the grounds of All Saints'
Cathedral in Zamalek.

Luuma $$

Spacious west-facing Nile-front terrace dining
in Zamalek, with a menu that bounces from
Egyptian to international, including family-
sized breakfast platters.

 Caffeine Fix

Sip $

Hip coffeehouse with minimalist millennial
vibes (dusty pink accent wall, on-table succu-
lents) near Cinema Radio in Downtown Cairo.

Zahrat Al Bustan

Sufi Cafe & Bookstore $

Young Cairenes tap on their laptops while
sipping coffee amid the creaky wood-floored
rooms rimmed by shelves of old books at this
artsy cafe in Zamalek.

Falak $

Cafe, bookshop and gallery on the ground floor
of a villa on a quiet square in Garden City.

After Dark

Zahrat Al Bustan $

Do as the Cairenes do: smoke shisha, drink tea
and watch the world go by on the streets of
Downtown Cairo.

El Horreya $

Downtown's most famous *baladi* (local) bar,
with an interior of high ceilings, mirrors and
vintage drinks signs.

Shinko $$$

In a sleek New Cairo spot, mixologists craft
cocktails with inventive ingredients like pink
peppercorn distillate, bee pollen gin, and
stout reduction inside an upscale residential
compound.

NORTHERN NILE VALLEY

ANCIENT RUINS | COPTIC CULTURE | ADVENTURE

Lake *Qarun* Tamiya

Qasr Qarun Girza

Abshaway **Medinat Al Fayoum**

Qalamshah El-maimun

Beni Suef

Zafarana

Biba

Maghagha

El-sheikh
Fadl

Shusha

*Gebel At
Teir*

Minya

Abu Qirqus

Al Ashmunein

Dairut

'arab
Miteir

Beni'Adi elBahariya
& Beni'Adi el Qibli **Asyut**

Abu Teeg

Aulda
Ismail **Sohag**

El-manshah

Al Balyana **Qena**

Dishna

Nag Hammadi

ebel Az Zuqaq El-harra

Bawiti

*Black
Desert*

*Western
(Libyan)
Desert*

*White
Desert
National
Park*

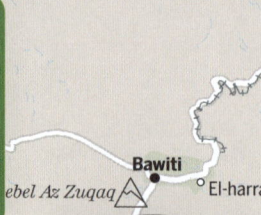

Scour the desolate
Wadi Al Hitan
for the bones of
33-million-year-old
whales (p84)
🚶 1½hr from Tunis
Village

*Eastern
(Arabian)
Desert*

Explore the vast, remote
ruins of Akhenaten's **Tell Al
Amarna** (p89)
🚗 1½hr from Minya

Admire some of Egypt's
most sublime Coptic art at
the **Red Monastery** (p95)
🚗 20min from Sohag

Experience Abydos' ethereal
light in the magnificent **Temple of Seti I** (p97; pictured
above left)
🚶 1½hr from Sohag

Glimpse ancient
Egypt's brightest
colours at Dendara's
Temple of Hathor
(p99; pictured
above)
🚗 15min from Qena

Nile Valley

Gulf of Suez

NORTHERN NILE VALLEY
Trip Builder

*Great
Sand
Sea*

Most travellers pass 'Middle Egypt' by on trains
between Luxor and Cairo. But stick around to explore
an untold wealth of Pharaonic riches and Coptic
heritage sites. Virtually free of crowds, the Northern
Nile Valley is Egypt's best-kept secret.

*Western
(Libyan)
Desert*

Limestone Plateau

Lake Nasser

0 ——— 100 km
0 ——— 50 miles

Practicalities

ARRIVING

Train The stations of Minya, Asyut and Sohag are well connected to Cairo and Luxor.

Bus Bus companies like Go Bus link Cairo with all Nile Valley hubs.

MONEY

Book online where possible and carry cash, including 10 and 20 Egyptian pounds for tips, expected by site guardians and police escorts.

POLICE ESCORTS

While you're free to explore, police generally insist on providing an escort for excursions between Al Fayoum and Qena.

WHERE TO STAY

Place	Pro/Con
Minya	Middle Egypt's best base, with excellent-value hotels in the centre for all budgets.
Abydos	A pair of comfortable options just opposite the temple complex.
Tunis Village	Good spread of guesthouses brimming with rural charm.
Qena	Budget options by the station. Luxury along the Nile.

EATING & DRINKING

A regional favourite breakfast spread stars *asal eswad* (molasses), also known as 'black honey', boiled from locally grown sugarcane and served with *fiteer* (flaky pastry) and fermented cheese. As elsewhere, juices and elaborate smoothies (pictured left) reign in Middle Egypt while alcohol is especially sparse; even larger cities here are entirely dry.

Best grills Orkeed, Minya (p100; pictured left)

Must-try kushari Koshary Goha, Sohag (p100)

GETTING AROUND

Car Private car is best. Security protocols make renting your own more hassle than it's worth, and hardly less expensive than hiring a driver, easily arranged by agencies and at most hotels.

Train Though slow and expensive, trains are the best (and only) public transport option here.

Microbus Only microbuses (generally off-limits to foreigners) link the region's towns to each other.

TOP: ALEXANDER FARNSWORTH/GETTY IMAGES BOTTOM: MOHAMED ABD ELKAREEM ALI/SHUTTERSTOCK

DEC–FEB	**MAR–MAY**	**JUN–AUG**	**SEP–NOV**
Chilly nights and occasional clouds, but pleasant afternoons	Ideal, sunny weather for outings, particularly in April	Heat can limit outdoor activity for much of the day	Perfect weather, with soft light, a photographer's boon

08 Fayoum
ESCAPE

ART | HISTORY | ADVENTURE

A wound-down retreat for Cairenes, Al Fayoum makes an excellent base for off-road exploring beyond its fertile radius, with smatterings of temples, slumping pyramids, colour-shifting lakes and strange desert formation. Stranger still is its famous trove of 33-million-year-old whales.

🗺 How To

Getting around You'll need 4WD for a number of highlights (including Wadi Al Hitan). Public transport links villages, but it's best to join a private tour or hire a driver.

When to go Spring or fall (weekdays

are best); late November for the ceramics-centric Tunis Village Festival; winter solstice for the magical solar alignment within Qasr Qarun.

Top tip Swing by Al Fayoum's pyramids on the way to or from Cairo.

Village Life

Near the picturesque shores of Lake Qarun, the tiny, arty Tunis Village is the ideal base in Al Fayoum. Its guesthouses overflow with bougainvillea and rustic charm. Sharing the walkways with donkey carts and egrets, and spotting clay pigeon towers en route, duck into the **Fayoum Pottery School** on a stroll down Sharia Porret, named for the school's late Swiss founder. This ceramicist settled in the village in the 1960s. Her multigenerational legacy now thrives in the workshops of her talented local students. While soaking up this slice of rural Egypt, try your hand at the pottery wheel or go boating or horseback riding, but don't pass up the chance to explore further afield in Al Fayoum.

📖 Cult of Sobek

Fayoum was a major centre for the ancient cult of Sobek, the crocodile god. Dozens of temples kept sacred crocodiles in pools, later embalmed and worshipped for their divine blessings of fertility to both land and people.

Top left Wadi Al Hitan (p84)
Left Fayoum Pottery School
Above Fayoum Pottery School

NORTHERN NILE VALLEY EXPERIENCES

The 'Oasis' & Beyond

You can bike to **Qasr Qarun**, a small temple of Sobek, but you'll need 4WD for the far more expansive remains of the goddess cult centre at **Medinat Madi**, the 'City of the Past'. This was built by Amenemhat III, the 12th-dynasty pharaoh responsible for Al Fayoum's ancient (and still functioning) canal. Though it's often referred to as an oasis, Al Fayoum's fertile pocket has always been fed by the Nile. For more recent waterworks, head to the heart of Medinat Al Fayoum to glimpse Ottoman-era **waterwheels**.

Deep in the Desert

Al Fayoum's star attraction lies deep in the dunes of the reserve of Wadi Rayyan, where a long, sandy track will land you at **Wadi Al Hitan**, a boneyard of whales dating back to the Eocene Epoch. The varied landscapes that speckle the reserve are striking and worth a detour, featuring fortress-like sandstone

◉ The Waterwheels of Al Fayoum

Approximately 20 water-driven wheels remain out of the 200 once scattered across Al Fayoum to irrigate its farmlands. While the current design of Fayoum's waterwheels may have been developed during the time of Muhammad Ali, their origins in the region likely date back to Roman times, much like the famous waterwheels of Hama, Syria. At the centre of Medinat Al Fayoum, four waterwheels remain, now a tourist attraction. Another easy place to see them is at Mandara village, where three 6m-high waterwheels sit beside the main road.

 By **Mahmoud Kamel,** a researcher and founder of Explore Fayoum tours @explorefayoum

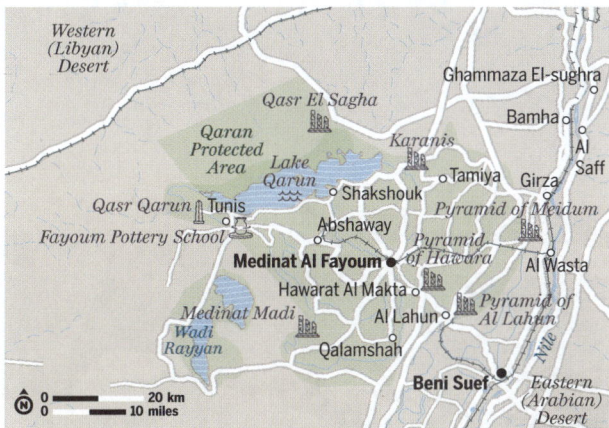

Left Waterwheel, Al Fayoum
Below Dimeh El Sabaa, Al Fayoum

bluffs and the three artificial lakes that lure the big weekend crowds from Cairo.

Stranger desert scenery awaits in the lonely expanse just north of **Lake Qarun**. Spot flamingos on the shores of the track to the towering, mud-brick walls of **Dimeh El Sabaa,** the 3rd-century CE temple complex of Soknopaiou Nesos ('the island of Soknopaiou', another name for Sobek). Nearby, admire the mammoth jigsaw stones of the mysterious Middle Kingdom temple of **Qasr El Sagha**, linked to a quarry by the faint but quite visible remnants of the oldest paved road in the world.

Highway Highlights

Along the road linking Cairo, wander the roadside ruins of Ptolemaic **Karanis**, ducking into the on-site Kom Aushim Museum for a few of the famous Fayoum portraits. Alternatively, wrap eastward from Medinat Al Fayoum to take in the area's trio of open pyramids, including the **Pyramid of Ha-wara**, built by Amenemhat III just beside his canal. Further along, don't miss the adrenaline-pumping descents into the tomb chambers of the pyramids of **Al Lahun** and **Meidum**.

09 Minya's Nile-Side DRIVES

HISTORY | CHURCHES | TOMBS

▬▬▬ After decades off the radar, friendly Minya – the 'Bride of Upper Egypt' – appears ready for the limelight as the Capital of Egyptian Culture in 2025. Commanding a historical gem-studded stretch of the Nile, this is Middle Egypt's best base.

🗺 **How To**

Getting around Hiring a private car through an agency or your hotel is the best option here. Taxi drivers are generally happy to be hired for the day.

When to go Autumn and spring are ideal weather-wise. On 22 August, Gebel At Teir swells with pilgrims for the Feast of the Assumption.

Top tip Get an early start for Tell Al Amarna, allowing time to combine with a visit to Tuna Al Gebel.

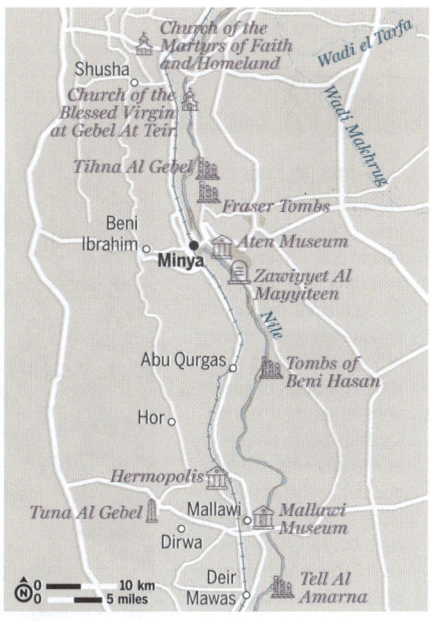

Cotton-Country Capital

Basing in Minya, home to the region's best hotel selection by miles, wander its compact core, from the railway station to the Corniche, one of Egypt's most pleasant. Along the way, admire the elegant villas of 19th-century cotton magnates. It was the surrounding countryside's cultivation of 'white gold' that fuelled this provincial capital's boom.

Along the water, take in the pretty Nile views while savouring grills at Orkeed (p100) or sipping a smoothie aboard C-Boat (p100). Beyond the pyramid-shaped **Aten Museum** (built in 2010 but yet to be opened), a thin strip of farmland hugs the base of the limestone cliffs beyond, pockmarked with tombs, temples, quarries and ancient churches begging to be explored.

Top left River Nile, Minya
Left Aten Museum

The Road North

Facing fields of sugarcane and sunflowers, the Old Kingdom **Fraser Tombs** were carved into the cliffs roughly 4500 years ago. Another nearby cluster of Ptolemaic-era temples is huddled around a chisel-scarred hump in the ridge known as **Tihna Al Gebel**, overlooking the town of the same name. Through a locked gateway, you'll spot several mummified crocodiles in situ.

Atop **Gebel At Teir** (Bird Mountain), one of Egypt's most celebrated Coptic **churches** is believed to house a sacred cave where Mary and Jesus rested on their flight into Egypt. Opposite the Nile, the far newer **Church of the Martyrs of Faith and Homeland** honours mostly local Copts, murdered by the Islamic State on a Libyan beach in 2014.

ⓘ Security Escorts

Throughout Middle Egypt, foreign travellers can expect police to insist on providing security escorts for excursions beyond city boundaries or, particularly in Sohag and Asyut, even within the cities themselves. Sometimes this means a separate police vehicle with armed officers in tow or a one-person detail riding along in your car. Either way, show only appreciation, even if this long-observed protocol causes some delay. To minimise hassle, try to clearly convey your itinerary before setting out. The fact that the police allow tourists to roam within Minya is another point for it being the region's best base.

🏛 The City of Akhenaten

Despite the profound impact of the heretical Akhenaten's break from old tradition, his city, Akhetaten ('Horizon of the Sun') survived as Egypt's capital for less than 15 years. The vast settlement, now known as Tell Al Amarna, was abandoned a decade after the pharaoh's death.

The Road South

Only a short hop from Minya, the Muslim necropolis of **Zawiyyet Al Mayyiteen** forms a sea of mud-brick domes, bounded to the south by what's left of a 4th-dynasty step pyramid. Climb the ridge here for spectacular views, then continue to the tombs over the village of **Beni Hasan**, wonderfully decorated as testaments to the power of Middle Kingdom nomarchs (governors). At nearby **Speos Artemidos**, a smattering of ancient quarries and cave temples guard the mouth of a wadi.

Mark off a separate day for **Tell Al Amarna**, a widely scattered site. During the 18th dynasty, it was this desolate stretch that was chosen by Pharaoh Akhenaten – perhaps the world's first monotheist – for his short-lived city, named for and devoted to the sun god Ra alone. The sunlit ruins are scant, but the tombs carved into the valleys' walls are worth the slog to reach, not least the **Tomb of Ay**, Akhenaten's vizier and successor to Tutankhamun, Akhenaten's son.

Across the Nile, peruse the rich finds at the **Mallawi Museum** and the open-air museum of ancient **Hermopolis** (encircled by modern Al Ashmunein) en route to the West Bank necropolis of **Tuna Al Gebel**. Vast catacombs lie buried beneath the sand here, built for untold baboons and birds.

Left Zawiyyet Al Mayyiteen
Top right Tuna Al Gebel
Above Tihna Al Gebel

Coptic
ICONS

01 St Mark
The evangelist is honoured as the founder of the Coptic Church, believed to have arrived in Alexandria in 48 CE.

02 Tawadros II
The 118th pope since St Mark, Tawadros II has held the title of Patriarch of Alexandria since 2012.

03 St Anthony
Revered as the father of monasticism, this desert-dwelling hermit is depicted in the traditional garb of a monk.

04 Coptic cross
As an indelible mark of identity, many Coptic children have this symbol tattooed on their inner wrists.

05 Coptic language
Still used in the liturgy today, the Coptic language descends directly from the ancient tongue of the pharaohs.

06 Iconostasis
The wooden screen that separates a church's sanctuary from the nave is often embellished with geometric patterns and ivory inlay.

07 The Holy Family's flight

The biblical story of the flight of Mary, Jesus and Joseph into Egypt is key to the Coptic tradition.

08 St George

The 'Prince of Martyrs' is easily recognised, most often depicted on horseback slaying the dragon, symbolising triumph over evil.

09 St Barbara

Beheaded by her own father, this storied Christian martyr is popular among women, believed to bestow strength, protection and resilience.

10 Abu Sifin

This beloved 3rd-century martyr is seen wielding his namesake pair of swords, one miraculously gifted by the Archangel Michael.

11 Theotokos

As in other Eastern Christian traditions, images of Mary as 'Mother of God' or 'God-bearer' are widespread in Coptic churches.

10 Asyut's Mountain
MONASTERIES

CHURCHES | HISTORY | ARCHITECTURE

A wealth of ancient tombs and quarries sprinkle the cliffs bounding modern Asyut to the west. Tracing the ridge north or south from here, you'll discover a pair of particularly hallowed monasteries, the eminence of each in the Coptic tradition still drawing steady streams of pilgrims: Al Muharraq, at the foot of Gebel Qusqam, and Deir Dirunka, halfway up Gebel Asyut.

How To

Getting around Security protocols make private transport for Asyut's outlying sites the only viable option, easily arranged at hotels or with taxi drivers. Expect to be assigned an escort.

When to go Pilgrims filter through year-round, but converge in their tens of thousands on Deir Al Muharraq in late June and Deir Dirunka in late August.

Top tip While long day trips from Minya are (barely) doable, you'll be rewarded by basing yourself in Asyut.

Top left Ancient quarry above the Tombs of Al Hammamiya
Bottom left Iconostasis, Deir Al Muharraq

The Burnt Monastery Revered as a 'Second Bethlehem', **Deir Al Muharraq** is where, according to Coptic tradition, the Holy Family made their longest stop in Egypt. Slipping past its fortress-like walls, you'll veer right to the signposted 'ancient church'. Inside, admire the right-side iconostasis (wooden screen), adorned with inlaid-ivory crosses. According to believers, it was beneath the red carpet right here that one of Jesus' wells once miraculously bubbled. The plain yet striking iconostasis to the left belongs to an erstwhile Ethiopian church, which was crammed onto the building's rooftop until it was razed in 1936.

Monastery of the Virgin Mary At least as alive is **Deir Dirunka**, the sprawling monastic complex just south of Asyut. Past more giant gates, a 22m-tall statue of Mary welcomes pilgrims, while at the end of the steep road is the entrance to the cavernous Church of the Virgin Mary. It has certainly made the most of an already impressive Pharaonic quarry cutting deep into the side of the mountain.

While you're here In sharp contrast to these two living landmarks are two silent clusters of Old Kingdom tombs. The **Tombs of Mir**, half-buried in dunes, a short hop from Deir Al Muharraq, hide spectacular painted scenes bursting with colour, while carved into the Nile Valley's eastern walls are the rarely seen **Tombs of Al Hammamiya**.

Terminus of the Holy Family Trail

In a 5th-century vision, the Coptic Pope Theophilus recounted the flight of the Holy Family – Mary, Joseph and the infant Jesus – into Egypt, escaping the wrath of King Herod on a zigzagging route that has become a pilgrimage path: the Holy Family Trail, stretching from the Delta southward, deep into Upper Egypt.

According to Theophilus' vision and the monks at Deir Dirunka, it was here that an angel informed the Holy Family of Herod's death, advising that the coast was clear for their safe return. Deir Dirunka's rival claim, however, places their journey's end about 50km further south.

11 Sublime
COPTIC ART

ART | CULTURE | HISTORY

On the doorsteps of Sohag, squeezed between deep green fields and the desert are the ancient Red and White Monasteries – two of Egypt's most breathtaking Coptic Christian achievements, built in part with the blocks and columns of nearby Ptolemaic temples. It's inside the glorious, newly restored sanctuary of the Red Monastery in particular that you'll feel yourself entranced.

ANTHON JACKSON/LONELY PLANET

🗺 How To

Getting around Sohag's central train station is well linked up and down the Nile. Private transport, the only viable option for exploring beyond town, is easily arranged via hotels or directly with taxi drivers.

When to go Avoid summer and start your day early to elude peak heat.

Sohag police Security protocols in and around Sohag are the strictest in Middle Egypt. Expect an escort on excursions even within the city.

ANTHON JACKSON/LONELY PLANET

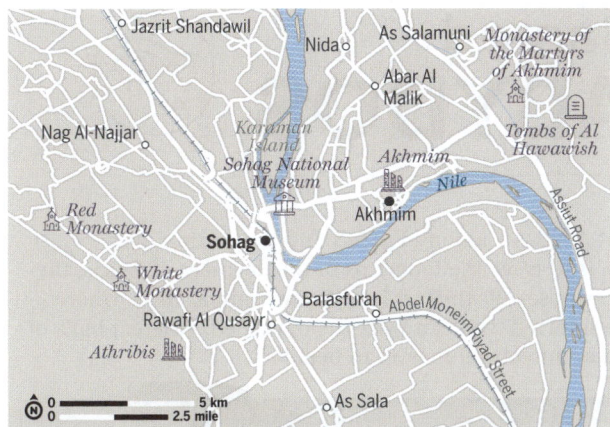

Top left Red Monastery
Bottom left Tombs of Al Hawawish

Celebrated monasteries A half-hour drive from Sohag stands a pair of hauntingly beautiful remnants from late antiquity. The **Red Monastery's** Sanctuary of St Bishoi and St Bigol, constructed around 500 CE, was until recently blackened by centuries of smoke. Painstakingly restored in 2018, they again enliven the space's apses, niches and columns, most of them painted in the 6th and 7th centuries CE. Far fainter reliefs remain in the open-air courtyard outside, formerly the church's nave.

The sanctuary of the **White Monastery**, 3km to the south, though somewhat plainer, feels every bit as ancient, studded with shell-capped niches and frescoes, most dating back to the 12th century CE. Founded in the 5th century by the hermit St Shenoute, it's named for its recycled limestone blocks. Circling its outer walls, you'll spot hidden hieroglyphs, flipped upside-down just to spite the old gods.

Both monasteries are free to enter. Remember to leave your shoes outside the sanctuaries.

While you're here It's worth the short hop south of the monasteries to the Ptolemaic-era ruins of **Athribis**. Its temple to the lion-headed goddess Repit was a source for the monasteries' building materials. At Sohag's **museum**, peruse a good sampling of the area's Pharaonic finds, then admire the **colossi of Akhmim**, standing 11m tall at the centre of Sohag's satellite city. Continue eastward to climb to the rock-hewn **Tombs of Al Hawawish**, an Old Kingdom cemetery.

East Bank Monasteries

Overshadowed by Sohag's famous monasteries to the west is an eastern cluster on the opposite banks of the Nile, eight in total and equally esteemed among faithful Copts for their martyrs' relics. While these span many centuries, the most famous instance of blood-letting here is believed to have occurred in the 4th century CE, when the Roman general Arianus oversaw the slaughter of 8140 Christians. Only recently exhumed, the supposed remains of a portion are displayed in these East Bank monasteries, with a particular preponderance of glass-encased corpses crammed into the **Monastery of the Martyrs of Akhmim**.

12 Sacred ABYDOS

TEMPLES | ART | HISTORY

A journey to ancient Abydos – among Egypt's and the world's most venerable pilgrimage sites, is to trace the footsteps of the devotees of Osiris, the murdered, resurrected god whose cult thrived here for millennia. Here, where the earliest pharaohs were interred, you can walk the darkened, ethereal halls of the Temple of Seti I, a true architectural marvel to behold.

ANTHON JACKSON/LONELY PLANET

🗺 How To

Getting here Most visitors arrive on bus tours, but independent travellers can alight at Balyana's railway station, 10km east of Abydos, then hail a tuk-tuk or taxi.

Where to stay Choose between the basic **Flower of Life** guesthouse and the upscale **House of Life**, each within a short walk of the temple complex.

Beat the crowds Your best odds for solitude are before 10am and after 3pm.

MERLIN74/SHUTTERSTOCK

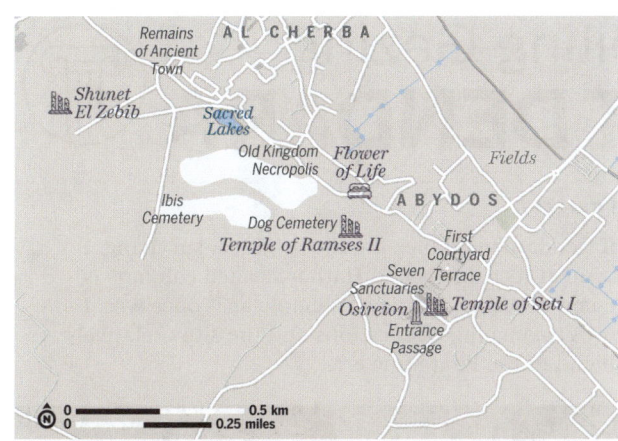

Top left Temple of Ramses II
Bottom left Temple of Seti I

NORTHERN NILE VALLEY EXPERIENCES

Temple of Seti I In approaching the Temple of Seti I, you'll cross a pair of broad courtyards and stair ramps constructed by Seti's son Ramses II, who's also responsible for the portico ahead, adorned with reliefs depicting his military glories.

Stepping inside, allow your eyes to adjust as you walk amid the 24 pillars of Ramses' hypostyle hall. Yet another stair ramp leads to the hypostyle hall of Seti I, supported by 36 pillars and featuring some of the finest reliefs found anywhere in Egypt. Beyond these, the sanctuaries of the temple's gods lay, with Osiris' shrine placed third from the right. Exiting to the left, you'll spot the famous sequence of pharaohs known as the **Gallery of the Kings**. Beyond this a staircase leads up to the right, exiting the temple to a ledge overlooking the mysterious **Osireion**, a sacred island of unadorned megaliths of granite, believed to have been built as a cenotaph of Seti I as the resurrected Osiris.

Temple of Ramses II Few take the short desert path running north of here to the smaller Temple of Ramses II, of which relatively little remains. Still, basking in full sunlight, its surviving reliefs are an impressive sight.

Shunet El Zebibb History buffs may wish to continue to the much older remains of Abydos' original complex, highlighted by the hulking, mud-brick enclosure of Shunet El Zebib.

📖 Omm Seti

Abydos has served as a sacred place of pilgrimage for millennia, a role that's been somewhat revived in recent times with a stream of eclectic seekers, each discerning a special, magnetic energy to Seti I's great temple. Pioneering the trend was London-born Dorothy Eady (1904–81), having spent her last decades as a draughtswoman here, where older villagers remember her as Omm Seti, the 'Mother of Seti'. Since as early as age four, she'd felt an affinity for Abydos, believing it to have once been her home. Indeed, her work drew on old 'memories' of a life as a temple priestess and Pharaonic concubine.

13 Ceiling Gazing AT DENDARA

ARCHITECTURE | HISTORY | RELIEFS

The striking blues of Dendara's complex are the brightest surviving from ancient Egypt. Gazing up at its ceilings and Hathor-headed columns is perhaps the closest you'll come to seeing an ancient temple as it once was. Its remarkable preservation owes to ongoing restorations and the site's relatively late construction at the tail end of the Pharaonic era.

ANTHON JACKSON/LONELY PLANET

🗺 How To

Getting here It's a 15-minute taxi ride from Qena's railway station to the temple. When you're done, the tourist police can call a taxi for your return.

When to go Arrive at opening time to beat the big buses; with luck, you'll have the place all to yourself.

Temple roof and crypts It's worth the extra cost to reach the temple's highest and lowest points.

ANTHON JACKSON/LONELY PLANET

YASEMIN OZDEMIR/SHUTTERSTOCK

Far left Reliefs, Temple of Hathor
Left Temple of Hathor

Last of the native Pharaohs On your right, a pair of *mammisi* (birth houses) mark the approach to the enormous temple. The second of these is the oldest structure around, built by Nectanebo II (358–340 BCE), the last Egyptian pharaoh before Ptolemaic (Greek) rule. The first is Roman. In between them, look for carved crosses from a 5th-century Christian basilica.

The reliefs Accentuated by a steady supply of sunlight, the most vivid of Dendara's colours adorn the ceilings of the temple's first enclosure. Right of the entrance, over the far-western aisle, find the sky goddess Nut preparing to swallow the sun disc. Built by the Roman Emperor Tiberius, the enclosure is encircled with reliefs of imperial offerings to the gods, conveying a continuation of tradition despite foreign rule. Around the back of the temple is the sole surviving relief of Cleopatra, standing beside her son, Caesarion, by Julius Caesar.

The goddess Hathor Crowning the columns in both the first and somewhat gloomier second enclosure, built by the Ptolemies, are columns of four-sided heads of Hathor, the goddess of beauty, fertility and love, depicted either with the head of a cow or a woman wearing a sun disc as a headdress between cattle horns. On the New Year, the goddess' image was brought from the temple sanctuary to greet the first rays of the sun god Ra.

☆ The Dendara Zodiac

The best-known of the Hathor temple's bas-reliefs is an extraordinary ancient map of the stars, a large stone slab that adorned the ceiling of a chapel situated on the temple's roof. Sketched during Napoleon's Egyptian campaign, the carving stirred controversy in Europe for its supposed vintage, perhaps even exceeding the age of Earth according to the Bible. In 1821, a French thief used explosives to dislodge it from the ceiling, carting it off to France. Its age has since been pinpointed to approximately 51 BCE, thanks to depictions of a pair of eclipses known to occur only once in a thousand years.

Listings

BEST OF THE REST

 Local Flavours

Ibis Restaurant $$

International favourites served in a serene garden overlooking Lake Qarun in Tunis Village. Swiss chef Markus Iten's on-site cooking school has trained a generation of local chefs.

Kom El Dikka Restaurant $$

This Tunis Village favourite is best known for its farm-to-table succulent roasted duck, but there are also excellent pigeon and chicken dishes.

Orkeed $$

Minya's local pick for traditional Egyptian meals, including pigeon, *molokhiyya* (garlicky leaf soup) and kebabs, is enjoyed alongside lofty Nile views.

Abou Shakra $

At the centre of Asyut, you'll find all of Egypt's classic grilled-meat plates (kebab, kofta and *shish tawooq*) plus *tagens* (stew cooked in a clay pot) and desserts.

Koshary Goha $

Best *kushari* in Sohag; separate seating for women and families. Unless you're starving, order a small to leave room for *ruz bi laban* (rice pudding).

 Stylish Stays

Holy Family Hotel

Just opposite the ancient church atop Gebel At Teir, a short drive from Minya, this hotel boasts fabulous Nile views and a wonderful rooftop terrace with a pool.

Omar El-Khayam Hotel

On a quiet, leafy side street near Minya's Corniche, this immaculate hotel sets the standard, with all manner of mod cons and extremely helpful, English-speaking staff.

Savoy

The pick of the khedives a century ago, just opposite Minya's railway station, was lovingly restored and offers spectacular value, with elegant rooms and a rooftop restaurant.

C-Boat

Minya's budget pick, with small, well-appointed rooms floating off the Corniche and breakfast on the deck's cafe.

Diamond Azur Hotel

Sohag's best-value accommodation, its rooms fitted with balconies facing the Nile. The breakfast buffet is excellent, and the staff are friendly and proficient in English.

Flower of Life

Friendly Ameer's family-run guesthouse in Abydos village offers spartan rooms, home-cooked meals (half-board), and a rooftop view over the adjacent ruins of the Temple of Ramses II.

House of Life

Abydos' most luxurious offering is a short hop up the road from the temple entrance.

House of Life

The mock-Pharaonic decor is excessive, but there's a wellness centre, a nice pool and sparkling rooms.

Hathor Hotel

Qena's recently revived Nile-side resort, complete with a pool and restaurant overlooking the water, is by far the most comfortable accommodation option in town.

Grand Hotel Qena

Solid budget pick in Qena with clean, bland (but noisy) rooms within an easy walk of the train station. If full, try the nearby, nearly identical Dream Hotel.

More Middle Egyptian Heritage

Al Qaitbey Mosque

In the heart of Medinat Al Fayoum, this 500-year-old mosque is one of a trio of Mamluk-era mosques on this stretch of the Bahr Yusuf Canal, only a short walk to the west of the city's famous waterwheels.

Monastery of the Archangel Gabriel at Naqlun

At the southeastern fringe of the Fayoum, this 4th-century monastery is a worthwhile detour from the Desert Road, where a Polish team is working to restore its 11th-century frescoed walls.

Al Babein Quarry

North of Gebel At Teir near Minya, Al Babein Quarry shows where New Kingdom and modern quarries meet. Look for a locked Hathor shrine and a Ramses II stele.

Deir Rifeh

South of Asyut's Deir Dirunka, more Middle Kingdom caves in the same ridge house a monastery devoted to martyr Prince Tadros. Alert the village custodian before heading up the mountain road.

Basuna Mosque

Tombs of Al Bahnasa

Between Cairo and Minya, this Muslim cemetery features domed mausolea of *sahaba* (Companions of the Prophet Muhammad), said to have died here in large numbers during the 7th-century Arab conquest.

Basuna Mosque

Built in 2019, this innovative mosque in the centre of tiny Basuna drew acclaim for its ground-breaking design. It's worth the 19km drive north of Sohag for enthusiasts of modern architecture.

Mosque of Sidi Abd Al Rahim Al Qenawi

Qena's most celebrated mosque, dedicated to 12th-century saint Abd Al Rahim Al Qenawi, hosts the city's *moulid* (birthday celebration of the saint), drawing pilgrims and culminating on the 14th of Sha'ban.

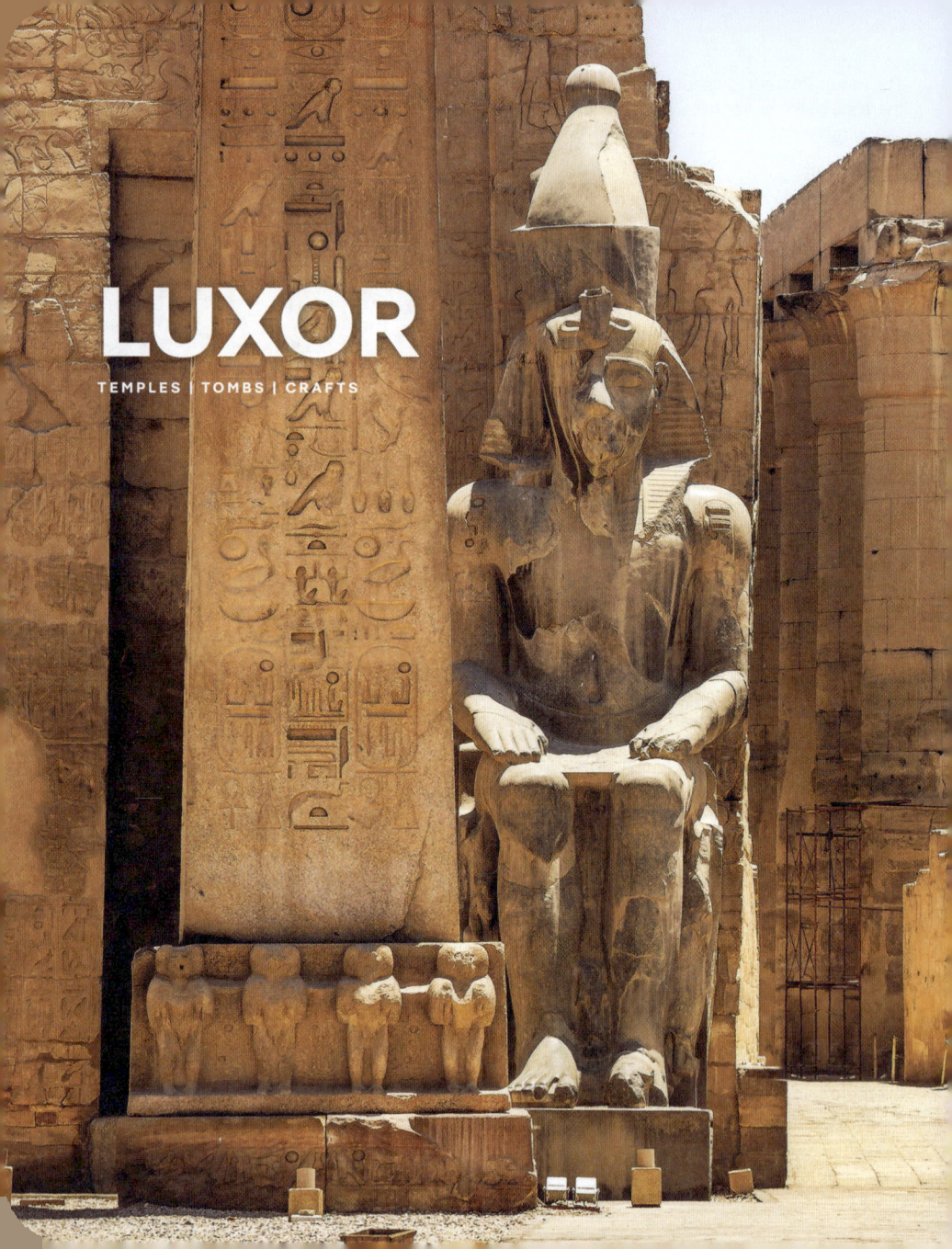

LUXOR

TEMPLES | TOMBS | CRAFTS

Descend into painted tombs (pictured right) in the **Valley of the Kings** (p116)
🚢 20min from west-bank ferry

Valley of the Kings

A L Q U R N

Assasif Tombs

Float to the heavens above **Thebes** in a balloon (p120)
🚗 10min from west-bank ferry

D R A A B U ' L N A G A

Cemetery

Tombs of the Nobles

Explore craftwork, ancient and modern, around **west-bank temples** (p122)
🚢 10min from ticket office

O L D G U R N A

D E I R A L M E D I N A

Fields

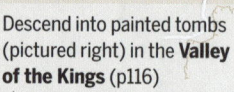

Valley of the Queens

Cycle between **west-bank temples** from the Colossi (p118)
🚲 20min from west-bank ferry

K O M L O L A H

Fields

N E W G U R N A

LUXOR
Trip Builder

Famed for elaborate last rites, Luxor has in fact always been less about dying and more about celebrating life. Equally today, a balloon ride or strolling along the Corniche is likely to be as memorable as touring tombs and temples.

0
0
2 km
1 mile

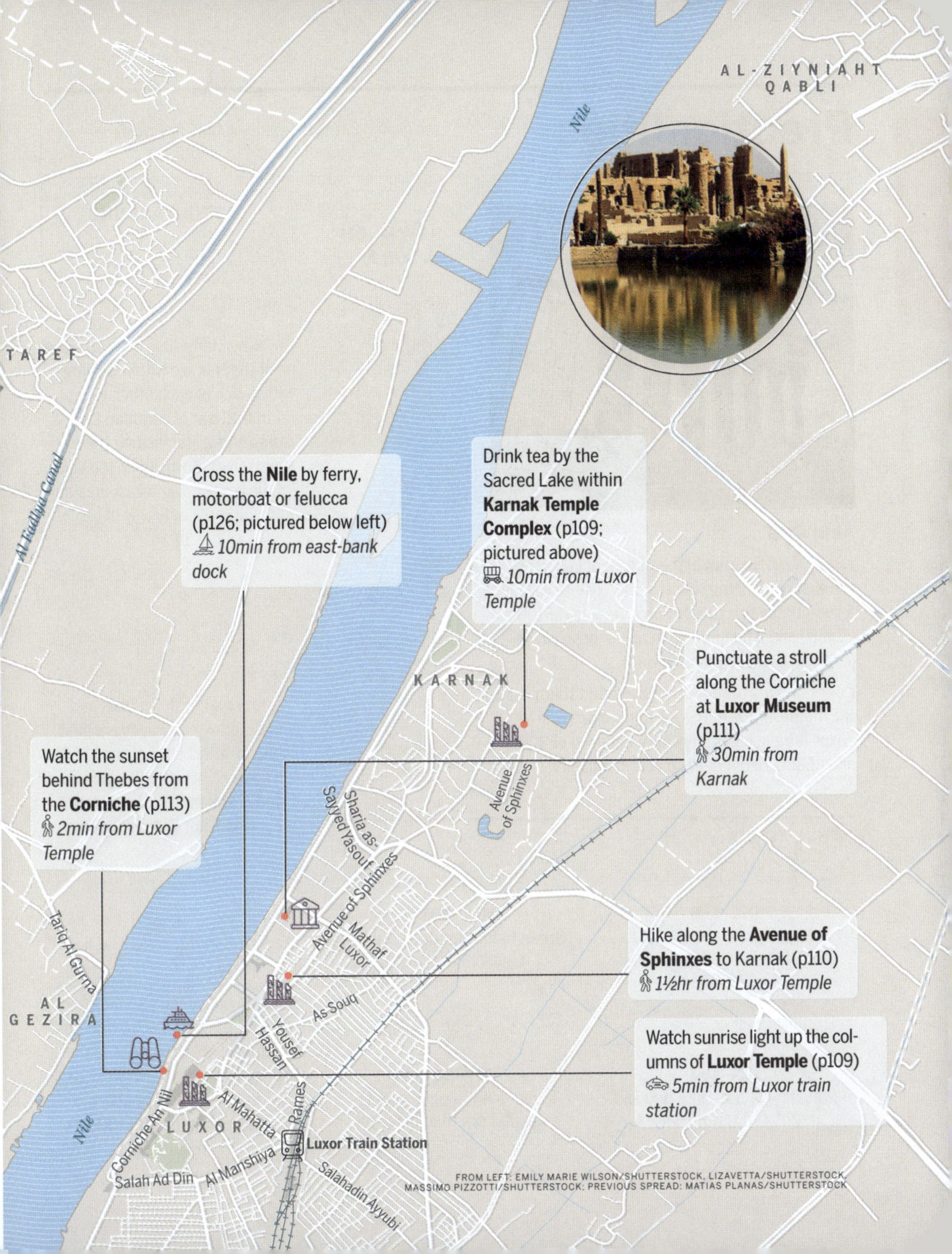

AL-ZIYNIAHT
QABLI

TAREF

Cross the **Nile** by ferry, motorboat or felucca (p126; pictured below left) ⛵ *10min from east-bank dock*

Drink tea by the Sacred Lake within **Karnak Temple Complex** (p109; pictured above) 🚋 *10min from Luxor Temple*

Punctuate a stroll along the Corniche at **Luxor Museum** (p111) 🚶 *30min from Karnak*

KARNAK

Watch the sunset behind Thebes from the **Corniche** (p113) 🚶 *2min from Luxor Temple*

Avenue of Sphinxes

Sharia as-Sayyed Yasouf

Hike along the **Avenue of Sphinxes** to Karnak (p110) 🚶 *1½hr from Luxor Temple*

Tariq Al Gurna

AL GEZIRA

Mathaf Luxor

As Souq

Watch sunrise light up the columns of **Luxor Temple** (p109) 🚗 *5min from Luxor train station*

Nile

Corniche An Nil

Yousef Hassan

Al Mahatta

Rames

Luxor Train Station

LUXOR

Salah Ad Din

Al Marnshiya

Salahadin Ayyubi

Al Fadilya Canal

Practicalities

COLINMTHOMPSON/SHUTTERSTOCK

ARRIVING

Luxor Train Station In the middle of Luxor, on the east bank of the Nile. It's a 15-minute walk or a five-minute taxi ride to Luxor Temple (LE100 to LE450) and a further five minutes' drive to the jetty for ferries to the west bank.

Luxor International Airport Located 10km from the middle of town. The 20-minute taxi ride to Luxor Temple costs anywhere between LE200 and LE800, depending on your bargaining skills.

HOW MUCH FOR A

Egyptian cotton T-shirt LE2500

Felucca sunset ride LE500

Sakara beer LE350

GETTING AROUND

Walking Many sites on both sides of the Nile are within walking distance of each other, except in the heat of summer. Save some energy for visiting the sites themselves. Karnak and the Valley of the Kings cover a vast area and walking is the only way to explore them.

Taxi and calèche Taxis and horse-drawn carriages are available for short hops (from LE50) on the east bank but bargain hard and check that 'pounds' means Egyptian, not British currency.

Boat A public ferry service (single/return LE50/60; 10 minutes) runs from jetties close to the centre of the east- and west-bank Corniches. Motorboats cover the same journey (LE100; five minutes).

WHEN TO GO

DEC–FEB
Cold nights, warm days, perfect for walking; high season

MAR–MAY
Green fields, hot days, balmy nights; high season

JUN–AUG
Punishingly hot, both day and night, but fewer visitors

SEP–NOV
Golden fields, cooler nights; fewer visitors than in winter

EATING

If you've ever fancied sampling stuffed pigeon, baby aubergines (pictured bottom right) and other Egyptian delicacies, Luxor is a good place to do so, with regional favourites such as duck, rabbit and bitter-leaf soups amplifying the menu. Restaurants housed in heritage buildings add an antique charm to the traditional cuisine.

For a more modern experience, the newly landscaped Corniche on the east bank has cafes and restaurants catering for more international tastes. Many hotels have roof terraces for watching the sun set behind Thebes.

Best cocktails Winter Palace Hotel (pictured top right; p124)

Must-try traditional dishes Sofra (p124)

CONNECT & FIND YOUR WAY

Wi-fi Readily available, but in budget hotels free access is only available in communal areas.

Navigation Luxor is split between the modern, busier east bank (with temples of Luxor and Karnak, tour agents, banks and most restaurants and hotels) and the more rural west bank, site of temples and the Valley of the Kings. Ferries and motorboats connect the two.

WHERE TO STAY

Most visitors stay on Luxor's east bank, convenient for the temple sites of Karnak and Luxor. For the full Luxor experience, though, sharing time between both banks is a must.

Neighbourhood	Pro/Con
East bank	Top-end accommodation is more readily available on the east bank, with many international chains represented. Convenient budget options are near the train station.
West bank	Tranquil budget and midrange options are spread around the west bank. These make it easier to go ballooning and reach the temples and tombs of Thebes.
Luxor fringe	A couple of beautiful traditional houses have been converted to hotels a taxi-ride from Gezira on the west bank.

LUXOR PASS

Purchasable only from Karnak and Valley of the Kings, this pass (premium normal/student US$250/130) is valid for five days and covers all archaeological sites. Payable in dollars or euros cash only. Passport photo required.

MONEY

Carry lots of small change in Egyptian pounds for tips, which are expected for all services including illuminating dark tombs. Dollars or euros are necessary for some permits and passes.

Two Top
TEMPLES

PHARAOHS | TEMPLES | SHOWTIME

In a town boasting 30% of the world's antiquities (at least by some estimates), it's difficult to select just two of Luxor's many Pharaonic temples to visit. Spend a morning at Karnak Temple Complex, with its forest of lotus columns, and the evening at atmospherically lit Luxor Temple, and you'll have experienced two of the Nile-side best.

ALEXANTON/SHUTTERSTOCK

🗺 How To

Getting here The two temples are located close to the Nile, on Luxor's east bank, and can be reached by *calèche* (horse-drawn carriage), taxi or on foot.

When to go Two weeks before the start of Ramadan, the Moulid of Abu Al Haggag festival takes place around Luxor Temple.

Cost Tickets to the Karnak Temple Complex (visitor/student LE600/300; 6am to 4pm) and Luxor Temple (LE500/250; 7am to 7pm) are only payable by card (or use Luxor Pass).

BIST/SHUTTERSTOCK

Top left Luxor Temple
Bottom left Karnak Temple Complex

A temple 'most esteemed' Within view of the Nile, **Karnak** is a spectacular complex of decorated temples, protected behind massive, monumental gateways (pylons). Built by many great pharaohs over 1500 years in honour of their gods, Karnak – 'the most esteemed of places' – was Egypt's most significant point of worship. Today, walking through its clustered pillars in the famous **hypostyle hall** is a highlight of a visit to Luxor.

Exploring this vast complex can prove bewildering. Hiring a guide (available from the ticket office; US$10 per person) helps, but so does some planning. Use the model in the ticket hall to select your own points of interest and navigate the site. Make sure to include a stop at **Abydos Oasis** beside the **Sacred Lake** – the only place inside the complex serving refreshments.

The city's temple namesake Visiting the smaller but beautifully proportioned **Luxor Temple**, it's easy to see how Luxor earnt the sobriquet of 'greatest open-air museum in the world'. Likely to be the first monument you'll see on a visit to Luxor, it has become part of the city's iconography, gracing the Corniche beside the Nile.

Once the focus of annual ritual during the inundation of the Nile, the temple known as Al Uqsur (fortifications) in Arabic, and from which the city's name derives, continues the tradition of celebration. *Aida* renditions take place in October and festivities during the **Moulid of Abu Al Haggag**.

☼ Sound & Light Show

The soundtrack may be dated but that won't matter once you enter through the first pylon of Karnak's great temple and watch as treasures emerge from the blackness of night. Running since 1972, Karnak's nightly sound-and-light show continues to delight visitors, providing the only chance to visit this world wonder at night.

Shows in English start at 7pm, with tickets bought from the kiosk outside the complex entrance. It gets very cold walking through the grounds in winter, so bring a warm layer.

Not to be outdone, Luxor Temple is also beautifully lit at night, albeit without an accompanying show.

Walking the
SACRED WAY

WALKING | MUSEUMS | NILE

The two great temples of Luxor's east bank were once linked by an esplanade. Today's **Avenue of Sphinxes**, excavated through the town centre, follows its course. Walking this route and returning along the **Corniche** reunites ancient Luxor with its modern incarnation.

MOONFISHB/SHUTTERSTOCK

🗺 Trip Notes

Getting around Flat and pedestrian-only, the Avenue of Sphinxes (3km; 1½ hours) is shorter than the Corniche (3.5km; three to four hours, including museum visits).

When to go The unshaded Avenue of Sphinxes opens at 6am – the coolest time of day.

Admission The Avenue of Sphinxes is included in the Luxor Temple ticket but only as far as the **Misr Public Library**. A kiosk here sells onward tickets to Karnak (grand entrance pictured above).

🏛 Temple Treasures

In 1989, workers found 26 beautiful statues in the Temple of Luxor, buried by priests in Roman times. Look out for these, 16 of which are on display in the Luxor Museum, just off the Corniche. Among them is an exquisite rendering of the temple builder himself, kilted and muscular Amenhotep III.

03 If you've had enough of Shank's pony, opt for a horse from the **calèche stand** outside Karnak. For walkers, the landscaped Corniche is shaded with trees and dotted with Nile-side cafes.

K A R N A K

Nile

Calèche Stand – Karnak

Mut Temple Enclosure

Avenue of Sphinxes

04 Halfway along the return, you'll come to **Luxor Museum**. A gem among Egypt's many fine collection of antiquities, it houses some exquisite pieces.

Sharia as-Sayyed Yasouf

Sharia Serb

02 Pause to inspect ancient wine presses or rest on a shaded bench along the Avenue of Sphinxes (pictured left) en route to Karnak. You'll arrive at the seldom-visited **Mut Temple Enclosure** (separate ticket) by the 10th pylon.

05 End your Corniche stroll at the tiny **Mummification Museum** (pictured above). Detailing embalming rituals, it displays mummified animals among the fascinating exhibits.

Luxor Museum

Maabad Al Karnak

Avenue of Sphinxes

Mummification Museum

Al Montazah

Hatshepsut

Avenue of Sphinxes

Luxor Temple

As Souq

Mostafa Kamel

01 Start your walk at **Luxor Temple** (pictured right). Signboards describe the splendour of the annual Opet celebrations, when colourful processions carried statues of the gods between the ram's-headed sphinxes.

L U X O R

Al Mahatta

Ramses

Mohammed Farid

Corniche An Nil

Al Manshiya

Salah Ad Din

Luxor Train Station

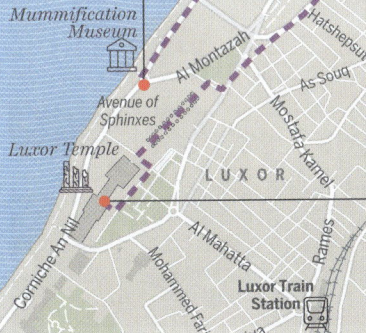

N 0 _____ 0.5 km
   0 _____ 0.25 miles

16 Making the Most of
MODERN LUXOR

SHOPPING | CAFE CULTURE | FOOD

On a trip to Luxor, the past looms large on every visitor's itinerary – so large, in fact, that it can completely overshadow the present. But focusing only on tombs and temples misses the point – ancient Thebes was all about the excitement of life and the desire to prolong it. Balance your Luxor experience, then, by engaging with the town of today.

🗺️ How To

Getting around Luxor's shopping and nightlife is mostly within walking distance, or a short *calèche* (horse-drawn carriage) ride from Luxor Temple.

When to go The east bank goes to sleep around lunchtime and comes alive from sunset onwards, when families stroll the Corniche and shop in town souqs.

Bargaining Bargaining is a must when shopping. The price is whatever you're willing to pay balanced against the vendor's expectation – in other words, a flexible concept.

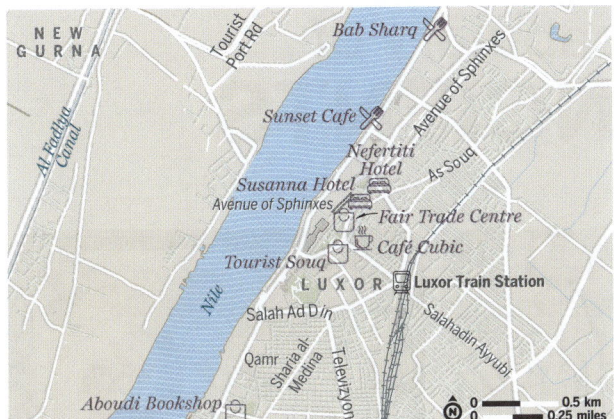

Top left East bank of Nile River, Luxor
Bottom left Tourist Souq, Luxor

Art of buying well However resolved against buying souvenirs, however small your bag, you'll find it almost impossible to escape without making some kind of purchase as you explore the shops and souqs of east-bank Luxor.

The trick to enjoying the experience rather than feeling bamboozled into a sale is to engage in the process. Sip the hospitality tea, chat about the vendors' family and let your eye roam over the goods on offer – the locally grown saffron and peppermint, the perfumes of pure essence, Egyptian cotton hand-loomed on the west bank, faience jewellery as lovely as a queen's necklace. The pressure to buy generally decreases with every minute spent 'just looking'.

Genuinely local goods are on offer at fixed prices in the **Fair Trade Centre**; **Aboudi Bookshop** sells publications and maps in English; and just about everything else can be found in the colourful **Tourist Souq** – all within a stone's throw of the Temple of Luxor.

Cafe culture While you're out shopping, spare time for a Turkish coffee or mint tea in **Café Cubic** in the Tourist Souq. Slowing the pace down is part of the Luxor experience, and all over town there are attractive cafes where it's fun just to while away time. Sit at the floating **Sunset Cafe** or **Bab Sharq** on the Corniche, and you can watch the public ferry shuttling across the Nile and feluccas heading upstream in the afternoon wind.

Best Nile Views

The east-bank Corniche is a great place to watch the morning sun lighting up the Nile with a backdrop of balloons, but to feel the Nile, you have to ride it. Take a felucca from either bank and watch fishermen in their boats with kingfishers flying alongside.

At around 4pm the sun begins to go down. The Nile fills with colour as motorboats and feluccas crowd the water for the sunset trips. For land-side views, sit at a Corniche cafe or the roof terraces of the **Nefertiti** and **Susanna** hotels, and watch the sunset.

■ **By Captain Ali** of Mona  Lisa east-bank felucca (*WhatsApp +20-10-6248-0567*)

Visual Vocabulary of
THE ANCIENTS

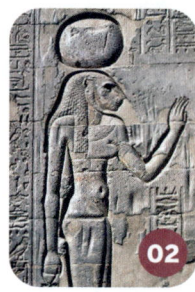

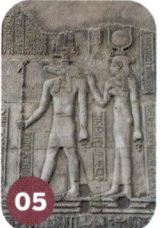

Prominent Pharaonic Gods

01 Atum
Thought by ancient Egyptians to be the first god and creator of the world, Atum fathered gods Tefnut and Shu.

02 Tefnut
Connected with water and dew, Tefnut (represented as a lion-headed woman) was attributed the power to bring rain.

03 Nut
In Egyptian mythology, Nut protects dead souls, swallowing the sun every night and giving birth to it each morning.

04 Isis and Osiris
Isis (healer and god of magic) and Osiris (god of fertility and the afterlife) were married siblings.

05 Hathor and Sobek
Hathor was goddess of love, joy, music and beauty, while Sobek, the crocodile-headed god of the Nile, controlled the inundation.

06 Horus
Falcon-headed Horus (associated with sky, hunting and war) was worshiped as the protector of Egypt and is pictured in many tombs.

07 Seth and Anubis
Seth was the god of storms and chaos, while gentle jackal-headed Annubis, god of

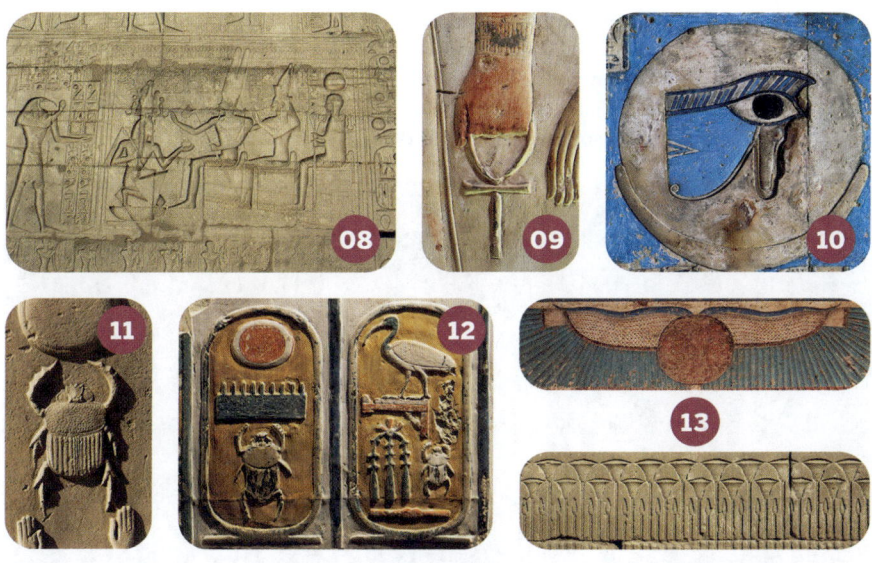

mummification, was associated with grief and mourning.

08 Trinity of Luxor gods

Amun, his wife Khonsu and son Mut were worshiped at Karnak. During annual Opet celebrations, their statues were taken to Luxor Temple.

Common Hieroglyphic Symbols

09 Ankh

The 'key of life' represents eternity and, as symbol of the Nile, the union of Isis and Osiris.

10 Eye of Horus

Still believed by some to ward off evil, envy and ill-health, the eye of Horus

is found in temple, tomb and town.

11 Scarab

Associated with protection, this powerful symbol was worn as an amulet by the ancients; it's now given for good luck.

12 Cartouche

An ancient nameplate protecting a person's 'ka,' or

life force, cartouches identified owners with their pharaonic monuments.

13 Winged sun and lotus

Lotuses represent rebirth and, like the double red-and-white crown, the unification of Egypt – also symbolised as the midday sun.

Descending into the
AFTERWORLD

TOMBS | MUMMIES | ARTISTRY

With temples and monuments, the Nile and walkable Corniches, Luxor is rich in treasures – but arguably the main excitement lies underground, in the Valley of the Kings. This honeycomb of decorated tombs has attracted visitors for centuries and remains the west bank's main destination. Naturally, it's perennially busy. Let the crowds create the atmosphere, or escape to quieter nearby tombs.

JAKUB KYNCL/SHUTTERSTOCK

📖 How To

Getting around Buggies ferry visitors from the ticket office to the main tomb area in the Valley of the Kings. Descending the shafts of any tomb requires physical effort. Tuk-tuks (LE50 for a short ride) travel between sites.

When to go Being at tomb sites before 6am helps beat the crowds.

Admission Tickets (card only) are bought at the Valley of the Kings and Valley of the Queens. For all other tombs, visit the Antiquities Inspectorate Ticket Office.

EVRENKALINBACAK/SHUTTERSTOCK

Map labels:
Entrance Gate & Ticket Office for Tutankhamun's Tomb
Valley of the Kings
Tomb of Ramses VI (KV-9)
Howard Carter's House & the Replica Tomb of Tutankhamun
Assasif Tombs
DRA ABU'L NAGA
Cemetery
TAREF
Tomb of Nefertari
Tombs of the Nobles
Deir Al Medina
Valley of the Queens
OLD GURNA
Fields
Al Fadiya Canal
Antiquities Inspectorate Ticket Office
NEW GURNA
0 1 km
0 0.5 miles
N

Top left Tomb of Ramses VI
Bottom left Deir Al Medina

Top Tomb Tips

- Download the **Theban Mapping Project** (*kv5.com*) website to your mobile phone for free, comprehensive guides to individual Valley of the Kings tombs.

- Spend the extra fee for **KV9**, the lesser-visited tomb of Ramses V/VI, with beautiful, well-preserved decoration.

- Bring a guidebook and torch to fully appreciate the Tombs of the Nobles, showcasing domestic rather than religious scenes.

- The Tomb of Nefertari, although expensive, is the Valley of the Queens masterpiece.

- Visit **Howard Carter's House** for a faithful facsimile, and cheaper experience, of Tutankhamun's tomb.

■ **By Professor Kent Weeks**, celebrated Egyptologist (*thebanmappingproject.com*)

Tombs of royalty Yes, it's likely to be crowded. Yes, there will be impolite fellow visitors, elbowing their way through tomb shafts or stopping for endless selfies. But should that put you off? Enter the first tomb in the **Valley of the Kings**, sniff the dust of ages and let your eye alight on a string of painted or carved hieroglyphics, and the answer is clear.

The tombs of Egypt's ancient pharaohs are elaborate poetry to life, rather than a celebration of death, and as such were the dedicated work of thousands of engineers, labourers, painters, scholars and clerics. The Valley of the Kings was therefore a place of noise, artistry and mischief, where one tomb was being robbed even as another was being hidden in the honey-coloured cliffs.

Fit for a queen If you really can't hack the crowds, then a visit to the **Valley of the Queens** is likely to be a slightly quieter experience. Some of the most exquisitely decorated tombs in all Thebes (including the separately ticketed **Tomb of Nefertari**) are here.

Best of the rest Spare some energy to visit **Deir Al Medina**, the workers' village where artists decorated their own path to the afterlife. These, and the **Tombs of the Nobles**, are scattered around the mountainside and depict the best scenes of local life in ancient times.

New find In 2025, there was considerable fanfare at the discovery of a new tomb. Belonging to Tutmosis II, it was discovered in the West Valley by the first British archaeological team to have found a tomb since Howard Carter.

18 Cycling the
GREEN FRINGE

CAFES | CRAFTS | COUNTRYSIDE

There's bound to come a point in a trip to Luxor's west bank when even the most dedicated lover of antiquities has seen one monument more than their interest can absorb. Time to hire a bike and go shopping instead.

RICHARDBAKEREGYPT/ALAMY

🗺 Trip Notes

Getting around Roads are flat, paved and quiet, except in the centre of Gezira.

When to go Cycling is feasible all year round. Go in the early morning or late afternoon in summer.

Where to hire A range of bikes are available from **Mohammed Setohe Bike Rental**. Hiring a bike from **Marsam Hotel**, near the Ramesseum, avoids cycling through Gezira. **Go Luxor Tours** offers five-hour cycling trips of the west bank.

👁 West Bank for Free

Entry fees to tombs and temples quickly mount up, but not all west-bank pleasures cost money. There's no charge to walk around the Colossi of Memnon, a star attraction near Gezira, and the Tuesday market, **Souq At Talaat**, near the Temple of Seti I, makes a fun stop on a bike ride.

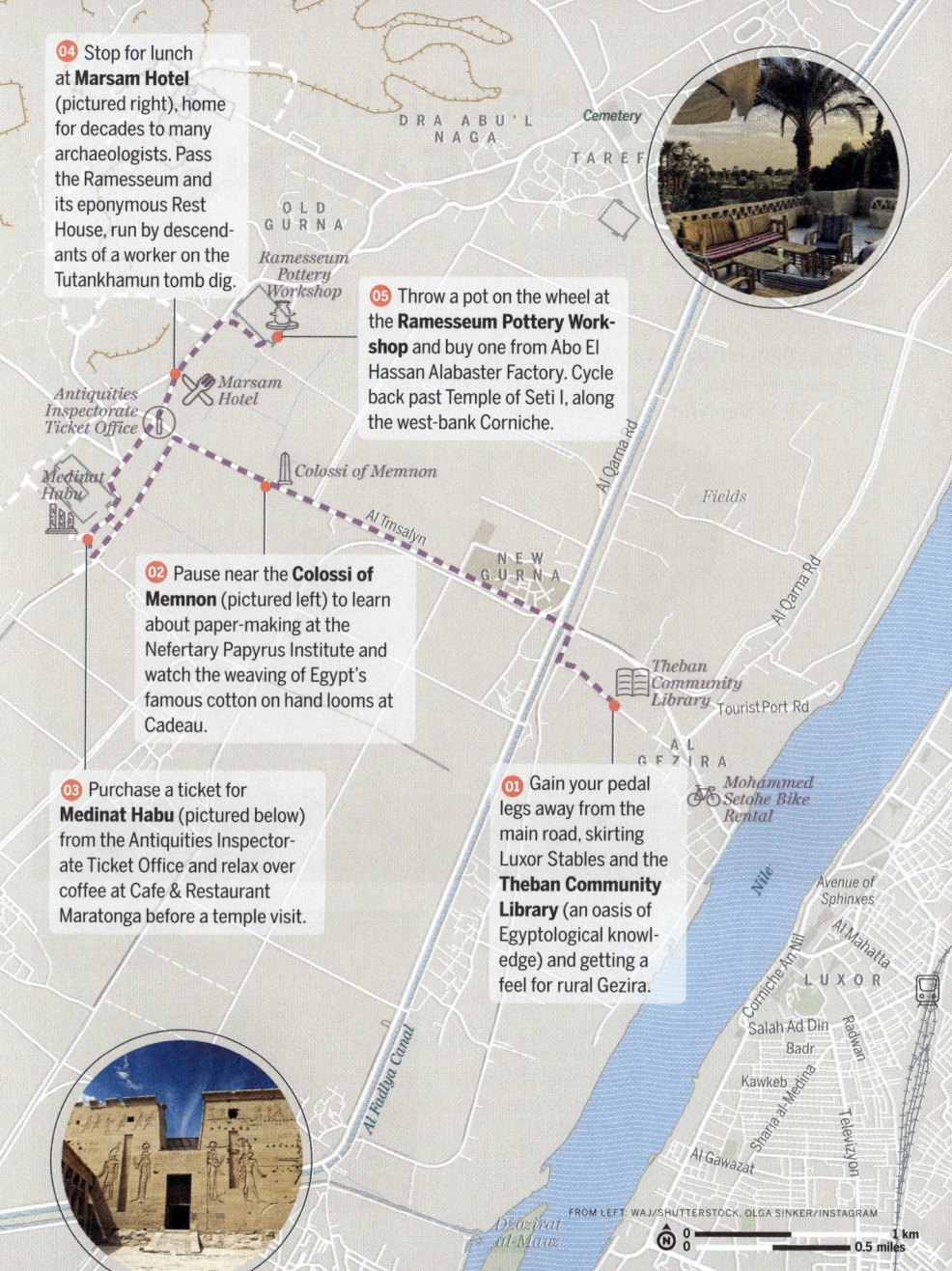

04 Stop for lunch at **Marsam Hotel** (pictured right), home for decades to many archaeologists. Pass the Ramesseum and its eponymous Rest House, run by descendants of a worker on the Tutankhamun tomb dig.

05 Throw a pot on the wheel at the **Ramesseum Pottery Workshop** and buy one from Abo El Hassan Alabaster Factory. Cycle back past Temple of Seti I, along the west-bank Corniche.

02 Pause near the **Colossi of Memnon** (pictured left) to learn about paper-making at the Nefertary Papyrus Institute and watch the weaving of Egypt's famous cotton on hand looms at Cadeau.

03 Purchase a ticket for **Medinat Habu** (pictured below) from the Antiquities Inspectorate Ticket Office and relax over coffee at Cafe & Restaurant Maratonga before a temple visit.

01 Gain your pedal legs away from the main road, skirting Luxor Stables and the **Theban Community Library** (an oasis of Egyptological knowledge) and getting a feel for rural Gezira.

Cemetery

DRA ABU'L NAGA

TAREF

OLD GURNA

Ramesseum Pottery Workshop

Marsam Hotel

Antiquities Inspectorate Ticket Office

Medinat Habu

Colossi of Memnon

Al Tmsalyn

NEW GURNA

Al Qarna rd

Fields

Al Qarna Rd

Theban Community Library

Tourist Port Rd

AL GEZIRA

Mohammed Setohe Bike Rental

Nile

Avenue of Sphinxes

Al Mahatta

LUXOR

Corniche An Nil

Salah Ad Din

Badr

Radwan

Sharia al-Medina

Televizyon

Kawkeb

Al Gawazat

Al Fadiya Canal

Dsazirat al-Mauz

1 km
0.5 miles

19

Ascending into
THE HEAVENS

BALLOONING | VISTAS | DESERT

Look out of the window at sunrise, and you'll find the sky above the west bank is full of abstract shapes, rising and falling against the cliffs of Thebes. Ballooning here has become such big business, up to 50 take flight each morning. Floating through the heavens in one of these gentle crafts is a serene way to view the Nile and necropolis.

SERGII FIGURNYI/SHUTTERSTOCK

🧭 How To

Getting around The launching site is near the Ramesseum on the west bank of the Nile. All ballooning agencies collect clients from their hotel.

When to go Balloons fly every day (weather permitting) in two shifts – at sunrise and one hour later. The second shift may be less romantic but the colours are more intense.

Cost The dawn flight costs around US$75; the later flight is cheaper (around US$60).

RAMESH M THADANI/GETTY IMAGES

Preparing for takeoff The ballooning experience is a triumph of grassroots logistics. Reputable operators, such as **Magic Horizon**, **Salam Balloons** and **Alaska**, collect clients from their hotel (4am in summer) before dawn, serve breakfast on the boat or minibus, and take them to a balloon. There's quite a bit of waiting involved, which seems random but is in fact carefully choreographed to ensure all balloons have time and space to launch safely.

Boarding Nothing quite compares with the excitement of the launch site as great hulks of limp canvas start to fill with hot air and rise off the ground. Getting into the basket takes some manoeuvring, but once aboard, the moment of liftoff is magical as the balloon silently becomes airborne.

Flight path Each 40-minute flight is different, depending on wind speed and direction. It may involve a vertical ascent high above the mountains, while breezier days may dictate a more horizontal course across Medinat Habu to the desert beyond. Whichever route wind and pilot skill determine, the highlight is viewing the Nile from above, flanked by a glory of palm fronds and green fields.

Soft landing Unable to steer, the pilot aims for a piece of desert and passengers brace below the rim of the basket for what is generally a soft landing, before being met by their transport back to the hotel.

⬡ Safety First

Ballooning started life in Luxor as a means to assist archaeologists in mapping the sites of Thebes. Since then, and the first commercial flight for tourists in 1988, it has become almost as key to a Luxor experience as sailing in a felucca, with competition helping to reduce the cost.

Despite the slightly chaotic appearance, and learning from an accident in 2009, ballooning is carefully regulated, involving licensed 'pilots', traveller manifests and approvals by the Civil Aviation Authority. Ballooning is subject to weather conditions and if it's too windy, flights are cancelled. Age, height and weight limits also apply – check with your operator before booking.

20 More Mighty
MONUMENTS

TEMPLES | PHARAOHS | SUNSET

The pharaohs, in planning for their afterlife, constructed not only their burial tombs but also grand funerary temples – elaborate edifices for last rites, decorated with delicate reliefs and wall paintings. Scattered across the plain in front of the Theban necropolis, these semi-reconstructed temples create a broader context for the tombs and are a key part of the west-bank experience.

MIRKO KUZMANOVIC/SHUTTERSTOCK

🗺 How To

Getting around The temples are distributed across the west bank between the fields and mountainside, and reached by taxi, tuk-tuk or bicycle.

When to go Hatshepsut's temple is at its most beautiful early morning,

the Ramesseum and Medinat Habu in late afternoon.

Admission Entry to the Mortuary Temple of Hatshepsut is via the ticket office at the site. For all other temples, tickets are purchased at the **Antiquities Inspectorate Ticket Office**.

WAJ/SHUTTERSTOCK

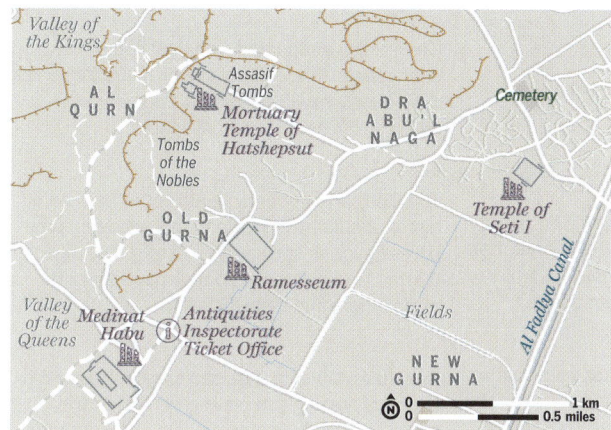

Far left Mortuary Temple of Hatshepsut
Bottom left Ramesseum

A temple most modern The stylish **Mortuary Temple of Hatshepsut** spreads across the Theban cliffs like the outstretched wings of Nekhbet, the vulture goddess, ascending the mountain in a series of three ramped terraces. Once graced with a fragrant garden, it was called the 'Most Holy of Holies' and befitted a woman celebrated as a powerful (and beautiful) queen in her day. Spare time to enjoy the view – this elegant temple was built to face Karnak on the east bank.

Look and despair Look for a pair of giant feet in the temple complex of the **Ramesseum**. Around them lie the remnants of the enormous stone trunk of Ramses II – a statue that lies prone and in pieces in front of the hypostyle hall. Known as 'Ozymandias' in Greek times, this great colossus of one of ancient Egypt's most powerful pharaohs inspired 19th-century British poet Shelley to lament the vanity of human endeavour. Oddly, though, Ramses II lives on in the beloved poem and has been most recently resurrected through contemporary culture, including the cult TV series *Breaking Bad*.

Golden at sunset If you're looking for a quiet corner for a picnic, the lesser-visited **Temple of Seti I** is shaded by palm trees, but for sunset, head to magnificent **Medinat Habu**. Golden in the afternoon light, this was the grand mortuary temple of Ramses III and one of the west-bank's treasures.

The Rebel Queen

Hatshepsut, the powerful rebel queen, was loved by some and hated by others. And if 'hate' seems too strong a word, take any image of the queen throughout her mortuary temple complex and you'll see that she has been systematically defaced. The act of her overshadowed co-regent (who also happened to be her stepson, son-in-law and nephew), Tuthmosis III, the despoliation speaks volumes not just of family intrigue but of prejudice too, towards a woman occupying the throne of kings. As a sop to conservative clerics, Hatshepsut is depicted dressed as a man in many temple representations.

Listings

BEST OF THE REST

Heritage Stays

Winter Palace Hotel $$$

One of Egypt's most famous historic hotels, on the east-bank Corniche near Luxor Temple, has just enough modernisation to make it comfortable without losing its aged atmosphere.

Al Moudira $$$

Some 12km from Gezira, on Luxor's east bank of the Nile, this gorgeous rambling complex of domes and arabesque details makes a luxury rural retreat from the hot and dusty city.

Marsam Hotel $$

Built in the 1920s as a residence for archaeologists, near the Ramesseum, this has been a family-run hotel since 1939 and remains a favourite for its home cooking and shaded courtyard.

Malkata House Boutique Hotel $$$

In a beautifully renovated old house in Gezira, behind Medinat Habu, this heritage hotel is stylishly decorated and makes the best of an upper terrace with temple views.

Nefertiti Hotel $$

Not vintage by Luxor's ancient standards, the east-bank Nefertiti has been in business long enough to win repeat customers, attracted by Oriental decor and rooftop views of Luxor Temple.

Traditional Eats

Koshari Alzaeem $

This local chain sells delicious *kushari* (mix of noodles, rice, black lentils, fried onions and tomato sauce), Egypt's fast food. Situated in the heart of modern Downtown, it brings focus to contemporary Luxor.

Sofra Restaurant & Café $$

Charmingly antiquated with tiled floors and chandeliers, this local east-bank favourite serves delicious Egyptian classics. It's popular year-round so it's best to reserve a table.

Gerda's Garden $$

The German-Egyptian couple at this east-bank bistro popular with international residents prepares Egyptian specials including grilled pigeon. It attracts consistently good reviews for both atmosphere and tasty dishes.

Marsam Restaurant $

Served on tables in a garden of palm trees, with a view of grazing camels in green fields, the home-cooked food at this popular restaurant near the Ramesseum is worth forgoing breakfast for.

Paris Restaurant $

With a terrace view of the Colossi, the Paris serves delicious home-cooked fare in a simple two-storey house, with an emphasis on soups and stews.

Top-Tier Tombs

Tomb of Tuthmosis III (KV 34)

This tomb, at the most southern reach of the Valley of the Kings, is ingenious in its design. Reached via a steep staircase rising 20m above the valley floor, it has hidden depths.

Tomb of Nefertari

Tomb of Seti I (KV 17)

Cut 137m into the rock and lavishly decorated, this tomb's astronomical ceiling was the first of its kind. Discovered in 1817, the tomb suffered from an early copying technique but is still magnificent.

Tomb of Tutankhamun (KV 62)

This small tomb was overlooked until Howard Carter's epic discovery in 1922. With the treasure now in museums, the sarcophagus containing the young pharaoh's mummy remains in situ.

Tomb of Nefertari

In this celebrated Valley of the Queens tomb you'll be under a canopy of golden stars. Nefertari is hypnotic in a transparent white gown and golden headdress, trailing a pair of vulture feathers.

Tomb of Ramses VII (KV 1) & Tomb of Ramses IV (KV 2)

Notice the Coptic crosses and inscriptions overlaying the painting near the entrance of either tomb. KV2, with its beautiful goddess Nut ceiling, was used as a hotel by 18th- and 19th-century visitors.

Tomb of Ay

Reached via West Valley, this lesser-visited Valley of the Kings tomb is a 2km walk from the ticket office. The route to the tomb leads rewardingly into a striking amphitheatre of honey-coloured rock.

 **Domestic Details**

Workers' Village

The craftspeople and officials responsible for building Thebes lived next to the Valley of the Queens. Many were buried at Deir Al Medina in beautifully decorated tombs of their own.

Howard Carter's House

EUGEN_Z/SHUTTERSTOCK

Ostraca Depository

Found in a dried-up well, beyond the workers' village, these clay fragments have huge historical significance, documenting daily life from medical treatments to water-carrying arrangements.

Tombs of the Nobles

For an inkling of daily life 3500 years ago, head to the 6th-dynasty Tombs of the Nobles. More funerary chapel than tombs, they're decorated with paintings (rather than reliefs).

Tomb of Nakht

With its famous images of a blind harpist and three dancers, hunting scenes and rural life, the Tomb of Nakht is the best preserved of the Tombs of the Nobles.

Howard Carter's House

See where British Egyptologist lived when his tireless digging led to the extraordinary 'luck' in finding the Tomb of Tutankhamun, a replica of which is on-site.

Souq At Talaat

Life goes on in Luxor with regular markets bringing the community together – including at the Tuesday open-air souq on the west bank.

21

Cruising the
NILE

**BOATING | ANCIENT MONUMENTS |
BUCKET-LIST ADVENTURE**

The world's longest river, its extraordinary temples and tombs, the fertile valley, the barren beauty of the desert, and the joy of slow travel in a fast-paced world add up to one of the highlights of a trip to Egypt.

GIVAGA/GETTY IMAGES

How To

Getting here/around
Most cruises travel between Luxor and Aswan, reachable by train or plane from Cairo.

When to go June to August brings extreme heat but also the lowest prices. Christmas and Easter are the busiest and most expensive. Spring and autumn are ideal.

Sailing time Many travellers are surprised by how little time is spent cruising – it's only about 240km between Luxor and Aswan.

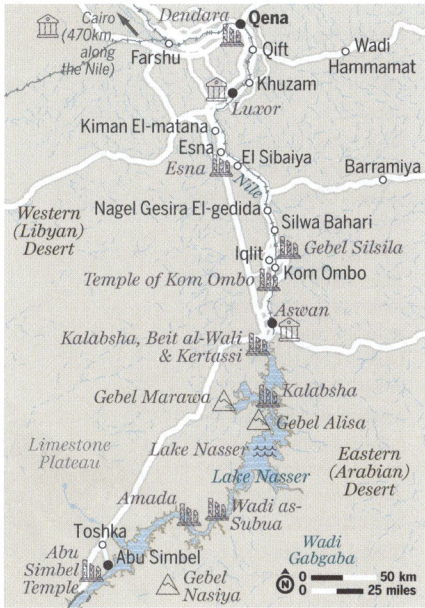

Standard Nile Cruise: Between Luxor & Aswan

The stretch of the Nile between Luxor and Aswan has the greatest concentration of well-preserved monuments in Egypt, making it a popular route for boats and tourists, cruising in both directions. Large cruisers stick to rigid itineraries, while dahabiyas can stop at small towns or antiquities sites, such as Esna and Gebel Silsila.

Pros Classic Egypt itinerary with stops at must-visit ancient monuments. Most cruises are three or four nights, so it's easy to slot into a wider Egypt visit.

Cons Popular and therefore busy, with multiple boats moored together in Luxor and Aswan – your view may be directly into another boat.

ERIC VALENNE GEOSTORY/SHUTTERSTOCK

Top left Nile cruiser
Left Dahabiya

Long Nile Cruise: Between Cairo & Aswan

Long Nile cruises take in the best of Egypt from the water, visiting popular archaeological sites between Luxor and Aswan and quieter locations between Luxor and Cairo, such as Amarna – the capital of the 'heretic pharaoh' Akhenaten – and the painted Middle Kingdom tombs at Beni Hassan.

Pros Stunning alternative to land-based itineraries, taking in ancient sites along the river.

Cons Takes 12 to 14 days. Infrequent departures; often just once a month, with none in summer. Few operators run these itineraries.

Lake Nasser Cruise: Between Aswan & Abu Simbel

Lake Nasser is the place to go if you would rather see empty landscapes than crowds of tourists. The lake was created by the 1960s construction of the High Dam near Aswan, and it now covers much of Egyptian Nubia, once rich with tombs, temples and churches. Some

⚓ Best Boats & Tour Operators

Viking (vikingrivercruises. com) Scandi-sleek boats with top-notch guides. Itineraries take in some lesser-visited sites, such as Esna and Dendara.

Nour El Nil (nourelnil.com) Beautifully decorated dahabiyas with candy-cane-striped sails that look straight out of a design magazine.

Jules Verne (vjv.com) Best variety of Egypt itineraries, including long Nile cruises, trips on Lake Nasser and even steamship journeys.

Aswan Individual (aswan-individual.com) Best way to book an overnight felucca trip from Aswan with excellent boat captains.

Oberoi (oberoihotels.com) This luxury brand brings its elevated style to the Nile aboard the *Philae* and *Zahra*.

Uniworld (uniworld.com) The SS *Sphinx* is pure eye candy with bright Middle Eastern–influenced designs.

⛵ Types of Boats

Nile cruisers Medium to large boats that carry 30 to 100 passengers.

Dahabiyas Small wooden vessels with double sails that carry about 15 passengers.

Feluccas Traditional sailboat for a few travellers, offering sunset cruises or overnight trips from Aswan.

monuments were relocated before the dam's creation and are now grouped at four sites: Kalabsha, Wadi As Subua, Amada and Abu Simbel.

Pros Quieter cruising experience with stops at rarely visited monuments, some of which are only accessible by boat. Short itineraries (three or four nights).

Cons Not many cruisers to choose from. Fewer customers, so more expensive than Nile cruises.

Feluccas

Except for swimming, taking a felucca journey is as close as you can get to the river. Though many travellers ride a felucca for just a sunset cruise or to get around the islands of Aswan, it's also an amazing way to travel downriver from Aswan to Kom Ombo, and maybe beyond if the winds are in your favour. These open-top sailing boats don't have cabins or toilets, so it's like camping on the river. Feluccas are not allowed to sail in the dark, so they stop at sunset and set up camp.

Pros Overnight trips are the best adventure on the Nile, with relaxed days, hearty meals cooked by the boat captain and nighttime stargazing.

Cons With no motor, feluccas are at the mercy of the wind, which means itineraries must be flexible and potentially cut short. No on-board facilities.

Left Felucca crew
Top Nile cruiser
Above Nile cruise, Nour El Nil

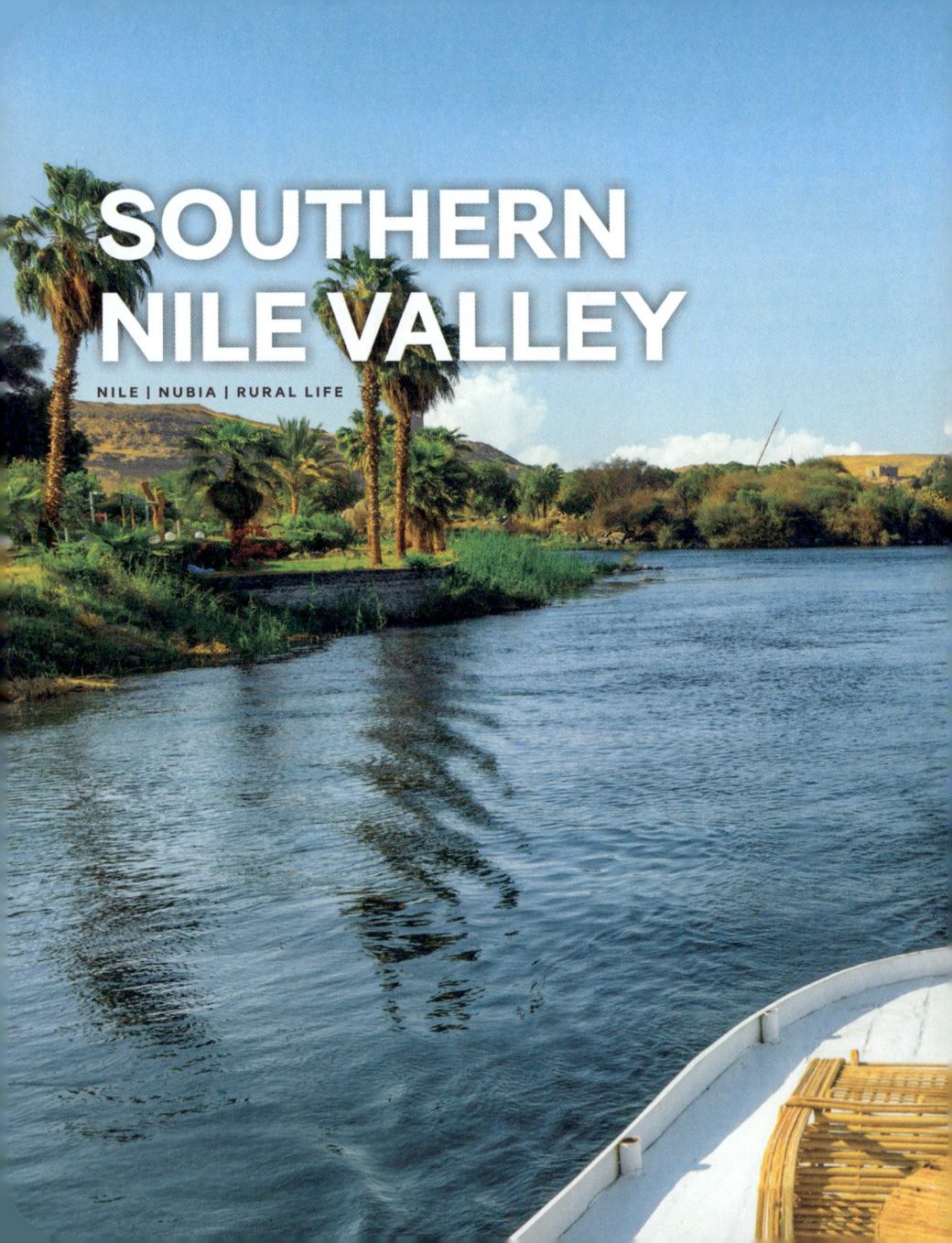

SOUTHERN NILE VALLEY

NILE | NUBIA | RURAL LIFE

SOUTHERN NILE VALLEY
Trip Builder

Sail on a felucca, dine on Nubian cuisine, chat with traditional weavers and marvel at exquisitely preserved ancient monuments in the Southern Nile Valley. This is Egypt's ultimate slow-travel destination where you can delve into the country's past and present against a timeless riverine backdrop.

Gebel Kattar

Red Sea Mountains

Gebel Ash Shayib

Qena

El-barahma

Qus

Khuzam

Eastern (Arabian) Desert

Al Kharga

Ginah

Ezbet Nasser

Western (Libyan) Desert

Ezbet Algeir

Bulaq

Gurmashin

Jaja

Baris

Ezbet Dush

Ezbet Maks El-qibli

Kiman El-matana

Esna Barrage El-deir

El Sibaiya

Nile

Edfu

Nagel-gesira El-gedida

Silwa Bahari

Iqlit Faris

Ibrim

Daraw

> Mingle with traders (pictured below) and sample traditional dishes in historical **Esna** (p134)
> 🚶 1hr from Luxor

> Discover Nubian civilisation at the **Nubia Museum** (p141)
> 🚶 5min from Aswan

Aswan

Philae

> Experience Aswan's tranquil side on a sunset **felucca cruise** (p138)
> ⛵ 5min from Aswan

Limestone Plateau

Lake Nasser

Gebel Marawa *Gebel Alisa*

STEVE HEAP/SHUTTERSTOCK, PREVIOUS SPREAD: GIVAGA/SHUTTERSTOCK

0   80 km
0   40 miles

Practicalities

ARRIVING

Aswan International Airport About 20km south of Aswan, with flights to/from Cairo and Abu Simbel.

Aswan Train Station In central Aswan, within walking distance to the market area and ferries.

MONEY

Aswan has a wide range of good-value accommodation. Dining local-style is both delicious and cost-saving.

FIND YOUR WAY

To get the most out of temple visits, consider a pre-arranged guide like the knowledgeable Mena Zaki (p140).

WHERE TO STAY

Area	Pro/Con
City centre (east bank)	Widest selection of accommodation; busy and bustling.
Elephantine Island	Offers a taste of rural Nubian life; frequent public ferries to/from town (five minutes).
West bank	Colourful Nubian-style accommodation. Boat and/or taxi to town takes up to 30 minutes.

EATING & DRINKING

Fish *sekhina* (pictured top left) is a delicately spiced Esna speciality. *Shamsi* ('sun') bread – let to rise in the sun – is best eaten warm. Southern Egypt has its own twist on the classic *molokhiyya* (pictured bottom left; garlicky leaf soup).

Best Nile-side dining
Terrace (p151)

Must-try meal
Okra Women's Kitchen (p134)

GETTING AROUND

Boat Public ferries link Aswan with Elephantine Island and the west bank. Charter a felucca by the hour for a short sail or book a multiday dahabiya or felucca trip.

Taxi In town, short-haul fares range from LE50 to LE200. Private taxis are good for longer excursions (from LE1000 for a one-way trip between Luxor and Esna).

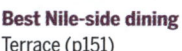

JAN–MAR
Peak-season prices in January; February's winds can be unreliable for sailing

APR–JUN
Comfortable temperatures and fewer crowds

JUL–SEP
Hot days, especially in July and August

OCT–DEC
A lovely travel time, although hotels fill in December

SOUTHERN NILE VALLEY FIND YOUR FEET

22 A Walk
THROUGH TIME

CULTURE | CUISINE | SHOPPING

Dine on home-cooked regional specialities, meet Esna residents and take a walking tour of this lively town with a multi-layered history. Esna provides a refreshing change of pace, offering the best of community-led tourism and an immersion into southern Egyptian life.

AHMED MOSTAFA/TAKWEEN-ICD

 **How To**

Getting here Esna is an hour from Luxor by private taxi. The boat dock is a short walk from the town centre.

Settle in A half-day is perfect for an introduction, but there's so much more to do for those who can linger for at least an overnight.

Plan ahead Discover **Esna** (facebook.com/discover.esna) is the hub of community tourism in Esna. Contact in advance to arrange guides, tours and meals.

TAKWEEN-ICD

Stroll Through the Centuries

A chat with vendors in Esna's **Al Qīsāriyya market** takes you back to 18th-century Egypt, when this market town – favourably set at the crossroads of major east–west and north–south trade routes – reached one of its many heydays. It is at its most atmospheric near the beautifully restored **Wakālat Al Jiddāwī**, the old caravanserai with its graceful arches, wooden latticework and vintage photos (the clean public toilets are an additional draw).

Nearby is a stamp maker who, in minutes, can carve a personalised design for you, harking back to the days when stamps and seals were all-important for authenticating letters. Or, try your hand at turning the sturdy wooden handle of Nasir Bakkur's **oil press**, where Esna's famous vegetable oils

TAKWEEN-ICD

✕ Esna's Culinary Heritage

Esna's culinary heritage was revived when Discover Esna sponsored a contest to identify local traditional dishes. A flood of recipes was ultimately the response. The best – all now refined and documented for future generations – feature on the menu of **Okra Women's Kitchen**.

Top left Esna
Left Wakālat Al Jiddāwī
Above Nasir Bakkur's oil press

have been pressed for generations. Next, watch as a local weaver crafts colourfully patterned scarves on a wooden loom at **Khnum** and browse neighbouring shops with their fine arrays of alabaster figures, wood-carvings, textiles and ceramics – all 100% Egyptian materials and designs.

At Esna's heart is the not-to-be-missed **Temple of Khnum**, with its magnificent hypostyle hall supported by 18 frescoed columns, lavishly detailed cosmological scenes on the ceiling and side panels telling the story of Khnum, the creator god.

A Multilayered History

Esna's prominence reaches back to at least the 4th century BCE, when it was capital of the Latopolite nome of Upper Egypt and an important administrative centre. Over subsequent centuries, it continued to be an attractive base for merchants and wealthy trading families, who flourished during the

🛍 Top Shops

Ali Baba Scarab charms (they bring good luck!), ankh carvings and more.

Iron Man High-quality *galabeyas* (men's robes) and traditional foot-ironing services.

Khnum Textiles and scarves, and a loom where you can watch the weaver at work.

King T-Shirts Save your souvenir T-shirt shopping for this place, with designs reflecting Egyptian history and Esna life.

Pottery Home Handcrafted ceramics and pottery, made from Nile clay and compact enough to take home in your luggage.

Pr.Ba Concept Store Lovely bags, scarves and handi-crafts, all locally designed and produced.

Seba Exquisite alabaster designs and locally carved woodwork.

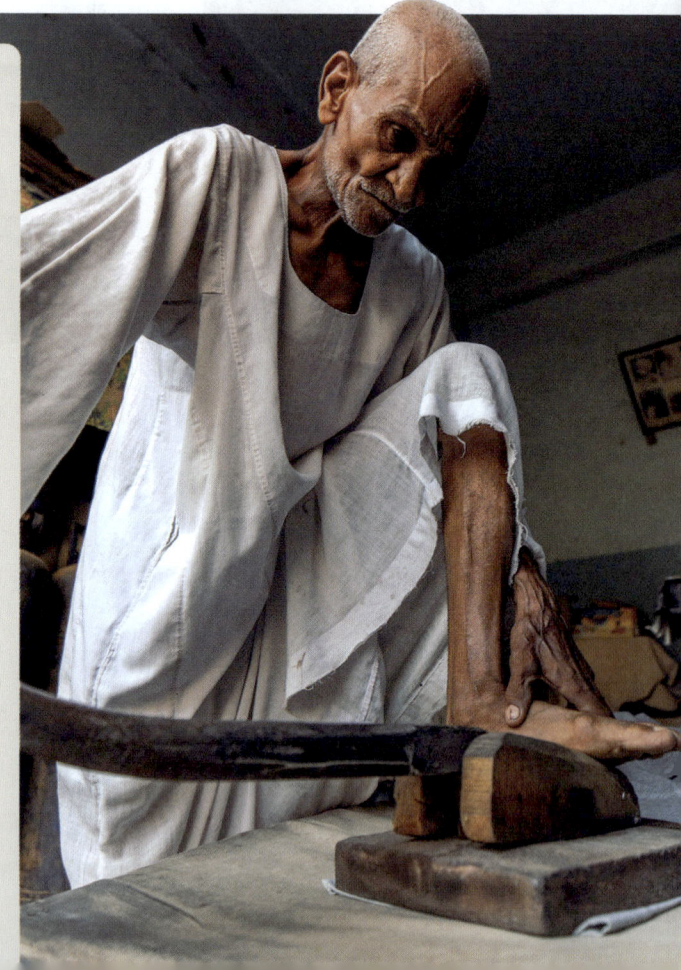

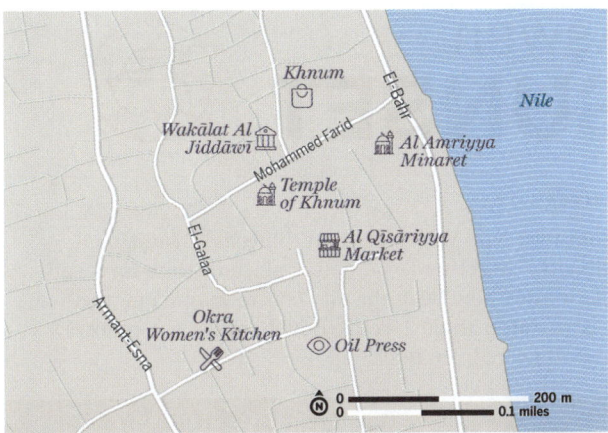

SOUTHERN NILE VALLEY EXPERIENCES

FROM LEFT: AHMED MOSTAFA/TAKWEEN-ICD, HEMRO/SHUTTERSTOCK

Left Iron Man, Esna
Below Temple of Khnum

Ottoman era and who continue to dominate the local economy.

Today, this historical lineage is best seen in Esna's architecture. In addition to the Graeco-Roman Temple of Khnum and the Ottoman-era Al Qīsāriyya market, there is the Fatimid **Al Amriyya minaret**, an imposing Coptic church and many carved doors and lintels hidden away in side streets. A two- to three-hour walking tour is a perfect way to start exploring before finishing up with a traditional southern Egyptian lunch at Okra Women's Kitchen (p135) and a chat with one of Esna's merchant families in their personal *diwan* (formal meeting room).

A Jaunt to the Countryside

Once you've experienced central Esna, head into the surrounding villages where you can pick and sample Esna's famous tomatoes, check out the geologically significant **Dababiya Natural Reserve** and have a village lunch. With more time, learn about the region's long Coptic roots on Discover Esna's **Coptic Experience** tour, stopping at shrines and monasteries and exploring the interplay of ancient Egyptian spirituality with Coptic Christianity. Esna's good budget hotels and trained guides make the town an ideal spot to linger longer and delve deeper into local life.

23 Aswan
SUNSET

SAILING | TRANQUILLITY | RIVER LIFE

It wouldn't be the Southern Nile Valley without feluccas – traditional, single-masted, wooden sailboats – and there's no better place or time for a sail than in Aswan at sunset. No matter how busy the city centre may seem, the bustle fades away as soon as you step aboard, settle down amidst the pillows and patterned carpets, and pull away from dock.

MURATART/SHUTTERSTOCK

🗺 How To

Getting here/around
Travel from Cairo by train, bus or plane, and from Luxor by train or private taxi. Ferries link central Aswan with Elephantine Island and Aswan Gharb (west bank). Taxis are plentiful.

Finding a boat Arrange a boat through your hotel, or with the operators listed opposite.

A felucca for yourself
Pricing is modest (about LE300 per hour), so consider splurging on a boat just for you and your group.

WARREN LEMAY FROM CULLOWHEE, USA/WIKIMEDIA/CC BY 0

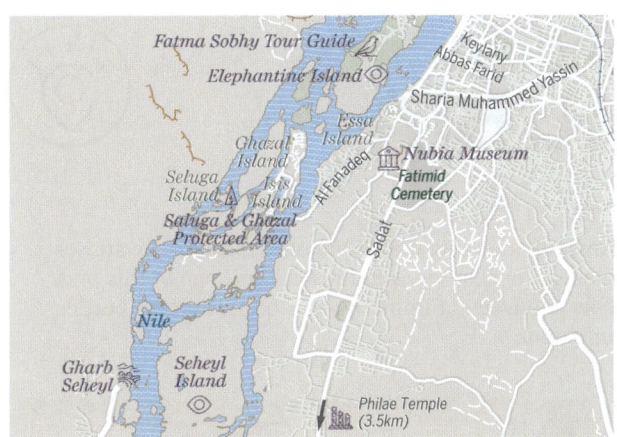

Top left Felucca
Bottom left Seheyl Island

Feluccas are Nile travel at its most elemental, and a felucca sail is never better than on an Aswan evening as the breeze picks up, the day's heat melts away and the sun starts to sink behind the Tombs of the Nobles. If you're hooked and want something longer, try a one- or two-night sail from Aswan towards the Temple of Kom Ombo, stopping en route at small villages. At night, the boat is moored and you drift to sleep under the stars after an evening bonfire on the riverbank.

Remember, though, that despite their romance, feluccas are working vessels and therefore frill- and cabin-free. Instead, you'll live, eat and sleep on a shaded deck. In winter it gets chilly, so bring a sleeping bag or check there are blankets aboard. Feluccas also have no plumbing, with toilet breaks taken on the riverbank behind a screen (bring your own toilet paper and a torch). Also, for longer trips, keep in mind that if there's no wind, you may need to finish part of your journey by road.

Recommended felucca contacts include **Captain Safy** (nubiansailing.com); **Captain Ziggy** (+20-120-856-2850); **JJ Jamaica** (facebook.com/jjjamaicafelucca); and Waleed at **Aswan Individual** (aswan-individual.com). Note that sailing the full stretch from Aswan to Luxor isn't possible. Trips to Edfu usually stop somewhat before town, with the remainder done by vehicle.

Bird-watching at Dawn

For a twist on the sunset felucca ride, try motoring at sunrise around the granite boulders and islands south of Elephantine Island, especially Saluga and Ghazal, which are part of a **protected area** that is a haven for migratory and breeding birds.

With luck, and guided by local ornithologist **Fatma Sobhy** (WhatsApp +20-11-5360-6770), you may see black ibises, vultures and swamp hens. You'll also pass **Seheyl Island**, domain of Anukis, goddess of the cataracts. As you cruise by its southern tip, look out for a cliff with over 200 inscriptions dating to the 18th and 19th dynasties.

24 Finding NUBIA

CULTURE | HISTORY | HERITAGE

A generation has grown up knowing old Nubia only through the stories of the elders, who strive to keep the customs and musical heritage of this once-powerful kingdom alive. Take a journey of immersion into this ancient border region straddling Egypt and Sudan.

LIZAVETTA/SHUTTERSTOCK

🗺 Trip Notes

Getting around All sites can be reached by foot, taxi or boat; hotels can help arrange transport. Alternatively, contact guide **Mena Zaki** (aswanluxortravel. com).

Angels of the Nile Nubians have a close relationship with the Nile, making offerings to the *malayket al bahr* (angels of the Nile) to seek intercession and blessings.

Nobiin language While walking around, listen for Nobiin, Nubia's endangered (and primarily oral) language that is sometimes written in both Latin and Arabic scripts.

◎ Land of the Bow

Known to ancient Egyptians as Ta-Sety (Land of the Bow), old Nubia dates back to at least 3800 BCE, when it flourished between Aswan (pictured left) and the Second Nile Cataract, alternately dominating and being dominated by its mighty neighbour. Despite massive displacement during High Dam construction, Nubian culture lives on, including in art, music and literature.

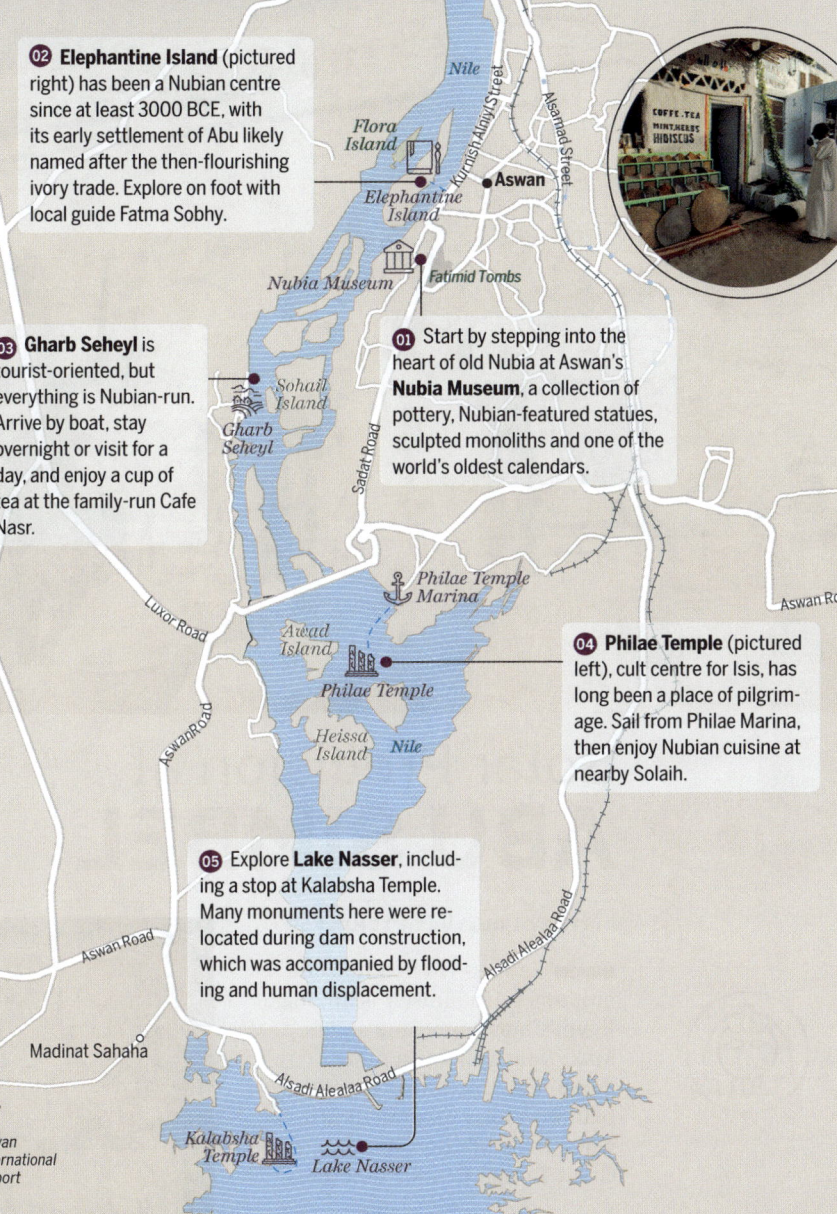

02 Elephantine Island (pictured right) has been a Nubian centre since at least 3000 BCE, with its early settlement of Abu likely named after the then-flourishing ivory trade. Explore on foot with local guide Fatma Sobhy.

03 Gharb Seheyl is tourist-oriented, but everything is Nubian-run. Arrive by boat, stay overnight or visit for a day, and enjoy a cup of tea at the family-run Cafe Nasr.

01 Start by stepping into the heart of old Nubia at Aswan's **Nubia Museum**, a collection of pottery, Nubian-featured statues, sculpted monoliths and one of the world's oldest calendars.

04 Philae Temple (pictured left), cult centre for Isis, has long been a place of pilgrimage. Sail from Philae Marina, then enjoy Nubian cuisine at nearby Solaih.

05 Explore **Lake Nasser**, including a stop at Kalabsha Temple. Many monuments here were relocated during dam construction, which was accompanied by flooding and human displacement.

Nile
Flora Island
Kurnish Alnury Street
Alsamad Street
Aswan
Elephantine Island
Nubia Museum
Fatimid Tombs
Sohail Island
Gharb Seheyl
Sadat Road
Luxor Road
Aswan Road
Awad Island
Philae Temple Marina
Philae Temple
Heissa Island
Nile
Aswan Road
Alsadi Alealaa Road
Aswan Road
Madinat Sahaha
Alsadi Alealaa Road
Aswan International Airport
Kalabsha Temple
Lake Nasser

SUN_SHINE/SHUTTERSTOCK

N
0
0
5 km
2.5 mile

25 Solar Precision at
ABU SIMBEL

HISTORY | CULTURE | TEMPLES

Ramses II's magnificent monument to himself is among Egypt's most imposing sights. Make your visit even more memorable by timing it with the biannual solar alignment festival, when the sun's rays illuminate the Great Temple's inner sanctuary.

How To

Getting here/around
Cruise down Lake Nasser, fly from Cairo or travel by road from Aswan. Once in Abu Simbel, walk, take a taxi or join a sunrise boat cruise.

When to go Anytime, but best just before and after the solar alignment festivals (22 February and 22 October); the actual festival days get crowded.

How long? Don't miss staying overnight to visit crowd-free and see the temples illuminated at the **sound-and-light show**.

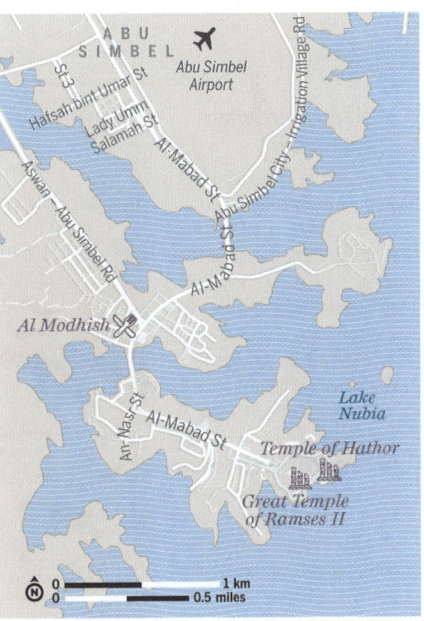

Master Ruler, Master Builder

Ramses II, one of the ancient world's greatest rulers, built the magnificent **Temples of Abu Simbel** in order to leave visitors travelling north past the Nile's 'great' (second) cataract with no doubt about Egypt's power. Millennia later, his message still echoes, with four colossal 20m-high statues of the pharaoh rising up from the desert and gazing out over the water in serene majesty. It's a breathtaking sight, whether you approach by boat or come around the final bend on the path from the ticket office on foot.

Just as impressive as Abu Simbel's mighty statuary is the alignment of the **Great Temple of Ramses II**. It is built so that twice yearly – currently on 22 February and 22 October – the rays of the rising sun pass through the massive doorway and penetrate deeply

Top left Great Temple of Ramses II
Above Temples of Abu Simbel

through the temple into the sacred inner sanctuary, where Ramses II sits flanked by the gods Amun-Ra, Ra-Horakhty and Ptah. The temple is aligned so precisely that the sunlight first illuminates the face of Ramses before spreading to Amun-Ra and Ra-Horakhty. Ptah, to the far left, remains in the shadows, emphasising his links with the underworld.

Exploring the Great Temple

The Great Temple's interior is rich in detail. As you make your way through the massive door into the **Great Hall**, you'll find yourself dwarfed by eight giant statues of Ramses II supporting a ceiling adorned with vultures, symbolising the protective goddess Nekhbet. Fabulous, deeply carved battle scenes fill every inch of the walls, including – on the northern side – a depiction of the Battle of

🏛 Happy Birthday, Ramses II?

Although it's often said that Abu Simbel's solar alignment festivals coincide with Ramses II's birthday and coronation day, scholars debate this. Slight changes to the sun's angle of approach over the millennia, plus the challenges of linking fixed calendar dates with cyclical natural phenomena, and the fact that the sun's rays have been observed hitting the inner sanctuary over a range of days, mean it is more likely the alignment dates were tied to the annual planting and harvest seasons. What is undisputed is that ancient Egyptians were masters of both astronomy and architecture.

🍴 Fresh Fish

For authentic local flavour, try a meal at **Al Modhish**, Abu Simbel's best seafood restaurant. Order *makla* (fried) or *meshwi* (grilled) and staff will do the rest, serving up fresh, delicious catch of the day with sides of rice and salad.

Kadesh (c 1274 BCE), in what is now Syria, where Ramses rallies his demoralised troops to defeat the Hittites. On the southern wall is an account of Ramses laying waste to Libyans and Nubians in his chariot.

As you continue inside, before reaching the inner sanctuary, you'll enter a four-columned **vestibule** where Ramses and his wife Nefertari are shown making offerings to the temple gods Amun-Ra and Ra-Horakhty.

Equal Partners

Immediately next to the Great Temple is the smaller **Temple of Hathor**, dedicated to Ramses' favoured wife, Nefertari, and to Hathor, the goddess of love, motherhood, fertility and music. In front are six 10m-high carvings of Ramses and Nefertari, who is dressed as Hathor. In a rare display of ancient equality, Nefertari is depicted at the same scale as Ramses, with her exalted place confirmed by an inscription stating that the pharaoh has cut this temple 'for his chief wife Nefertari...for whom the sun shines'. As you enter inside, the tale of spousal love and respect continues, with walls depicting scenes of Ramses II and Nefertari and Nefertari again shown as the equal of Ramses.

Left Temple of Hathor
Left Sunlit inner sanctuary, Great Temple of Ramses II **Below** Great Hall

26 Temple-Hopping on THE NILE

BOATING | HISTORY | TEMPLES

Experience the Southern Nile Valley's timelessness in comfort on a dahabiya cruise between Esna and Aswan, stopping en route at stunning temples and ancient sites. Thanks to the leisurely pace and the temples' small scale, you'll have plenty of time to linger on the details.

KAREL STIPEK/GETTY IMAGES

🗺 Trip Notes

Where to start Southbound dahabiya trips normally start with a road transfer from Luxor to the dock at Esna and end at Aswan's northern bridge.

How long Allow four to six nights for a cruise, depending on direction (northbound is faster) and itinerary.

Tip Try to avoid mid-morning stops, when the temples are often inundated with visitors from cruise ships.

Horus, Father of Pharaohs

Horus, son of Osiris and Isis, was the god of kingship, to whom pharaohs traced their lineage. Protected by his magic-wielding mother, Horus defeated his rival Seth, restoring cosmic order and facilitating Osiris' resurrection. This myth gave rise to the duty to protect and respect the pharaoh, Horus' earthly representative.

01 Al Kab (ancient Nekheb) was cult centre of the vulture goddess Nekhbet. While much of the site is off-limits, the New Kingdom tomb of Ahmose, with its well-preserved inscriptions, is worth a stop.

02 Edfu's imposing **Temple of Horus** brings Ptolemaic Egypt to life with extensive hieroglyphic inscriptions and massive wall reliefs. Other highlights: a perfume laboratory and a replica wooden barque in the inner sanctuary.

03 Gebel Silsila (pictured left), at the Nile's narrowest point, was a major source of sandstone for temple building. Its west bank is scattered with shrines; the quarry holds clues about ancient masonry techniques.

04 Picturesquely set **Temple of Kom Ombo** (pictured above) is dedicated to both Horus and the crocodile god Sobek, with two symmetrical temples along its main axis. The adjoining Crocodile Museum has mummified crocodiles.

Eastern (Arabian) Desert

El Sibaiya

Nile

Al Kab

El-saayda

El-kilh Gharb

Edfu

Temple of Horus

Nagel-gesira El-gedida

Silwa Bahari

Gebel Silsila

Kajuj

Faris

Iqlit

Temple of Kom Ombo

Ibrim

Kom Ombo

Daraw

Nile

0 — 10 km
0 — 5 miles

27 Off-Piste
ADVENTURES

HIKING | HISTORY | VIEWS

▬▬▬ For an offbeat excursion, head across the Nile to Aswan's west bank. The steep hillside there is scattered with dozens of tombs on its upper flanks and capped by the domed Qubbet Al Hawa (the tomb of a Muslim sheikh). To the south and west, the terrain flattens out, with a path of sorts leading to the ruins of St Simeon's monastery.

G.LUKAC/SHUTTERSTOCK

📷 How To

Getting here Take the Aswan Gharb public ferry from just west of the train station. Once across, it's a 10-minute walk uphill to the tombs.

When to go Early morning and late afternoon are ideal, with views over the Nile at their best around sunset.

Camel rides Cover the approximately 2km from the tombs to St Simeon's monastery on foot, or hire one of the camels lounging near the dock.

KAREL STIPEK/SHUTTERSTOCK

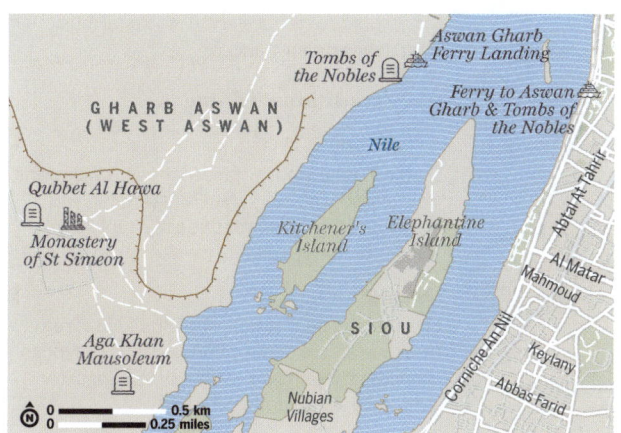

SIOU

Top left Tombs of the Nobles
Left Aga Khan Mausoleum

The **Tombs of the Nobles** – containing many Old and Middle Kingdom (2200–1750 BCE) burial sites for ancient dignitaries, priests and governors of Elephantine Island – can be visited on their own or as part of a half-day circuit also taking in St Simeon's monastery. From near the ferry dock, steep stairs lead up to the tombs, where there's a caretaker who will open them up for a tip.

Afterwards, hike further uphill to **Qubbet Al Hawa** for Aswan's best views before continuing on camel or on foot (about 30 to 45 minutes through deep sand; bring water and a hat) across the barren hilltop to the impressive ruins of the 7th-century **Monastery of St Simeon**. There are some rock caves, a church with remnants of frescoes of the Apostles and many reminders of the asceticism that shaped Egypt's long monastic tradition. Check out especially the monks' narrow stone beds with their built-in stone pillows – these will put your budget guesthouse bedding situation into a new perspective.

From the monastery, with its high walls that glow red and ochre around sunset, head down the hillside via the (closed) **Aga Khan Mausoleum** to the riverbank, where there are a few small restaurants and boats for hire back to Elephantine Island. Alternatively, return northwards for the ferry back to Aswan.

🏛 Nobility's Best

Only a few tombs can be visited. The best is Site 31 – the burial chamber of Sarenput II, a 12th-dynasty governor of southern Egypt. Statues of Sarenput guard its entrance chamber, while deeper inside is another burial room with paintings of Sarenput and his family. Also impressive is the double tomb of Old Kingdom governor Mekhu and his son, Sabni (Sites 25 and 26). Inside, impressive reliefs tell of Sabni's military campaign to Nubia to punish the tribe responsible for murdering his father. Site 34 contains the tomb of Governor Harkhuf and hieroglyphic texts detailing trading expeditions into Africa.

Listings

BEST OF THE REST

Angles on History

Aswan High Dam

Built to regulate Nile flooding and increase agricultural production and hydroelectric power, the dam is both a source of pride and – for Nubians – a symbol of loss.

Aswan Museum

Flanked by the ruins of ancient Abu, and the modern-day Nubian villages of Siou and Koti, this small museum contains an eclectic collection of Nubian and Egyptian artefacts.

Unfinished Obelisk

At 42m high, Aswan's obelisk – abandoned after a crack was discovered – would have been the tallest of its kind. Ancient masons carved these monuments from the bedrock.

Hotels with Heritage

El Salam Hotel

Part of the Discover Esna initiative, El Salam offers spotless, sun-filled rooms, Nile views and authentic Egyptian breakfasts just around the corner at Taghmest Ramadan.

Sofitel Legend Old Cataract

Built in 1899 by Thomas Cook, Aswan's Old Cataract has hosted a long line of dignitaries and celebrities, including Agatha Christie, who wrote *Death on the Nile* here in 1937.

Anakob

Be lulled to sleep by the lapping waters of the Nile on this comfortable riverboat moored off Elephantine Island's western side.

Eskaleh Nubian Ecolodge

Built by Nubian musician Fikry el Kashef, this lodge in Abu Simbel offers Nubian decor, meals on an outdoor terrace and occasional music and dance performances.

Traditional Dining

Omar's Coffee Shop $

Settle in on the colourful benches to enjoy mint tea, chilled hibiscus juice, French coffee and other local favourites at this cosy spot near Esna's Khnum temple.

Zalabia $

This small street stand near Esna's Hasheem mosque serves scrumptious *zalabya* (Egyptian doughnuts) with your choice of toppings; try cinnamon and powdered sugar.

Onaty Ka $

Tagen (stew), grills, local cheese and other Nubian favourites, together with Nile views from the upper terrace, are the draws at this brightly painted spot in Aswan.

Solaih Nubian Restaurant $$

On Bigga Island and overlooking Philae Temple, the rustic Solaih serves traditional Nubian dishes against a waterside backdrop. Some are cooked on an open fire. Book ahead.

Abeer $

This bustling local institution in central Aswan is known for its speedy service and tasty kofta

Aswan High Dam

and kebabs. Mains are generously sized and come with bread, soup and tahini.

El Masry $$

Waiters in ties and black-and-white photos lend a vintage touch to this longstanding Aswan eatery known for its stuffed pigeon and other traditional Egyptian dishes.

Meals with a View

Terrace $$$

Stunning views of the Nile, vintage decor and excellent service at the Old Cataract hotel. Famous for its old-school English high tea.

Panorama $$$

Enjoy North African cuisine or high tea with 360-degree views over Aswan and the Nile from the tower-top restaurant at the Mövenpick on Elephantine Island.

Kafana $

It's just you and the lapping waters of the Nile at this low-key restaurant on the quiet western side of Elephantine Island. Local favourites include kofta and homemade camel *tagen*.

Escape from the Bustle

Aswan Botanical Gardens

These peaceful 1km-long gardens on Kitchener's Island are particularly lovely at sunset, when the scent of jasmine floats on the breeze.

Fryal Gardens

Overlooking the First Nile Cataract, these public gardens fill with picnicking Egyptian families on holiday weekends. The main attraction is the Nile views.

Spices & Camels

Sharia As Souq

Aswan's atmospheric souq features everything from colourful mounds of spices to textiles. On warm evenings, Aswan residents come in droves to stroll its narrow lanes.

Aswan Botanical Gardens

RATNAKORN PIYASIRISORCST/GETTY IMAGES

Daraw Camel Market

A major station on the Forty Days Road caravan route linking Sudan with Egypt. Trading (Saturdays from 6am) is fast and furious; it's one hour north of Aswan.

Cruising Comforts

Nour El Nil

Nour el Nil runs a fleet of eight vintage dahabiyas in varying sizes and styles, with an emphasis throughout on relaxed luxury for their set and customised departures.

Nile Dahabiya Boats

Run by Luxor locals, this group has a fleet of four mostly smaller dahabiyas, each with five to six cabins and taking 10 to 15 passengers, with set and customised departures.

Dahabiya Nile Sailing

This environmentally aware operator offers a range of three- to five-night itineraries made special by the chance to kayak or fish and combine sailing with local excursions.

Saï Safari

A beautifully crafted boat that plies Lake Nasser between Aswan and Abu Simbel, with temple stops and nature-focused activities en route.

SIWA OASIS & THE WESTERN DESERT

LANDSCAPE | HISTORY | ADVENTURE

Siwa

SIWA OASIS & THE WESTERN DESERT
Trip Builder

With escarpments streaked caramel and vanilla and dunes rambling into infinity, the magnificent Western Desert is dotted with tiny, ancient oases clinging to life on the desert fringe. Sandboarding, camping and hot-spring dips entertain the adventurous in this remote region.

Float in blue pools in ancient **Siwa** (pictured below), Egypt's remotest oasis (p158)
🚌 12hr from Cairo

EGYPT

Hike past rock tombs in **El Arag Oasis** (p160)
🚙 2hr from Siwa

Great Sand Sea

LIBYA

Great Sand Sea

0 — 100 km
0 — 50 miles

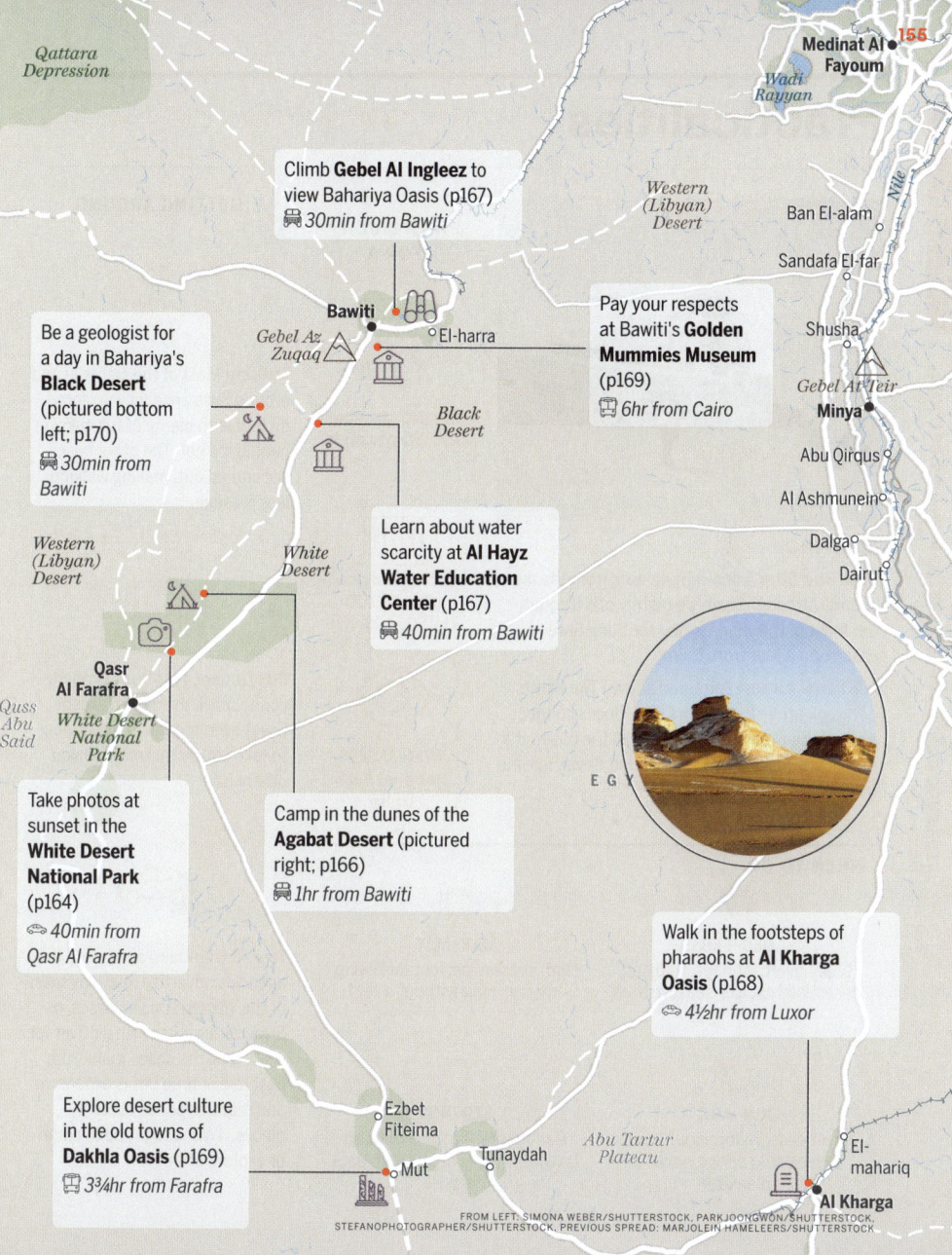

Qattara
Depression

Western
(Libyan)
Desert

*Wadi
Rayyan*

Medinat Al
Fayoum

Ban El-alam

Sandafa El-far

Climb **Gebel Al Ingleez** to
view Bahariya Oasis (p167)
🚌 *30min from Bawiti*

Shusha

Bawiti

*Gebel Az
Zuqaq*

El-harra

Pay your respects
at Bawiti's **Golden
Mummies Museum**
(p169)
🚌 *6hr from Cairo*

Gebel At Teir

Minya

Be a geologist for
a day in Bahariya's
Black Desert
(pictured bottom
left; p170)
🚌 *30min from
Bawiti*

*Black
Desert*

Abu Qirqus

Al Ashmunein

Dalga

Dairut

Learn about water
scarcity at **Al Hayz
Water Education
Center** (p167)
🚌 *40min from Bawiti*

*Western
(Libyan)
Desert*

*White
Desert*

*Quss
Abu
Said*

**Qasr
Al Farafra**

*White Desert
National
Park*

E G Y

Take photos at
sunset in the
**White Desert
National Park**
(p164)
🚐 *40min from
Qasr Al Farafra*

Camp in the dunes of the
Agabat Desert (pictured
right; p166)
🚌 *1hr from Bawiti*

Walk in the footsteps of
pharaohs at **Al Kharga
Oasis** (p168)
🚐 *4½hr from Luxor*

Explore desert culture
in the old towns of
Dakhla Oasis (p169)
🚋 *3¾hr from Farafra*

Ezbet
Fiteima

Mut

Tunaydah

*Abu Tartur
Plateau*

El-
mahariq

Al Kharga

Practicalities

ROLAND UNGER/WIKIMEDIA/CC BY-SA 3.0

ARRIVING

Siwa Bus Stop A one-minute walk from the main square. Although there's a nightly bus through-out most of the year, visiting far-flung Siwa is easiest on a tour from Cairo.

El Kharga Airport (pictured above) Two flights per week arrive here from Cairo. Buses connect each of the other oases. To tour all the oases, it's more convenient to book a car and driver, leaving from either Luxor or Cairo.

HOW MUCH FOR A

Desert camping US$150 per night

Archaeological sites LE100 (LE50 student)

White Desert National Park US$5

GETTING AROUND

Walking Most of the sights in and around Siwa are easily explored on foot with plenty of tuk-tuks on hand if it's hot. The other oases are spread out, making walking less feasible.

Bus Upper Egypt Bus Company connects all the oases (except Siwa) even though locals hoping to take you by taxi may tell you otherwise.

Tour/Car In Cairo and Luxor, tour agencies advertise multiday tours of the Western Desert oases, or Siwa. Hiring a car with a driver for visiting all the oases makes the best use of time but is expensive and requires police escort in places. 4WD is required to camp or explore off-road.

WHEN TO GO

DEC–FEB
Chilly overcast days, freezing desert nights; low-season rates

MAR–MAY
High season, perfect for hiking and camping without a tent

JUN–AUG
Fruit season; ferocious heat makes cold spring soaks a pleasure

SEP–NOV
Balmy weather; like-minded travellers for cost sharing; date harvest

EATING & DRINKING

Oasis food (pictured right) as served in hotels follows a pattern of soup, salad, chicken and rice, and can be a bit bland. Venture downtown and pick any busy-looking restaurant, and chopped livers and spicy green soups liven up the plate. In Siwa, the main-square restaurants serve as a social hub for travellers.

Some of the best food is prepared by Bedouin driver-guides (pictured right) during a camping trip. They muster delicious lentil soups and ember-baked bread with the minimum of fuss.

Best camel meat OLA Restaurant, Siwa (p173)

Must-try traditional dishes Wimpy Albasateen, Al Kharga Oasis (p173)

CONNECT & FIND YOUR WAY

Wi-fi Readily available but access is often restricted to communal areas.

Navigation The road connecting the oases of Bahariya and Siwa continues to be off-limits. Currently the only way of visiting Siwa is via Cairo, Alexandria and Marsa Matruh. The road from Luxor to Al Dakhla is seldom travelled – most people visit the oasis from Cairo, or Asyut on the Nile.

POLICE PERMITS & ESCORT

Police permits for travel beyond each oasis are obtained by the tour operator; book the day before. Police escorts are obligatory in many places – go with the flow and allow extra journey time.

WHERE TO STAY

Desert accommodation tends to be simple, even when it's boutique-chic. What hotels and camps lack in terms of luxury, they make up for in feeling closer to nature.

Town/Village	Pros/Cons
Siwa	The main hub of the oasis. Walking distance from main sights.
Bawiti	Central for transport and accommodation in the Bahariya Oasis. Lacks charm of desert camps.
Qasr Al Farafra	Nearer base than Bawiti for exploring White Desert National Park. On edge of old Qasr with camping in the Agabat Desert.
Mut	Centre of the Dakhla Oasis; good hub for exploring nearby antiquities by taxi.
Al Kharga	Best for staying, eating and onward connections, including south to Baris.

MONEY

Payment by credit card is limited. Payment for police permits (often covered by tour operators) is in US dollars only. ATMs work well in Siwa but are often bereft of cash elsewhere. High-season travel makes sharing transport costs easier.

28 Life in the
SHADOWS

OASIS | HERITAGE | DUNES

▬▬ In scorching summer heat, the presence of water in the desert seems miraculous. Springing from under the sands, water bubbles up in numerous places in and around Siwa, irrigating the oasis and its dense palm plantations. Pack a swimsuit and dip in and out of the date-palm shade to see how water has allowed life to flourish here for centuries.

SUN_SHINE/SHUTTERSTOCK

🗺 How To

Getting around Walk between Siwa's most visited springs or take a tuk-tuk in summer. A 4WD vehicle and police permit is needed to visit Bir Wahed.

When to go March to May and September to November are best

months for walking, but a dip in summer is refreshing. The springs are cold but less crowded in winter.

What to wear Respect local traditions and wear a T-shirt and shorts over swimwear.

MARK READ/LONELY PLANET

Top left Cleopatra's Spring
Bottom left Bir Wahed

Bathing beauties Keen swimmers are likely to want to hop into a tuk-tuk and head straight for **Cleopatra's Spring**. This gorgeous little spot, ringed by cafes and souvenir stalls, is a picture-perfect waterhole that's perennially popular.

Walking under date palms For those wanting to feel how springs impact the life of the oasis, it's possible to walk back to town from Cleopatra's Spring through the plantation, where citrus trees, pomegranates and olives also grow. Head for the **Temple of Umm Ubayd**, **Temple of the Oracle** and the tomb-riddled **Gebel Al Mawta** – each of which sticks up above the canopy of date palms, allowing for views across the expanse of green.

Lakeside sunset To see how a spring can become a lake, take a tuk-tuk to **Fatnas Spring**. A causeway across salt flats ends in a small, deep pool, perfect for a dip on a hot day. Pontoons jut into the surrounding lake, making a pleasant perch for a fruit juice at sunset, albeit in the company of coach-loads of others.

Water from under the sands For a quieter, warm-water dip, book a morning tour to **Bir Wahed**. Almost all visitors head out into the dunes that surround this tiny palm oasis at 3pm, when the main activity is dodging everyone else's 4WD. On a winter's morning, you'll have the place to yourself.

≈ Disappearing Water

A highlight of any visit to Siwa is the trip to Bir Wahed, where you'll be taken in a 4WD to a nearby cold-water lake – or at least it was a lake until 2024, when the water suddenly disappeared. At the base of a lake, the reeds have at length withered and died – a reminder that water in the desert is far from a given. A fossilised fish in the middle of the dunes nearby is further reminder, if any were needed, that nothing lasts forever – neither lake nor sea. Without water, the pharaohs, Romans and early Christians that once lived in and around the oasis would have had no reason to be here.

29 Discovering the Middle
OF NOWHERE

DESERT | PHOTOGRAPHY | WILDLIFE

Vast expanses of desert dwarf the tiny oasis of Siwa. Largely featureless, it occasionally breaks out into an extravagant magnificence that only those in the know are ever lucky enough to see. Visit El Arag Oasis and you'll be among their number.

DEA/V. GIANNELLA/GETTY IMAGES

🗺 Trip Notes

Getting around Few travel to El Arag, 130km southeast of Siwa, but Aloush Abou Kasse, at Nour El Waha Hotel, organises police permits and expert 4WD drivers.

When to go November to February to have the experience to yourself; March to May for warmer saltwater dips; June to October to experience the ferocity of desert heat.

Top tip Save money by sharing the cost of the 4WD trip with other travellers.

■ By **Aloush Abou Kasse**, tour guide and patron of Nour El Waha Hotel (*aloushabou kasse@gmail.com*)

⛺ A Greater Wilderness

Like El Arag's sense of being in the middle of nowhere? Then you'll love the **Gilf Kebir**, far to the south. It's not currently possible to get a permit to visit, but if the restriction is lifted, two or three weeks' camping in this wilderness is an experience you'll never forget.

03 At the (usually dry) **Donkey Lake**, keep an eye open for its eponymous inhabitants, particularly at sunset. These are the wild cousins of the donkeys seen carting loads around Siwa's oasis towns.

05 End a trip into the middle of nowhere with a dip at the **Salt Pools**; floating in these turquoise pools, hollowed out for the salt industry, is like bathing in the sky.

01 Stand between the **wind-eroded inselbergs** around El Arag Oasis (pictured far left) and you'll realise that all of Siwa region's 'mountains' are remnants of escarpment whittled away, rather than rocky outcrops protruding upwards.

02 Scoop some gravel from the dazzling white **fossil floor** around the escarpment, and you'll find it's made up of sand dollars – proof that the area was once under the sea.

Qara

Siwa

Siwa Salt Pools

Az Zeitun

Qattara Depression

Donkey Lake

Fossil floor

Wind-Eroded Inselbergs

Tomb Cliffs

Western (Libyan) Desert

04 Stop for a picnic lunch between the **Tomb Cliffs** (pictured left) flanking Donkey Lake. Streaked in colourful sedimentary layers, their soft-stoned base was hollowed out in Pharaonic times.

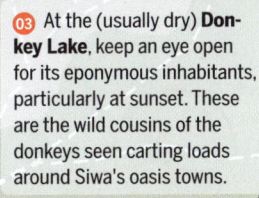

GEOFFREY PEERLESS/ALAMY

0   30 km
0   15 miles

The Desert & the Sown

OASES ARE DEFINED BY THE SURROUNDING DESERT

Before heading off into Egypt's Western Desert, it may help to know that what you go looking for on arrival is likely to be what you'll find. The desert, pared back of extraneous features, has a way of reflecting whatever we feel the need to project upon it.

Glimpses of Eternity

There's a reason why travelling in deserts feels good for the soul. The stark beauty of contrast, the rhythm of forms in a sea of sand, or the utter flatness of a rocky plain inspire contemplation of the infinite and give space for unencumbered thought. Little wonder that the first hermits of the Christian heritage, St Paul and St Anthony, made the Egyptian desert (near today's Hurghada) their locus of reflection and spiritual quest. For centuries they have been followed by explorers drawn to the Sahara, to which Egypt's Eastern and Western Deserts belong, to experience nature's extremes.

As recently as the late 1980s, the celebrated desert traveller Michael Asher and the photographer Mariantonietta Peru crossed the entire Sahara, from the Atlantic to the Nile, in a journey of over 7000km on foot and by camel. Though it's currently off limits, a few days travelling in the Gilf Kebir gives an inkling of their achievement. But, of course, they are not alone – people have in fact been testing human endurance here for centuries, travelling for trade and for pilgrimage. They mostly relied, as we do today, on the skills of the Bedouin to help them navigate a safe passage.

Desert & Sown

Even though most Bedouin tribes are now settled in oases, their culture is still rooted in the desert and they have much to teach – from their strong work ethic, sense of shared endeavour, avoidance of unnecessary risk, and responsibility towards those seeking their assistance. Retaining the parts of tribal life they still cherish, they tend to their cars with the same care once reserved for their camels, unafraid to use modern technology

Left Agabat Desert
Centre Bedouin man preparing tea
Right Group tour by camelback

SUN_SHINE/SHUTTERSTOCK

DANM/GETTY IMAGES

where it's helpful. Camping in their company in the Agabat Desert near Bahariya is a master class in adaptability – efficient, friendly and democratic, with a mobile phone as backup.

Settlement to the outsider may seem like a retreat from the desert – a selling-out, even, to the comforts of modern life. The oases themselves, shaded by date palms, fed by natural springs, seem to offer the communities of Egypt's western oases shelter from the great empty space between. But this isn't a local view. Desert, deserted, desolate – these are imported words that reinforce the binary notion of void and substance. They also reinforce the sense there is no great loss in filling in the negative space, of driving indiscriminately over delicate desert ecosystems or despoiling it through heavy industry. For those who live here, though, oasis and desert are not opposites but porous concepts that allow ebb and flow between them, inviting equal respect for both.

> Even though most Bedouin tribes are now settled in oases, their culture is still rooted in the desert and they have much to teach

Not an Empty Space

Watch a jerboa hop across the desert floor just before dawn, and your eye will be drawn to slivers of tracks in the sand. They belong to a gecko or a beetle, a big-eared fennec fox or more rarely a sand viper – these animals leave a light touch, the road maps of their existence smoothed over each day by the wind. It perhaps behoves us to do the same as travellers in their world.

🗺 The Forty Days Road

Travelling along the badly potholed road from Luxor to Al Kharga today, with its ridges of washboard making progress slow, it's hard to imagine a reason to stray from the Nile and its fertile banks. In fact, this currently seldom-used road arrives at the oasis of Al Kharga – once a major watering point on one of the Sahara's great trade routes. The **Darb Al Arba'een** (Forty Days Road) was so called because of the time taken to travel by donkey or camel caravan from today's North Darfur in Sudan to Asyut on the Nile. Visit Baris from Al Kharga, and you'll be following part of its course.

30 Dazzling DESERT

WIND-ERODED FORMS | DUNES | SUNSET

If there's one place in the whole of the Western Desert that you shouldn't miss, it's the White Desert National Park. Just 20km north of Farafra Oasis, the park encompasses a magnificent landscape of brilliant white inselbergs eroded into striking shapes by the wind. Officially, it's not permissible to overnight in the park, but there's wonderful camping nearby.

MOHAMED ABDELZAHER/SHUTTERSTOCK

🗺 How To

Getting here Although you can spot many formations from the bus window between Farafra and Bahariya, it's forbidden to enter the desert without a guide and only a 4WD trip does the area justice.

When to go The White Desert is spectacular year-round, but in winter the skies are blue rather than white with heat, making for spectacular contrasts.

Photography At sunset, the white stone turns pink – a superb time for photographs.

SAILINGSTONE TRAVEL/SHUTTERSTOCK

MICHAIL_VOROBYEVR/SHUTTERSTOCK

Far left, left White Desert National Park
Bottom left Crystal Mountain

Desert fantasia Throughout the **White Desert** (Sahra Al Beida), clusters of extraordinary wind-eroded shapes dot the desert floor. Once under the Tethy's Sea, the desert here was formed by the shells and bones of ancient marine animals deposited on the seabed over millennia. The softer layers of sediment were whittled away by the wind as the sea retreated, exposing harder rock that continues to be eroded into striking formations.

Local guides take delight in spotting zoomorphic likenesses among the scattered inselbergs, and a tour is not complete without ticking off the horse, camel and rabbit. It's the giant desert mushroom and accompanying chicken, though, that attract the crowds at sunset and which features as the national park's logo. It's here that park rangers come to collect tickets (US$5 per person) – usually included in the price of a tour.

Crystal clear Tour operators such as Rahala Safari Hotel (p173) in Farafra and guide **Mohammed Uosrri** (*WhatsApp +20-127-649-1454*) include **Crystal Mountain** in their White Desert itineraries. Comprised of quartz and with a hole blown out by the wind, this low bluff beside the Farafra–Bahariya highway glitters in the sun.

Take a look at the signboard beside Crystal Mountain to see the extent of the 300 sq km covered by the national park. Currently, only the portion east of the highway is open to visitors. This includes a large area of sand, called the **Karawin Dunes**, streaked with white pavement that's particularly beautiful at sunset.

Bedouin Memories

Take a moment to stargaze when you're camping in the desert. The Bedouin used to travel to the Nile (a 13-day journey), sleeping by day and navigating at night by the stars. Obviously, there was no Google then and the journey was really hard. During sandstorms, the guides would circle their camels and sleep in the middle, to shelter from the wind.

Despite the difficulties, though, the elders speak nostalgically of their old lives, enjoying the good health and teamwork. Escape modernity for a while, and you too can feel the benefit of a simpler life.

■ By **Ahmed Abed Abouda**, guide and documenter of Bedouin lives (*rahala-safari.com*)

31 Wandering in
THE WILDS

CAMPING | 4WD DRIVING | SWIMMING

One of the great joys of the Western Desert is camping out. The beautiful desert between Farafra and Bahariya oases offers plenty of opportunities for overnighting in spectacular landscape, while the journey to reach the campsite by 4WD provides the adventure. Throw in some hot-spring R&R, and little wonder exploring this area has become one of Egypt's top experiences.

KAZZAZM/SHUTTERSTOCK

🗺 How To

Getting around Tour operators in the oases offer trips to the Black Desert near Bahariya, White Desert National Park near Farafra (p164) and the Agabat Desert in between.

When to go Camping is possible year-round but very cold at night in winter.

What's included Police permits, 4WD transport, some dune driving by driver-guide, dinner by a campfire and dawn breakfast, with a spring dip if requested.

Plan ahead Some reports suggest you'll need to apply for police permits three weeks in advance for the Western Desert.

KATALEEWAN INTARACHOTE/SHUTTERSTOCK

ANTON_IVANOV/SHUTTERSTOCK

Left Bahariya Oasis
Far left Black Desert
Bottom left Agabat Desert

Under the night sky Imagining a night under the stars? The beauty of the real thing is that it exceeds all expectations. The lack of light and air pollution allows for skies that are so densely packed with stars they light up the desert floor even without a moon.

Camping trips can be organised from Cairo or, even better, through tour operators in Bahariya or Farafra. The driver-guides here know their patch intimately and ensure guests are discreetly camped and with the best views at dawn. A tent, thin mattress and bedding is supplied – even in winter, you're unlikely to feel cold, with a protective windbreak propped against the car and a roaring campfire.

Going off-road One-day camping trips generally include a visit to the **Black Desert** (Sahra Suda) with its striking landscape of black rock rising above yellow sands. Two-day itineraries from Bahariya may include **Gebel Al Ingleez** – an escarpment with fine views across Bahariya Oasis – and off-road driving through the magnificent **Agabat Desert** – the Monument Valley of Egypt.

Therapeutic waters An added pleasure of these desert trips is a dip in the medicinal waters of local springs. Near the Bahariya Oasis, there's **El Jaffara**, **Bir Al Ramla**'s sulphurous hot spring (45°C) and **Ain Gomma**. Call in at the excellent **Al Hayz Water Education Center** nearby, which charts the alarming drop in aquifer levels (all water now has to be pumped to the surface) while offering some water-saving solutions.

Less Pleasure, More Love

Want to drive like a Bedouin? Stay with us and we'll teach you how.

Looking for less pleasure, more love? Book a camel trip, 10km before lunch and 10km after, and feel the magic.

Car caput? We can fix it, in our garage of recycled parts.

Want some advice from Bedouin brothers? What you give, comes back, but don't forget we come with nothing and leave with nothing. In the meantime, where you put yourself, you'll find yourself.

 ■ **Talat Abdul Moulah** and his brother **Mohammed** have been tour guides for 33 years (edengardentours.com)

32 Walking HISTORY

PHARAOHS | FORTS | OASES

The beauty of the Western Desert is no secret, but few know about the region's more hidden treasures. Scattered throughout the oases are temples, tombs and forts. Visit some of these relics, and you'll be waking the warden up for the key.

CORTYN/SHUTTERSTOCK

🗺 Trip Notes

Getting around Buses link each of the oases, from Al Kharga to Bahariya. Taxis to the sites can be hired from each town.

When to go Sites are officially open 8am to 5pm daily but at lesser-visited sites, expect some variation – especially during Friday prayers.

What to wear Take a hat and wear comfortable shoes, as most of the sites involve hiking up or scrambling down on rough, unshaded terrain.

🏛 Golden Mummies

Discovered in the 1990s, the vast Graeco-Roman necropolis known as the **Valley of the Golden Mummies** lies beyond Bahariya Oasis and stretches over 3 sq km. More than 250 mummies have been unearthed, with possibly 10,000 yet to be excavated. The valley is closed, but a few mummies are displayed in Bawiti's museum.

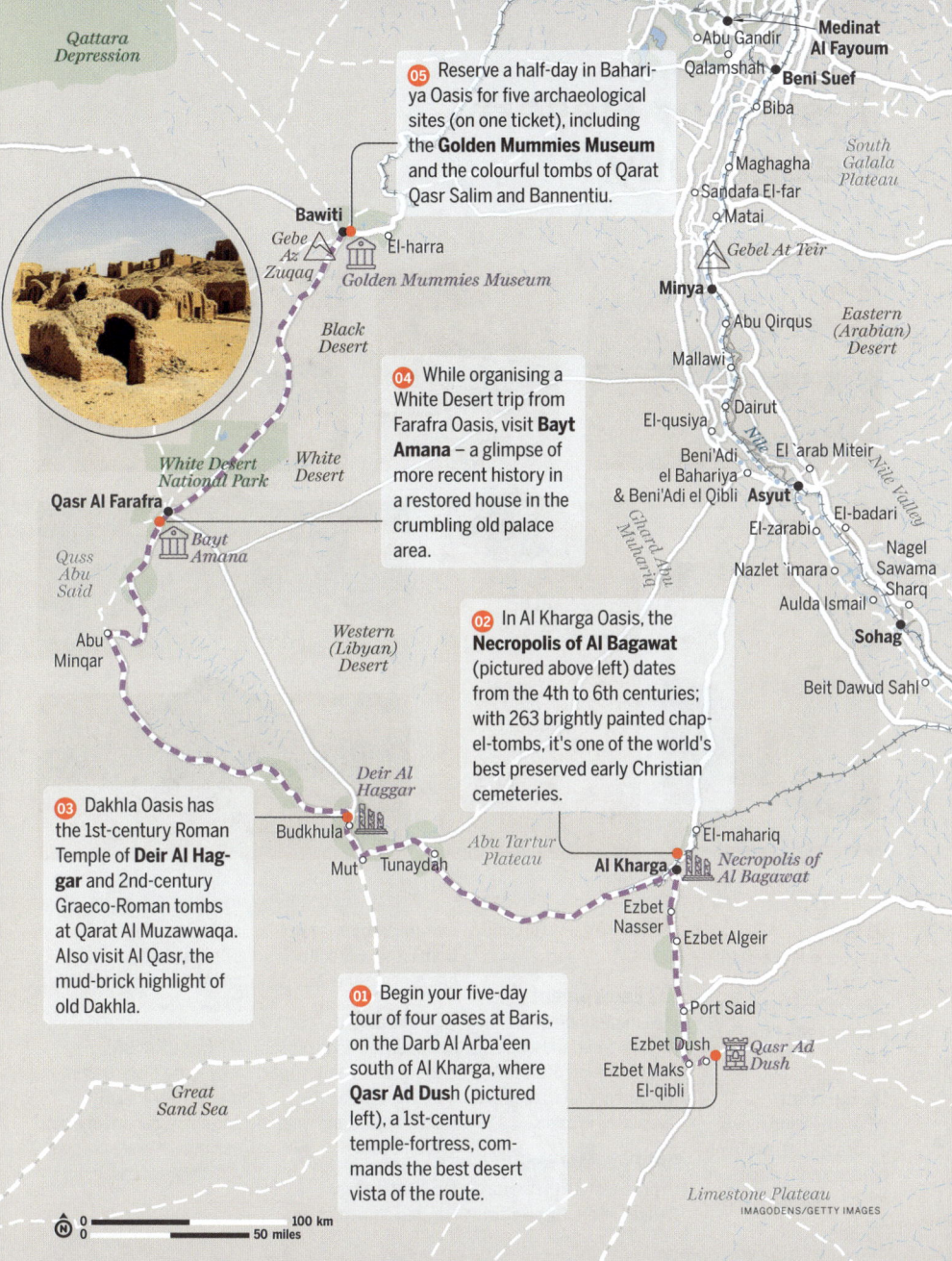

Qattara
Depression

Abu Gandir
Qalamshah

Medinat Al Fayoum
Beni Suef

Biba

05 Reserve a half-day in Bahariya Oasis for five archaeological sites (on one ticket), including the **Golden Mummies Museum** and the colourful tombs of Qarat Qasr Salim and Bannentiu.

Maghagha

South Galala Plateau

Sandafa El-far
Matai

Bawiti
Gebel Az Zuqaq
El-harra
Golden Mummies Museum

Gebel At Teir

Minya

Abu Qirqus

Eastern (Arabian) Desert

Black Desert

Mallawi

04 While organising a White Desert trip from Farafra Oasis, visit **Bayt Amana** – a glimpse of more recent history in a restored house in the crumbling old palace area.

Dairut

El-qusiya

El 'arab Miteir

White Desert National Park
White Desert

Beni'Adi el Bahariya & Beni'Adi el Qibli

Asyut

Qasr Al Farafra
Bayt Amana

El-zarabi

El-badari

Nagel Sawama Sharq

Quss Abu Said

Nazlet 'imara

Aulda Ismail

02 In Al Kharga Oasis, the **Necropolis of Al Bagawat** (pictured above left) dates from the 4th to 6th centuries; with 263 brightly painted chapel-tombs, it's one of the world's best preserved early Christian cemeteries.

Sohag

Abu Minqar

Beit Dawud Sahl

Western (Libyan) Desert

Deir Al Haggar

03 Dakhla Oasis has the 1st-century Roman Temple of **Deir Al Haggar** and 2nd-century Graeco-Roman tombs at Qarat Al Muzawwaqa. Also visit Al Qasr, the mud-brick highlight of old Dakhla.

Budkhula

Mut   Tunaydah

Abu Tartur Plateau

El-mahariq

Al Kharga
Necropolis of Al Bagawat

Ezbet Nasser
Ezbet Algeir

01 Begin your five-day tour of four oases at Baris, on the Darb Al Arba'een south of Al Kharga, where **Qasr Ad Dush** (pictured left), a 1st-century temple-fortress, commands the best desert vista of the route.

Port Said

Ezbet Dush
Ezbet Maks
El-qibli

Qasr Ad Dush

Great Sand Sea

Limestone Plateau

IMAGODENS/GETTY IMAGES

0   100 km
0   50 miles

Test Your Desert Geography

01 Erg
Egypt and Libya share a vast erg, or 'sea of sand', in the Gilf Kebir; its edge is just south of Siwa.

02 Barchan
When the wind blows across the desert in one predominant direction, it forms crescent-shaped dunes – as seen around Baris.

03 Escarpment
The mini 'mountains' that dot the Siwa landscape are what's left of an escarpment (flat-topped cliff caused by erosion).

04 Pedestal rock
A prize feature of Farafra's White Desert, these giant rock mushrooms result from erosion of softer layers of sedimentary rock.

05 Yardang
Pavements of long protrusions of sedimentary rock, fluted and grooved by sand abrasion and wind, in El Arag Oasis.

06 Inselberg
Isolated domes, pillars, rocks and other protrusions are imagined as animal forms in the White Desert.

07 Basaltic sill
Why is the Black Desert black? Near Bahariya, ancient volcanoes of black iron quartzite are capped with layers of basalt.

08 Desert rose
Desert 'roses' of gypsum crystal 'petals' are found near salt flats around Siwa. Other 'flowers' are formed from sand dollars.

09 Dollars and coins
El Arag is covered in fossilised sand dollars, formed of sea-urchin skeletons, and 'nummu-lites' (little coins), once used as currency.

10 White Desert
Why is the White Desert white? It's comprised of calcium, limestone and quartz crystals – as seen at Crystal Mountain.

11 Rock arch
Wind and sand some-times punch a hole through softer rock forming archways in the escarpment, notably in the Agabat Desert.

12 Watermelons and raspberries
Cannonball-shaped rocks of heavy chert sit on the limestone shelf near Al Fayoum. Tiny berry-shaped balls of framboidal pyrite are widely scattered.

13 Petrified wood
Petrified or fossilised wood is common in the Western Desert – look for small, heavy black 'sticks' of stone near the Agabat Desert.

Listings

BEST OF THE REST

 ## Oasis Hotels with Attitude

Al Babinshal Heritage Hotel

Seemingly integral to the mud-brick walls of Shali fortress, this gorgeous boutique hotel is part of a Siwa experience with its labyrinthine corridors and steep staircases.

Adrère Amellal

A stunning retreat 13km from Siwa, this chic eco-lodge has no electricity – the rooms and garden are lit by tilly lamps and candles. It's not cheap, but it is exclusive.

Qasr Al Bagawat

An eco-lodge with domed mud-brick rooms and local-style furnishings, this delightful Al Kharga guesthouse in a shaded garden gets consistently good reviews.

Sol Y Mar Pioneers Hotel

A pink confection of a building sprawling over a large plot, this grand hotel doesn't quite live up to its billing. That said, it's the best in Al Kharga and unusually has a bar.

Desert Lodge

Crowning a hilltop with a wonderful view of Dakhla Oasis and the desert escarpment, this old favourite resembles a mud-brick fortress with attractive common areas.

Bedouin Camp

The rooms of this attractive Dakhla guesthouse, run by Bedouin brothers, are in traditional brick-domed buildings, and there's a hilltop lounge with central fireplace.

Rahala Safari Hotel

Set in a garden of citrus fruit and shaded by date palms, this homely Farafra hotel is run by desert-knowledgeable owners and serves great food.

Al Badawiya Safari & Hotel

This Farafra institution, offering tours, has been in business for years and has slowly expanded up to its perimeter fence without losing any of its homeliness.

International Hot Spring Hotel

Run by desert expert, Peter Wirth, and his Japanese partner Mihru Shimazaki, this tranquil Bahariya hotel is set in a huge garden with a hot spring.

 ## In Ruins

Fortress of Shali

Built from *kershef* (salt blocks and rock, plastered with clay), this 13th-century mud-brick fortress looms up in the centre of Siwa offering fine views of the oasis.

Gebel Al Mawta

The tombs in this 'Mountain of the Dead' in Siwa date back to the Ptolemaic and Roman times of the 26th dynasty and include some striking tomb paintings.

Temple of the Oracle

Beside the ruins of Siwa's old town, Aghurmi, this 6th-century BCE temple was so renowned that Alexander the Great, it's believed, was declared the son of Amun here.

Qasr Al Ghueita

Some way south of Al Kharga Oasis, this massive garrison fort hides a beautiful 25th-dynasty temple, graced with a hypostyle hall and reliefs of Hapy, the pot-bellied Nile god.

Deir Al Haggar

On the edge of Dakhla Oasis, this well-restored temple was built in the 1st century. Look for the name of Gerhard Rohlfs and his

19th-century expedition team at the top of the once-buried column.

Ethnographic Museum

Just inside the main entrance to Al Qasr, this house formerly belonged to Sherif Ahmed and dates back to 1785. The ingenious wooden keys are still in use.

 Oasis Fare

Abdu Restaurant $

This is the traveller's meeting place in Siwa, with a wide menu of local favourites and some international dishes, served with free travel advice.

OLA Restaurant $$

This candle-lit garden is a magical place to enjoy desert nights while sampling tasty Siwa dishes, including camel-meat stews.

Wimpy Albasateen $

Molokhiyya (garlicky leaf soup) is served at this local Al Kharga favourite, along with generous portions of delicious grilled meats, rice, salad and *ta'amiyya* (fava-bean falafel).

 Touring with the Experts

Nour El Waha

One of the best Siwa tour operators, Aloush Abou Kasse, owner of Nour El Waha Hotel, can organise next-day trips with permits across the region, including El Arag Oasis.

Rahala Safari Hotel

Farafra-based, White Desert expert Ahmed Abed Abouda recently invited Bedouin elders back into the desert to document their memories. He shares their insights during camping trips with his guests.

Shahrazad Desert Camp

Beside the White Desert, this attractive camp has been operating since 2006. It

Deir Al Haggar

offers desert trips with accommodation in a permanent, tented camp for those less keen on roughing it.

Eden Garden Tours

Two highly experienced Bedouin brothers operate from an attractive camp on the edge of Bahariya Oasis. They remember walking between oases with their mother as boys and organise excellent multiday trips.

Badry Sahara Camp

Badry, of this delightful little camp on the edge of the Bahariya Oasis, is an old desert hand offering recommended 4WD tours and a traveller's vibe at his oasis camp.

Mohammed Uosrri

This experienced Bahariya-based local guide specialises in trips to the White Desert and the whole Bahariya area. (*WhatsApp +20-127-649-1454*)

Hesham Nessim

Although currently off limits, the Gilf Kebir and Great Sand Sea offer remarkable remote desert experiences. Record-breaking rally driver Hesham Nessim is the person to contact if the restrictions are lifted. (*@heshamnessim1*)

ANTON_IVANOV/SHUTTERSTOCK

ALEXANDRIA & THE MEDITERRANEAN COAST

ATMOSPHERE | URBAN MYTHS | BEACHES

ALEXANDRIA & THE MEDITERRANEAN COAST
Trip Builder

▬▬ Egypt's Mediterranean coast stretches 500km and is fringed by stunning beaches. At its heart stands atmospheric Alexandria, the storied city of Alexander the Great, which linked Europe with the old world of the pharaohs. It remains a city full of fascinating stories that reward the curious traveller.

Go bike riding and beach hopping in **Montazah Park** (p191)
🚲 30-50min from Saad Zaghloul Park

Enjoy tea and cake in vintage 1940s coffeehouses like **Délices** (p182)
🚶 15min from Misr Train Station

Discover surprising cosmopolitan legacies at **St Mark's Cathedral** (p183)
🚶 5min from Saad Zaghloul Square

Pay your respects at El Alamein's poignant **war cemeteries** (p193)
🚲 90min from Alexandria

Explore Alexander the Great's city at the **Graeco-Roman Museum** (p179; pictured left)
🚶 10min from Misr Train Station

Join Alexandrians in their favourite pastime – eating – on a **food tour** (p185)
🚲 10min from Saad Zaghloul Square

Mediterranean Sea

Aboukir
Abu Qir

Alexandria

Kafr El-dauwar

Arab's Gulf

El Alamein

El-hamman

Zawyet Sidi Abd El-ati

Western (Libyan) Desert

Wadi Natrun

FROM LEFT: MARINADA/SHUTTERSTOCK
PREVIOUS SPREAD: AHMED ELFIKY/SHUTTERSTOCK

0   30 km
0   15 miles

Practicalities

ARRIVING

Misr Train Station Located 1km from the central square, Midan Saad Zaghloul. Sidi Gaber Station serves the eastern suburbs.

Moaf Al Gedid Bus Station Served by Go Bus from Cairo. It's 7km from the city centre; a taxi costs LE450.

MONEY

There is no shortage of ATMs. Keep small notes handy for tips and taxis.

FIND YOUR WAY

Midan Ramla and Midan Saad Zaghloul are the central squares surrounded by the city's main shops, restaurants and hotels.

WHERE TO STAY

Area	Pro/Con
Downtown	The most convenient location with lots of options, including some historic addresses. Can be noisy.
Around Stanley Bridge	Midrange local chains cluster around Stanley Bridge; it's a 20-minute drive from Downtown.
Montazah Park	A lovely park surrounded by the best city beaches featuring luxury options; not much nightlife.

EATING

A highlight here is tucking into the fresh daily catch in one of the seafood restaurants (pictured below left) overlooking the harbour. Signature city dishes such as *kebda* (pictured left; beef-liver sandwiches) and *kushari* (mix of noodles, rice, black lentils, fried onions and tomato sauce) are also a must-try. The Corniche and markets are full of good-value street-food stalls.

Best seafood
White & Blue (p178)

Must-try ice cream with mastic Fahmy (p179)

GETTING AROUND

Walking Alexandria is made for walking, with people promenading the Corniche year-round. From central Midan Saad Zaghloul, all Downtown sights are a 20- to 30-minute walk away.

Taxi Needed for the 40- to 50-minute drive to Montazah Park and its beaches (LE50). Use Uber for fixed prices.

Tuk-tuk and tram More of a fun experience than a serious transport option. Less than LE10.

DEC–FEB
The coldest months with biting sea breezes; but there's Christmas

MAR–MAY
Perfect for seaside strolling and witnessing Coptic Orthodox Easter

JUN–AUG
Summer holiday season with a citywide festival and busy beaches

SEP–NOV
Balmy temperatures, empty beaches and poignant WWII remembrance services

ALEXANDRIA & THE MEDITERRANEAN COAST FIND YOUR FEET

33 Alexander the GREAT'S CITY

CLASSICAL TREASURES | CATACOMBS | RUINS

■■■■■ Founded in 331 BCE by Alexander the Great, Alexandria (Al Iskendariyya) is the stuff of legend, with its founding Ptolemaic dynasty being the longest – and last – line of pharaohs in ancient Egypt. Though much lies in ruins beneath the modern city, exciting explorations in gloomy catacombs, sunken ruins, and the glowing halls of the Graeco-Roman Museum bring it vividly back to life.

🗺 How To

Getting here The Graeco-Roman Museum and Kom Al Dikka are Downtown and walkable. Take a taxi to Kom El Shoqafa.

When to go May to June or September and October, when the weather is ideal for urban explorations.

Tickets Buy tickets online (egymonuments.com) or by card at the gate.

Fort Qaitbey
White & Blue
Eastern Harbour
SHATBY
Mohammed Koraiem
ANFUSHI
Midan Saad Zaghloul
Midan Ramla Tram Station
Champollion
Midan Orabi
Salah Salem
Sultan Hussein
Graeco-Roman Museum
An Nasr
Midan Tahrir
Al Nabi Daniel
Fouad
Bab Al Akhdar
Sidi Al Metwali
Kom Al Dikka
Mohafza
ATTAREEN
Misr Train Station
Sherif
Sidi al-Metwali
0   0.5 km
0   0.25 miles
Kom Ash Suqqafa

Understanding Alexandria

To get to grips with Alexandria's unique character, you have to start at the **Graeco-Roman Museum**. Fresh from renovation, it brilliantly conjures the city's glory days as a Hellenistic capital via unusual artefacts, recreated classical homes and temples, and unique exhibits of sculp-ture, tanagra figurines and Greek-Egyptian gods such as Serapis and Boubastis (a cat god worshipped by early Greeks).

With a model of the ancient city in your head, step out onto the Canopic Way, now Sharia El Horreya, and walk south to **Kom Al Dikka**, a sunken archaeological park surrounded incongruously by apartment blocks. Once a well-off residential area, it's littered with the remains of a university, public baths, villas and a Roman amphitheatre. The **Villa of Birds** retains a lovely floor mosaic of pea-cocks, quails and parrots.

Top right Kom El Shoqafa
Right Kom Al Dikka

ALEXANDRIA & THE MEDITERRANEAN COAST EXPERIENCES

🏛 The First Greek Pharaoh

At the tip of Alexandria's lovely curved bay, you'll spy a little crenellated citadel called **Fort Qaitbey**. It stands on the spot of the 3rd-century BCE Pharos of Alexandria (lighthouse), one of the Seven Wonders of the Ancient World. The lighthouse was built by Ptolemy I Soter (Ptolemy the Saviour), who also ordered the construction of the Library of Alexandria. Soter was one of Alexander's seven bodyguards and on his death in 323 BCE became the first Greek Pharaoh of Egypt. He asserted this claim by acquiring Alexander's body and burying it in Memphis.

Then jump in a taxi to **Kom El Shoqafa**, the largest Roman burial site in Egypt. Here, in gloomy underground chambers, you'll witness the syncretism of Pharaonic and Hellenistic beliefs, particularly in the principal tomb, where Anubis, the Egyptian god of the dead, is depicted as a Roman legionnaire and sports a serpent's tail, representative of Agathos Daimon, a Greek divinity.

Finish at the **Greek Club**, a hub for the Greek Alexandrian community, where you can have a fine seafood lunch on the terrace of White & Blue (p194).

UCG/GETTY IMAGES

INNERPEACESEEKER/GETTY IMAGES

34 Ottoman ALEXANDRIA

MAMLUK FORTS | MOSQUES | MARKETS

While Downtown Alexandria is dressed in 19th-century belle époque architecture, Anfushi and Bahari – the old Mamluk-Ottoman quarter – remain untouched, an indigenous district that contrasts with the new cosmopolitan city. This is where once-stuffy Alexandria came to let down its hair, and even today, its labyrinthine streets teem with markets, mosques and traditional *ahwas* (coffeehouses).

ALEXANTON/SHUTTERSTOCK

🗺 How To

Getting here Take a taxi to Fort Qaitbey and tour its ramparts. Then walk around the headland to the docks, turn into any side street, and walk east.

When to go Late morning is a good time to explore, when markets bustle. Then settle down for lunch in a local restaurant.

Local snack Try *kebda Eskandarany*, a sandwich of beef liver sautéed with garlic, ground chillies and spices.

CHERRIA KENZO/SHUTTERSTOCK

ALEXANDRIA & THE MEDITERRANEAN COAS EXPERIENCES

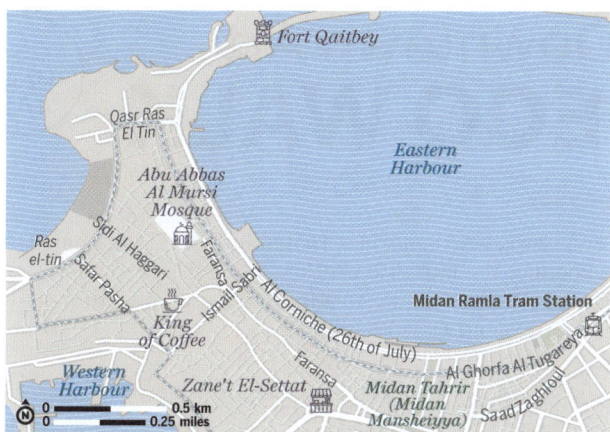

A deep dive into Anfushi Fort Qaitbey (egymonuments. com) sits at the tip of the peninsula, guarding Alexandria's eastern bay, and is a perfect Mamluk military fortification. It was built in the 1470s by Sultan Al-Ashraf Qaitbey. Spot the red granite pillars reused from the Pharos lighthouse around the exterior, then visit the antique mosque within, and finish on the ramparts, which offer the best views of the city.

In the shadow of the fort, Anfushi is the remains of the Mamluk and Ottoman city (1250–1914); a warren of tiny streets separate apartment blocks like urban canyons. Walk down the western bay to see shipbuilders at work, then dive in. A good street is Saqer Basha, lined with cafes, veg shops and barbecue stalls. Then head up Ras El Tin, have a Turkish coffee at **King of Coffee**, and drop into Mosque Square. Here you'll find **Abu Abbas Al Mursi**, a neo-Mamluk mosque rising over the 13th-century tomb of an Andalusian Sufi saint. Outside prayer time, you can visit the gorgeous interior, and on summer nights, there's a carnival atmosphere around the mosque.

Souq shopping Zigzag southeast from the mosque down Ras El Tin and Ibrahim Zaghloul streets to experience the city's fantastic souq district. It's one long, heaving bustle of produce stalls, barbecue stands, bakeries, cafes and sundry shops selling every imaginable thing. **Zane't El Settat**, the 'women's souq', is famously full of buttons, braid, baubles, bangles and beads.

Egypt's First Serial Killers

Lawrence Durrell's *Alexandria Quartet* made Anfushi famous as the shady side of the city, where he and other soldiers frequented seedy brothels and bars. During the wars, Alexandria was a renowned hot spot for prostitution, fuelled by the extreme poverty many Egyptians faced. Raya and Sakina were the city's most infamous 'madams', who ran several brothels. When competition grew stiff and profits thinned, they allegedly killed 17 women with their husbands, stole their gold jewellery, and buried them under their homes. Discovered and sentenced to death in 1921, they became the first women in Egypt to receive the death penalty.

Learn more about this extraordinary story on Karim Serrie's **ghost tour** (+20-10-0261-7885).

35 A Downtown Art
DECO WALK

ARCHITECTURE | CAFES | CULTURE

▬▬▬ The character of contemporary Alexandria is rooted in Pasha Mohammed Ali's modernising building boom of the late 19th century, when the city had a beautiful belle époque makeover. Take a wander to admire the era's beautiful villas, banks, coffeehouses, theatres and apartment blocks.

JOHN WREFORD/SHUTTERSTOCK

🗺 Trip Notes

Getting around Alexandria is flat and easily walkable, although take care crossing roads given unpredictable tuk-tuks and mopeds.

When to go April to October is best weather-wise. To avoid rush-hour traffic, hit the streets between mid-morning and early afternoon.

Top tips Pre-book synagogue tours and bring your passport as security is tight. Have lunch at vintage **Santa Lucia**, once a high-society favourite.

■ By **Rasha Aggag**, an Alexandrian tour guide (*@rashaaa9434*)

☕ Cafe Culture

Alexandria's two heritage cafes are **Trianon** and **Délices**. Trianon, opened by Greeks Andrea Drikos and George Pericles in 1935, charms with its beautiful interior. Délices, a 1922 landmark, is famous for traditional Greek sweets, breads and biscuits.

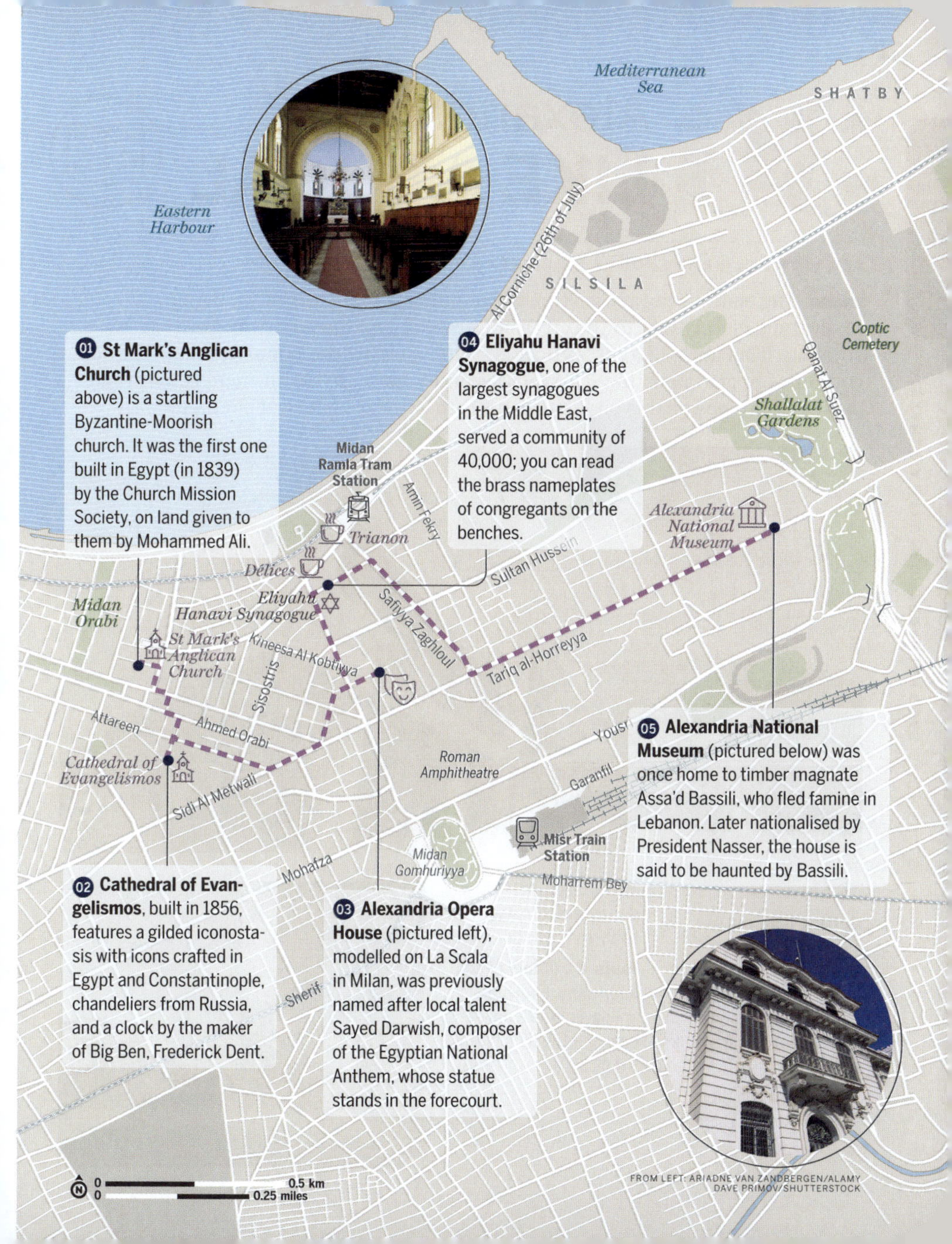

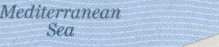

Mediterranean Sea

SHATBY

Eastern Harbour

SILSILA

Al Corniche (26th of July)

Coptic Cemetery

Qanat Al Suez

Shallalat Gardens

01 St Mark's Anglican Church (pictured above) is a startling Byzantine-Moorish church. It was the first one built in Egypt (in 1839) by the Church Mission Society, on land given to them by Mohammed Ali.

04 Eliyahu Hanavi Synagogue, one of the largest synagogues in the Middle East, served a community of 40,000; you can read the brass nameplates of congregants on the benches.

Midan Ramla Tram Station

Amin Fekry

Trianon

Délices

Sultan Hussein

Alexandria National Museum

Midan Orabi

Eliyahu Hanavi Synagogue

Safiyya Zaghloul

St Mark's Anglican Church

Kineesa Al Kobtuya

Sisostris

Tariq al-Horreyya

Attareen

Ahmed Orabi

Yousri

05 Alexandria National Museum (pictured below) was once home to timber magnate Assa'd Bassili, who fled famine in Lebanon. Later nationalised by President Nasser, the house is said to be haunted by Bassili.

Cathedral of Evangelismos

Sidi Al Metwali

Roman Amphitheatre

Garanfil

Mohatza

Midan Gomhuriyya

Misr Train Station

Moharrem Bey

02 Cathedral of Evangelismos, built in 1856, features a gilded iconostasis with icons crafted in Egypt and Constantinople, chandeliers from Russia, and a clock by the maker of Big Ben, Frederick Dent.

Sherif

03 Alexandria Opera House (pictured left), modelled on La Scala in Milan, was previously named after local talent Sayed Darwish, composer of the Egyptian National Anthem, whose statue stands in the forecourt.

0   0.5 km
0   0.25 miles
N

36 Alexandria
LIKE A LOCAL

SEA VIEWS | LIBRARY TOURS | ICE CREAM

■■■■ Alexandria's library isn't just a monument to history, it's a living institution, closely tied to the city's cultural life and university. It draws students from across Egypt, as does the city itself, whose population of 6 million continues to grow, making it Egypt's second-largest city. With them comes the dynamism to power this city of dreams into its next historical chapter.

LUIS DAFOS/GETTY IMAGES

🧭 How To

Getting here You can walk the length of the 18km Corniche from Fort Qaitbey to Montazah Park in four hours. The library is one hour's walk from the fort.

When to go The Biblioth-eca Alexandrina (bibalex.

org) is a cultural hub during the summer fes-tival, from July to August.

Tours The library offers daily tours, bookable online. For museum ac-cess, get the all-inclusive ticket.

LESHIY985/SHUTTERSTOCK

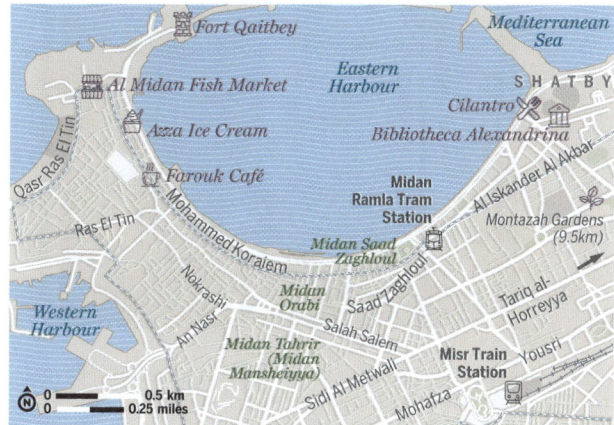

Top left Bibliotheca Alexandrina
Bottom left Corniche

A Library, Promenade & Feast

The **Bibliotheca Alexandrina** is the city's cultural heart, its 2500-seat reading room catering to various universities and institutions. Library tours illuminate the building's symbolism, modelled after an Egyptian sun disc and carved with symbols from more than 120 human scripts. Meanwhile, in subterranean galleries you'll find archaeological artefacts, historic manuscripts (including the only surviving scroll from Alexandria's ancient library), and some great modern Egyptian art.

Enjoy an iced latte at **Cilantro** cafe, set on a terrace beside the library overlooking the **Corniche**. Beloved by locals, the Corniche is a constant feature of daily life as people drift up and down enjoying the sea view, drinking tea at pop-up cafes, and snacking on grilled corn or ice cream from mobile stalls. You can walk the length of the city along it, which takes four hours from **Fort Qaitbey** to **Montazah Park**.

Alexandria's other claim to fame is the city's food scene. To access the best of it, join Rasha Aggag on a **food tour** (+20-10-6208-8282). She'll introduce you to the best street stalls, hole-in-the-wall restaurants, vintage cafes like **Farouk Café**, and locally loved ice-cream parlours like **Azza**, which serves chewy Alexandrian gelato. Definitely, don't miss the fish market, **Al Midan**, where you can browse the daily catch and have it grilled on the spot.

📖 The Great Library of Alexandria

Built in the 3rd century BCE by Ptolemy I to enhance Alexandria's prestige, the original Library of Alexandria was one of the greatest intellectual centres in antiquity. Known as the Mouseion (Shrine of the Muses), it functioned much like a university. To create the great collection – which estimates place as high as 400,000 scrolls – Ptolemy I ordered manuscripts to be confiscated from docking ships and sent merchants to scour Mediterranean markets for scrolls in Babylonian, Persian, Assyrian, Hebrew and Indian. The scale of the Ptolemies' ambition to create a repository of all human knowledge was unmatched at the time. It endured for six centuries until fire and political upheaval saw to its ruin.

The Cleopatras

EGYPT'S EXTRAORDINARY FEMALE PHARAOHS

Cleopatra VII's dramatic life and legendary beauty lead us to think she was a unique figure. But in truth, she was the last in a long line of female pharaohs, seven of whom shared her name, meaning 'the glory of her father' or 'her country's renown'.

Left Cleopatra VI Tryphaena
Centre Cleopatra II relief, Temple of Kom Ombo (p147)
Right Cleopatra VII relief, Temple of Horus (p147)

CHRONICLE/ALAMY

Cleopatra VII's position as the undisputed queen of Egypt was possible thanks to the extraordinary legacy of seven previous Ptolemaic queens, who cast off roles as mothers and wives to claim the same power as their husbands. Because of their wily politicking, in 34 BCE, when Egypt was the richest kingdom in the world, Cleopatra VII was able to call herself 'Queen of Kings'.

Their story begins with Alexander the Great's death in 323 BCE. It left three powers vying for control of the eastern Mediterranean: the Macedonians in Greece, the Seleucids in Syria, and the Ptolemies in Egypt. Cleopatra I, known as Cleopatra Syra (193–176 BCE), was a Seleucid princess, and her marriage to Ptolemy V formed part of a peace treaty that shored up Egyptian security. When her husband died (possibly murdered by her), she became sole regent of Egypt at the age of 24. She cancelled the war with the Seleucids that Ptolemy had planned, uniquely assumed the role of Vizier, and had coins minted in her name.

Meanwhile, Cleopatra II married two full-blood brothers (incest was a Ptolemaic custom to avoid hypogamy and dilution of power), led a rebellion against her second husband, and was the first Ptolemaic queen to be confirmed as female pharaoh. Her daughter, Cleopatra III, subsequently ruled as regent for her son, Ptolemy IX, until she expelled him from Alexandria in 107 BCE. She replaced him with her second son and made herself Priest of Alexander, an unprecedented position for a woman. She ruled for four decades until she was murdered by her son in 101 BCE.

The murders and marriages continued throughout the second century BCE. Cleopatra IV and her sister Tryphaena

wed Seleucid kings engaged in civil war, causing Tryphaena to have her sister executed in the sanctuary of Daphne in Antioch. Then, she herself was murdered by Cleopatra VI's husband. The Ptolemies' penchant for incest and multi-generational co-rule had by this point created the perfect power-struggle storm.

When Berenice III (also known as Cleopatra) ascended the throne, she did so as sole female pharaoh – the first time a woman gained the crown without marriage. As the monarchy was considered a dual male-female role, she quickly sought a husband, which the Romans furnished in the form of her much younger step-nephew, Ptolemy XI. They hated each other on sight and Ptolemy killed her after just 19 days of marriage, a foolish decision. The Alexandrians rioted on 22 April 80 BCE and killed Ptolemy, thus clearing the path to the throne for Cleopatra V Tryphaena. Little is known about this late Cleopatra other than she was the mother of the most famous Cleopatra of all, Cleopatra VII.

> The century and a half of the Cleopatras' rule was an extraordinary historical anomaly

The century and a half of the Cleopatras' rule was an extraordinary historical anomaly. Each wielded absolute power, and all were shrewd and capable rulers. Styling themselves as goddess-queens, they held power through arcane rituals, political savvy and unparalleled wealth. They navigated political turmoil and court intrigue, led armies into battle and commanded ship fleets, and dispatched their dynastic rivals.

The Real Cleopatra VII

Roman propaganda portrayed Cleopatra VII (69–30 CE) as an irresistible *femme fatale*. The reality is quite different: contemporary records note that Cleopatra was an exceptional stateswoman rather than a great beauty. She was multilingual and a gifted scholar, scientist and philosopher. She was also an astute politician focused on protecting Egypt against Roman aggression. She had a son with Julius Caesar and an affair with his protégé Mark Anthony, who fought to protect her throne against Octavian (later Emperor Augustus), Caesar's adopted son. Finally defeated at the Battle of Actium in 30 BCE, it's widely accepted that she took her own life rather than be paraded in Rome as a prisoner.

 Some Cosmopolitan
SURPRISES

CHURCHES | TEMPLE | CEMETERIES

▬▬▬ Alexandria is as much a place of imagination and memory as a concrete city on the Mediterranean. Its legendary tolerance, pluralism and cosmopolitanism run deep. Founded as a bridge between Europe, Africa and Asia – with its library a beacon of learning, its port a trade hub, and its cosmopolitan population a model of neighbourliness. Even today, the city is famous for its laid-back character.

JIM DAVID/SHUTTERSTOCK

🧭 How To

Getting here Although churches are open to the faithful, it's best to visit them on a tour, given tight security. Visits to the synagogue must be booked, and you'll need to show your passport.

When to go Easter is a joyful time, as the

celebration coincides with the ancient spring festival of Sham An Nessim, held the day after Easter Sunday.

Souvenir Buy some famous chocolate-covered Manolidis dates from Crystal Sweets (p195).

WILROOIJ/WIKIMEDIA/CC BY-SA 4.0

ALEXANDRIA & THE MEDITERRANEAN COAS EXPERIENCES

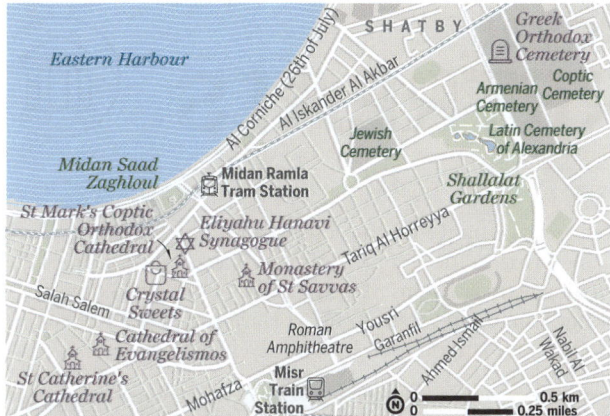

Top left St Mark's Coptic Orthodox
Cathedral
Bottom left Cathedral of
Evangelismos

Legacies of Faith

St Mark's Coptic Orthodox Cathedral was founded by the
apostle St Mark in 42 CE, and he remains the patron saint
of Egypt. Spot his name at the top of the list of patriarchs in
the church's peaceful interior before descending to see his
desolate tomb, which was robbed by the Venetians in 828 CE.
Thieves Buono da Malamocco and Rustico da Torcello carried
the relics away in a barrel of pork to elevate their then-insignif-
icant city of Venice.

In 451 CE, the Orthodox Church split into two branches,
the Coptic Orthodox and the Eastern (or Greek) Orthodox
patriarchates. The latter decamped to the **Cathedral of
Evangelismos**, richly decorated with a gilded iconostasis,
chandeliers and stained-glass windows. The patriarch is still
enthroned here. Meanwhile, at the frescoed **Monastery of St
Savvas**, the Academy of St Athanasios the Great continues to
train African priests.

For Catholics, there's the baroque **Cathedral of St Catherine**, once a Franciscan community that served pilgrims on
their way to the Holy Land. Italy's exiled King, Victor Emanuele
II, was buried here in 1947 in a lavish tomb until his body was
repatriated in 2017.

Finally, take a tour of the **Eliyahu Hanavi Synagogue**, an
Italian Revival structure with 28 pink marble columns. It was
the most important synagogue among the 20 that served a
40,000-strong community in the 1940s.

Stories from the Grave

Pasha Mohammed
Ali gifted Alexandria's
cosmopolitan Christian
community a feddan of
land in Shabty to bury
their dead. There you'll
find the **Greek Orthodox
Cemetery**, the **Coptic
Cemetery**, the **Cemete-
rium Latinorum Terra
Sancta** (Latin Cemetery
of Alexandria), the **Anglican Cemetery** and the
Armenian Cemetery. It's
a fascinating place full of
Gothic, Art Nouveau and
neoclassical funeral sculp-
tures commemorating the
great and the good, such
as Botty, the first director
of the Greek Museum, and
poet Constantine Cavafy.
Researcher **Zahraa Adel
Awad** (+20-10-0272-
4324) leads insightful
tours and assists many
émigrés to trace their
relatives and explore their
Alexandrian heritage.

38 Royal RETREATS

GARDENS | BEACHES | JEWELS

▅▅▅▅ At Alexandria's eastern edge, you'll find the 1.5-dq-km Montazah Park, the largest green space in the city. Prior to the 1952 revolution, it was royal property, where the last Ottoman khedive, Abbas Helmy II (1874–1944), built the Salamlek hunting lodge and where King Fouad later added the Al Haramlek Palace. The park is beloved by Alexandrians and surrounded by the city's best beaches.

CAVAN IMAGES/SHUTTERSTOCK

🗺 How To

Getting here Montazah Park is 17km from Downtown, so grab an Uber. Golf carts and bikes are available in the gardens.

When to go Beach clubs are open between May and September.

Montazah Park is open 24 hours and is busy late into the night in summer.

Take a break In the garden stands King Farouk's tea pavilion, housed in a Roman-style structure set on a tiny island with sea views all around.

HAZEM OMAR/SHUTTERSTOCK

For 147 years, Muhammad Ali's dynasty ruled Egypt, during which time they amassed extraordinary wealth, built lavish palaces, and were assiduous collectors of fine art and jewellery. During this royal era (1805–1953), Alexandria was a decidedly Mediterranean city – its fortunes inextricably tied to the web of relations around it.

It's this cosmopolitan culture that **Montazah Park** and its fantastic Euro-Orientalist palaces reflect. The smaller **Salamlek Palace** (now a five-star, heritage hotel) was inspired by Austrian hunting lodges, while the main **Haramlek Palace**, built in 1932 by Ernest Verrucci, is a Byzantine-Italianate palazzo modelled on Florence's Palazzo Vecchio. Later, King Farouk added a Roman-style **Tea Pavilion** on Nelson's Island, and there's also a Victorian-style **greenhouse** harbouring exotic botanical specimens.

It's a beautiful place for a stroll or a picnic, and the headland is surrounded by Alexandria's best beaches – Aida, Nefertiti, Cleopatra, Semiramis and Marmoura – which you can access via beach clubs and hotel passes.

While the Haramlek Palace remains closed to visitors, you can get a glimpse of the extravagant taste of Egypt's royal family at the **Royal Jewellery Museum**. It is housed in the Art Deco villa of Princess Fatma Al-Zahra and includes King Farouk's gold-and-diamond-studded chessboard, gold and sapphire coffee cups, and dazzling diamond sets designed by Boucheron and Van Cleef & Arpels.

Top left Haramlek Palace
Bottom left Montazah Park

Beach Clubs

If you want to get in the water, there are plenty of beaches along Alexandria's waterfront. However, the shoreline near the Eastern Harbour is packed in summer and not always clean, so it's best to head to Montazah. The best beach clubs include the private section of Semiramis Beach, reserved for guests of the **Helnan Royal Palestine Hotel**; **Mamoura Beach** beside Montazah Park, which has a boardwalk, food stalls and a private area for **Paradise Inn Beach Resort** guests; and the hyper-luxe **Four Seasons Beach**, where passes cost LE1850 to LE2400 per person.

39 Excursions Beyond
ALEXANDRIA

WWII CEMETERIES | MEMORIALS | BEACHES

For a brief period in 1942, El Alamein commanded the world's attention, because it was here that the Allies won control of North Africa in WWII at the cost of thousands of lives. Nowadays, Alamein is looking to the future with the billion-dollar New Alamein City and a string of luxury beach resorts set along the stunning white sands of Sidi Abdel Rahman.

RICHARD WALKER MEDIA/SHUTTERSTOCK

🗺 How To

Getting here El Alamein is a 1½-hour drive (115km) west of Alexandria. The best way to get here is to hire a car and driver who will take you between the war museum and the cemeteries.

When to go Remembrance services are held on 23 October. Summer resorts open between June and September.

Guide Karim Serrie (+20-10-0261-7885) runs informative Alamein tours, which include transport and lunch in Alamein.

THOMAS W'NESS/SHUTTERSTOCK

Top left Commonwealth War Cemetery
Bottom left Military Museum

A Storied Theatre of War

Like Dunkirk and Passchendaele, El Alamein is one of history's most significant battlegrounds and is home to one of the largest WWII cemeteries in the world. More than 80,000 soldiers were killed in the battles fought between German and Allied forces here. That's because Alamein was the last defensible position before Cairo – and the critical Suez Canal – and the city's war cemeteries are a reminder of the high price paid to hold that line.

The **Commonwealth War Cemetery** is the largest, with thousands of tombstones stretching as far as the eye can see in impeccable rows interplanted with cacti and neatly clipped crimson bougainvillea bushes. After contemplating the poignant scene, head to the comprehensive **Military Museum**, which features a garden filled with tanks, anti-aircraft machine guns, and fighter planes.

Then drive 7km west of El Alamein and you'll see an octagonal sandstone fortress atop a promontory overlooking the sea. It is the **German War Memorial**, its blank facade embracing a peaceful interior surrounded by panels listing the names of over 4000 German servicemen. **Moneim Raouf** (*+20-12-2351-3401*) is the guardian and one of the people responsible for the ongoing burial of lost soldiers whose bodies are occasionally still recovered in the desert. He has a wealth of information and can arrange tours beyond Alamein to strategic desert battlegrounds, like Ruweisat Ridge.

Resort Land

Thirty minutes (40km) west of Alamein, a happier scene of fine white-sand beaches and heavenly turquoise water signals you've arrived in the resort town of **Sidi Abdel Rahman**. It's a favourite summering ground for the Egyptian elite with luxury resorts encompassing pristine, bikini-friendly beaches. Here you can indulge in jet-skiing, parasailing, kayaking, tennis, and cycling around gorgeous resort gardens, artificial lagoons, and some of the finest beaches in the Mediterranean. Marassi runs the standout **Al Alamein Hotel**, although **Casa Cook North Coast** is a more affordable alternative, just 700m from lovely Amwaj Beach.

Listings

BEST OF THE REST

 **Superb Seafood**

White & Blue $$$

The Greek Club's restaurant has sweeping views of the bay. Grilled fish is the highlight.

Samakmak $

Cute checked tablecloths and delicious specials like spicy crayfish and crab *tagen* (stewed in a clay pot).

Sidi $$

A foodie find with views of the Abu Abbas mosque; come here for fried shrimp and calamari, crab, and seafood *tagen*.

Jamboojo $$

A swish restaurant with views over the docks out to sea from the 1st floor. Choose fish from the ice counter or go for the soup or shrimp.

 **Cultural Nights Out**

Alexandria Opera House

Musical and theatrical performances from Egypt's top talent, national orchestra and foreign ensembles in a vintage auditorium.

Bibliotheca Alexandrina

Numerous concerts, talks and cultural events are hosted at the library, particularly during the July Book Fair and the summer festival.

Amir Cinema

Opened in 1952 with *All About Eve,* it's now part of the film festival circuit and screens original-language global blockbusters.

Local Favourites

Mohammed Ahmed $

A famous diner serving *fuul* (fava bean paste)

since 1957. The *fuul iskandarani* (mashed with lime juice) is delicious.

Kebda El Fallah $

A favourite for its beautifully arranged liver sandwich 'bouquets' in Viennese buns seasoned with green peppers and tahini.

Koshary 'Ala Sokhn $

Dedicated to crafting the perfect *kushari* (mix of noodles, rice, black lentils, fried onions and tomato sauce) with signature lemon and chilli sauce.

Teatro Eskandariya $$

Popular with local artists and creatives, Teatro serves honest, simple food in a lively atmosphere.

Characterful Digs

San Giovanni Stanly Hotel

An old Italian hostelry with a colourful Egyptian makeover, offering charming service and a restaurant with views of Stanley Bridge.

Steigenberger Cecil Hotel

Built in 1930, this Alexandrian institution is a memorial to the city's raffish 1940s heyday. It's perfectly located overlooking the sea.

Rixos Montaza Alexandria

The swish new kid in Montazah Park offers plush suites and chalets surrounded by beautiful gardens and the city's best beaches.

Steigenberger Cecil Hotel

Pastries & Ice Cream

Talaat Patisserie $

So-called 'pioneers of delight', famous Talaat makes the best traditional sweets such as *basbousa*, *harissa* and *kunafa*.

Fahmy $

An unmissable Alexandrian treat is the lemon or chocolate ice cream from Fahmy's. Take it to the Corniche to enjoy it with sea views.

Genoise Le Cafe $$

A popular patisserie dishing out doughnuts, hazelnut frappes and all manner of cakes. Good coffee and wi-fi, too.

Drinking Dens & Terraces

Cap d'Or $

A time capsule and one of the only surviving typical Alexandrian bars. Beer flows freely among the bohemian crowd.

Spitfire Bar $

Probably the best bar in town with a rough-and-ready feel, rocking soundtrack and very cheap beer.

Sky View Restaurant $$$

The rooftop restaurant of the Metropole Hotel is a great spot for sundowners with spectacular views of the bay.

 Multicultural Meals

Sidra By the Citadel $$$

A chic Lebanese restaurant with views of the harbour. Delivers Levantine favourites, such as *fattoush*, vine leaves and *kibbeh*.

Chez Gaby Au Ritrovo $$

Going strong since 1979, Gaby's has checked tablecloths, great pizzas and an '80s French soundtrack. Alcohol served.

Spitfire Bar

OBIE OBERHOLZER/AFRIPICS/ALAMY

Jeeda's $$$

A smart modern Spanish restaurant with slick decor, authentic tapas and a great signature seafood paella. Alcohol served.

Santa Lucia Restaurant $$

A vintage restaurant once popular with Italian actors and singers, still serving risottos and *vitello tonnato* (cold veal with tuna sauce).

Notable Shopping Experiences

Souq Al Attarine

Vintage hunters will have a blast exploring the warren of alleys in the antiques market.

Zane't El-Settat

A web of alleys where you can find anything from clothes and perfume to jewellery and belly-dancing gear.

Melbalad for Egyptian Arts & Crafts

Handmade heritage crafts, such as embroidered scarves, hand-painted pottery, jewellery and leather bags.

Crystal Sweets

A charming vintage sweet shop filled with treats, including the famous Manolidis chocolate-covered dates.

40 Side Trip to the SUEZ CANAL

HISTORY | MUSEUMS | SEAFOOD

Since 1869, when the launch of the Suez Canal brought this sliver of Egypt into the global spotlight, its trio of waterfront hubs – Port Said, Ismailia and Suez – has been crucial to the national story, yet remains well off the tourist map. Linger here, in sight of the world's largest tankers, and be met by a raft of historic charms.

NANCY PAUWELS/SHUTTERSTOCK

🗺 How To

Getting here/around
Buses, trains and microbuses connect Cairo and Alexandria to the canal's three hubs (and the hubs to each other). For the best views along the canal, the train is worth the splurge.

When to go Come in the spring or fall for the best walking weather; late summer for Ismailia's mango season.

Insider tours Get under the skin of the Canal Zone with the passionate, local guides of **Semsemia Tours**.

BYVALET/SHUTTERSTOCK

Top left Port Said
Left Suez Canal

Founded in 1859 as the canal's portal, breezy **Port Said** is named after the *khedive* (viceroy of Egypt) responsible for granting the canal's concession to Frenchman Ferdinand de Lesseps. Among the town's trove of old-world traces, only the plinth of the original De Lesseps statue remains by the water. The statue itself, seen as a colonial symbol, was toppled with the canal's nationalisation in 1956.

South of here, the streets linking the canal with the arcaded backbone of the European quarter are particularly rich with wooden, four- and five-storey **verandas** unique to the city. Follow the locals aboard the free ferry *(ma'adiya)* across the canal, admiring the twin skylines of Port Said and its sister city, **Port Fouad**.

Just over an hour's journey south is the Zone's halfway point: the garden city of **Ismailia**, named for Khedive Said's successor in 1863. The old Canal Company headquarters were repurposed in 2024 as the fabulous **Suez Canal Museum**, which showcases the canal's deep-rooted history. One of its treasures stands 6m tall in the courtyard: Port Said's De Lesseps statue.

The canal's southern terminus of **Suez**, an industrial port decimated in the conflicts of 1967–73, offers less historical appeal, though its **National Museum** is worthwhile, and its **Port Tawfiq**, guarded by statues of snarling tigers, is one of the best places to catch the big ships rolling by.

◎ Three Cities

Wandering around certain neighbourhoods – Port Fouad in Port Said, the Golf Club in Ismailia, or Port Tawfiq in Suez – you'll notice the same villas, gardens and trees, with the blue Suez Canal Authority flag flying alongside the Egyptian flag. This uniformity is by design: a cohesive, modern landscape envisioned by the original Canal Company. Yet each city's story is also shaped by subtle but significant realities of change. To grasp this layered history, explore from key vantage points: Port Said's Sharia Mohamed Ali, Ismailia's Sharia El Talatini (Gomhoreya), and the intersection of the Corniche and Sharia 23 July in Suez.

■ **By Mohamed Yehia**

 Kamel Elsayed, founder at Semsemia Tours, Ismailia
@semsemiatours.eg

RED SEA COAST

DIVING | DESERT | MONASTERIES

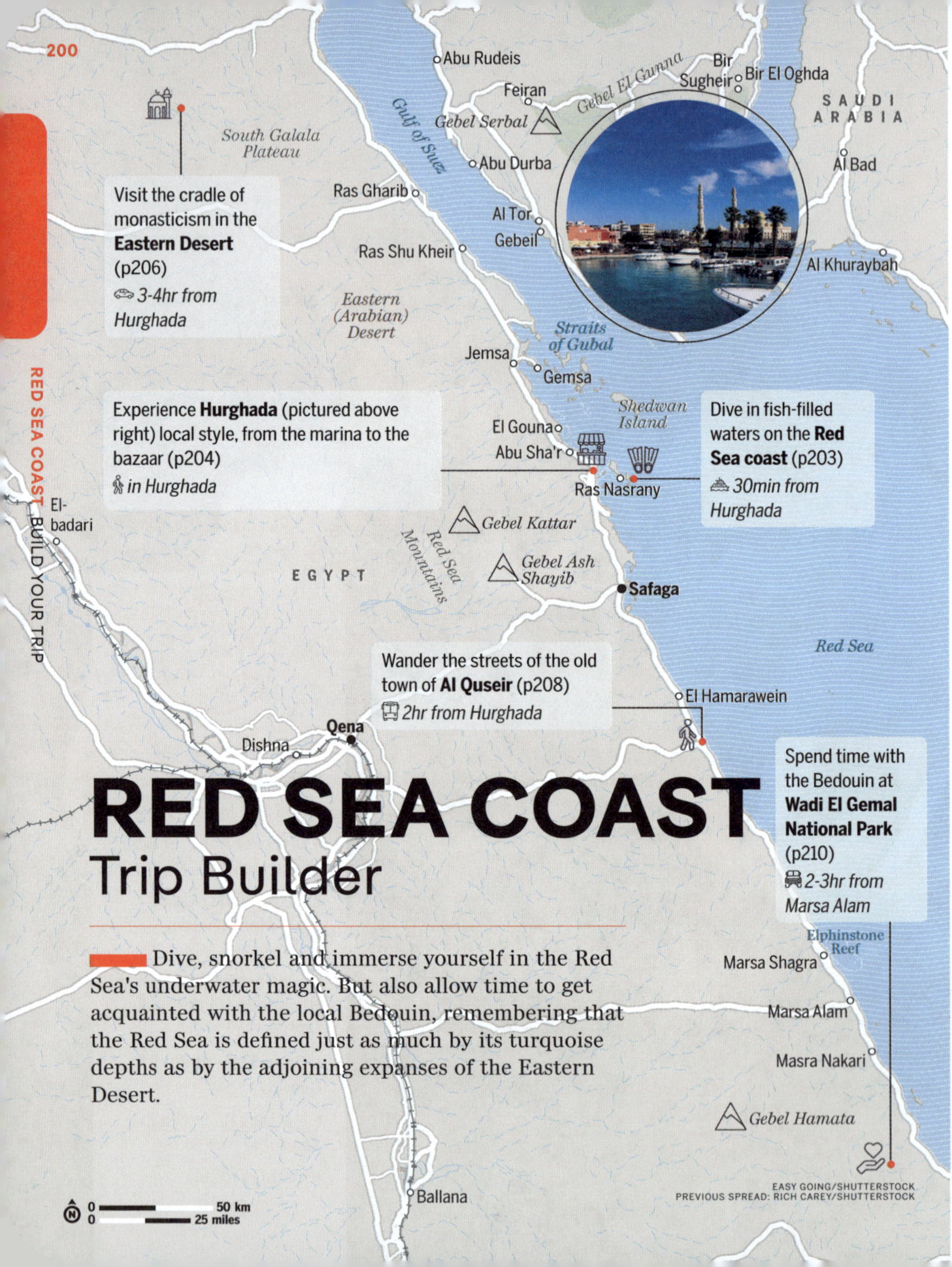

Visit the cradle of monasticism in the **Eastern Desert** (p206)
3-4hr from Hurghada
Experience **Hurghada** (pictured above right) local style, from the marina to the bazaar (p204)
in Hurghada
Dive in fish-filled waters on the **Red Sea coast** (p203)
30min from Hurghada
Wander the streets of the old town of **Al Quseir** (p208)
2hr from Hurghada
Spend time with the Bedouin at **Wadi El Gemal National Park** (p210)
2-3hr from Marsa Alam
Abu Rudeis
Feiran
Gebel El Gunna
Bir Sugheir
Bir El Oghda
SAUDI ARABIA
Gebel Serbal
Gulf of Suez
South Galala Plateau
Abu Durba
Ras Gharib
Al Bad
Al Tor
Gebeil
Ras Shu Kheir
Al Khuraybah
Eastern (Arabian) Desert
Straits of Gubal
Jemsa
Gemsa
Shedwan Island
El Gouna
Abu Sha'r
Ras Nasrany
El-badari
Gebel Kattar
Red Sea Mountains
EGYPT
Gebel Ash Shayib
Safaga
Red Sea
El Hamarawein
Qena
Dishna
Elphinstone Reef
Marsa Shagra
Marsa Alam
Masra Nakari
Gebel Hamata
Ballana
0 50 km
0 25 miles

RED SEA COAST

Trip Builder

Dive, snorkel and immerse yourself in the Red Sea's underwater magic. But also allow time to get acquainted with the local Bedouin, remembering that the Red Sea is defined just as much by its turquoise depths as by the adjoining expanses of the Eastern Desert.

EASY GOING/SHUTTERSTOCK
PREVIOUS SPREAD: RICH CAREY/SHUTTERSTOCK

Practicalities

ARRIVING

Hurghada International Airport About 12km south of Hurghada (taxi LE250 to LE400); flights to Cairo and international destinations.

Marsa Alam International Airport About 70km north of Marsa Alam (taxi LE1000 to LE1200); international connections.

MONEY

Carry cash for souq shopping, local dining and tipping. There are ATMs (accepting Visa) in major towns and some larger resorts.

CONNECT

Hurghada International Airport has kiosks where you can buy a local SIM card. Vodacom's network tends to be best.

WHERE TO STAY

Town	Pro/Con
Hurghada	Main hub with easy transport connections but plenty of bustle.
El Gouna	Low-key tourist and residential complex north of Hurghada suited for independent travellers; cafe culture.
Marsa Alam	On the doorstep of Wadi El Gemal National Park; ideal for diving and desert excursions.

EATING & DRINKING

Hurghada is a seafood paradise, with a wonderful array of restaurants. Think twice before booking an all-inclusive resort package, as dining out is one of Hurghada's highlights.

Best seafood experience Halaka Fish Market (pictured above left; p205)

Must-try drink Bedouin coffee (pictured left), served by a campfire in the desert

GETTING AROUND

Taxi Short-hop fares within towns cost LE50 or less. Also the most efficient way to reach destinations south of Marsa Alam. Arrange 4WD excursions, for example with Marsa Shagra Village, to Wadi El Gemal.

Bus Go Bus connects Hurghada and Marsa Alam via Al Quseir and Marsa Shagra Village as part of its Cairo to Marsa Alam service.

RED SEA COAST FIND YOUR FEET

JAN–MAR	**APR–JUN**	**JUL–SEP**	**OCT–DEC**
Chilly weather; a thick, full-length wetsuit for diving required	The most clement season for a Red Sea visit	Intense heat along the coast; near-perfect diving conditions offshore	Cooler temperatures make desert excursions a pleasure

41 Red Sea MAGIC

DIVING | SNORKELLING | CORAL REEFS

Famed for its turquoise waters, stunning corals and exotic sea creatures, the Red Sea Coast (with Hurghada as its hub) has long attracted tourists by the thousands. While unfettered development has left its mark, genuine attempts are being made to ensure more responsible underwater activities. This, combined with Hurghada's ease of access, makes it the perfect port of call for a Red Sea adventure.

BOSHY911/SHUTTERSTOCK

🗺️ How To

Getting here Travel by Go Bus from Cairo (seven hours) or by air, domestically on Egyptair or from European hubs.

When to go Diving is possible year-round, but many divers favour the months from October through May for their combination of pleasant temperatures, optimum visibility and fewer crowds.

Planning tip Check the website of the **Hurghada Environmental Protection & Conservation Association** (HEPCA; preview.hepca.org) for conservation participation opportunities.

IMAGEBROKER.COM/ALAMY

Top left Giftun Islands
Bottom left Gota Abu Ramada

Despite being renowned as one of the warmest (and saltiest) seas in the world, the Red Sea can still feel chilly in winter and wading out, even in a wetsuit, takes determination. But then there's that wonderful moment when water suddenly washes over the face mask and you come face-to-face with this extraordinary vision of light, colour and movement. The water alone, with its exceptional clarity, is entertaining, with light playing through the shallows in intricate designs.

And then comes the marine life. The first sighting of lemon yellow on a butterfly fish, or the pennant-waving fin of a bannerfish, are thrilling experiences as colour and shape seem extra sharp, suspended in the cut-glass water. Of course, the accessibility of some of the world's finest reefs is one of the reasons why Egypt's Red Sea Coast has become a world-class destination. Even if water isn't your thing, it's worth at least donning a mask and wading in for a view or taking a trip on a glass-bottom boat.

For divers and snorkellers, the opportunities are legion. While the reefs immediately around Hurghada are damaged, there are still exceptional sites just offshore. The nearby **Giftun Islands**, for example, form part of a marine reserve with diving at depths of up to 100m, or there's neighbouring **Gota Abu Ramada**, suitable for novice and night divers and popular with underwater photographers. Pilot whales and large pods of dolphins make **Shedwan Island** another rewarding option, while wreck divers will enjoy the explosion of life around the coral towers of **Umm Qamar**.

🐚 Local Tips

If you want your diving to leave a positive eco-print, visit any of the three locations run by **Red Sea Diving Safari** (redsea -divingsafari.com). Its team has been working closely for several decades with HEPCA and the Red Sea Protectorate to build an environmentally friendly diving model, and you will immediately notice the efforts they make to protect the reefs in front of their camps.

My personal favourite is their **Wadi Lahami** location, with its peacefulness and the chance for both diving and windsurfing in the shallow lagoon. In the early mornings, the mangroves attract a variety of wild birds and it is fascinating to observe them.

■ **By Karima Saad**, a diver from Cairo. @_karima

42 Discover Another Side
OF HURGHADA

MARKETS | MOSQUE | MUSEUM

Hurghada is primarily known as a diving and watersports hub. However, once you've finished exploring its fish- and coral-filled depths, it's worth taking some time in town to mingle with residents, stroll through the souq, visit the impressive fish market, sample some of the excellent restaurants and get a feel for local life.

SURONIN/SHUTTERSTOCK

🗺️ How To

Getting around Central Hurghada is mostly walkable, and there are plenty of taxis around for longer stretches.

When to go Hurghada is a year-round destination, although summers are hot. Peak tourist season is from October to April.

Planning tip Leave exploring Hurghada until late afternoon and evening to avoid losing a day's sun and sea, and to enjoy the city at its liveliest.

PHKORSART/SHUTTERSTOCK

Top left Grand Mosque
Bottom left Hurghada Museum

With their all-inclusive packages, resorts make it hard to venture beyond the foyer – but for those managing to stray outside, Hurghada has much to explore. Three-hour guided tours are offered by hotels, but it's also easy to take a taxi and make up your own itinerary.

Start with a trip to the **Hurghada Museum** (open until 9pm) in the city suburbs. Housing beautiful artefacts from recent Egyptian history, it also showcases some gems of antiquity. Next, head to **Ad Dahar Souq** and join the throngs of local shoppers haggling for textiles, ready-made clothing and perfumes. In contrast to the cramped lanes of the bazaar, the pedestrianised **Hurghada Marina** in Sigala, Hurghada's visitor hub, offers a breezy sunset stroll and is a perfect spot for sundowners.

From the marina, it's a short hop to the impressive **Halaka Fish Market**, where you can see samples of the Red Sea's marine residents, choose your dinner and have it cooked to your liking on the spot (to eat in or take away). Afterwards, stroll past the **Grand Mosque**, which looks particularly striking at night. If you didn't already eat at Halaka Fish Market, finish up with dinner at **Star Fish** – a local institution – or one of Hurghada's other fine restaurants, and don't miss a dessert at one of the many nearby sweet shops.

A Hurghada Chef's Dining Recommendations

Star Fish Their calamari-and-shrimp tajine is a must-try.

El Halaka Fish Restaurant A family favourite. I recommend their bream fish with lemon.

Albalcona Their pastas are great, especially the white-sauce mushroom pasta.

Al Sonny A traditional restaurant; try the Egyptian beef-shank *fatteh* (with pita bread soaked in a garlicky-vinegary sauce).

El Esraa Known for their BBQ dishes – I recommend the BBQ chicken.

 ■ By **Amr Abd El Azeem**, owner of Hurghada's El Dar Darak restaurant. *fb.com/ eldardarak22*

43

In the Footsteps of Early
MONASTICISM

DESERT | HISTORY | ART

Egypt's Eastern Desert is the cradle of Christian monasticism. Visit two 4th-century Coptic monasteries in the desert's rugged northern mountains to see where it all began. While here, you'll get to climb 1804 steps to the cave of St Anthony (the founder of monasticism) and join pilgrims from all over the world who come to venerate St Anthony and his contemporary, St Paul the Anchorite.

IMAGODENS/GETTY IMAGES

📖 How To

Getting here Visit as a day trip from Hurghada on a tour (organised through most hotels) or by taxi. The monasteries are only 30km apart as the crow flies but over 80km by road; not all tours cover both.

When to go Year-round, although summer is uncomfortably hot.

Planning tip Check opening hours first, as access to the monasteries is restricted during Advent and Lent and they are closed at Christmas and Easter.

CORTYN/SHUTTERSTOCK

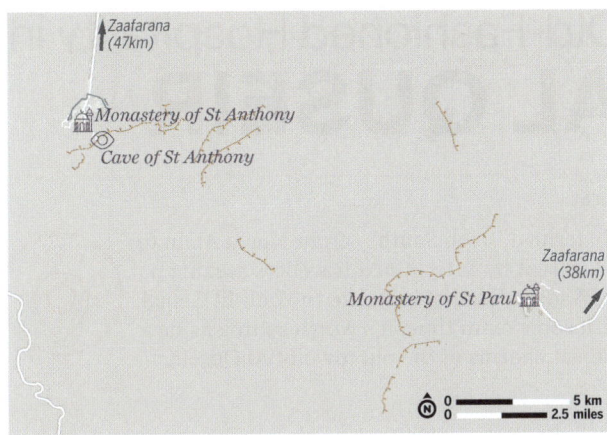

Zaafarana
(47km)

Monastery of St Anthony

Cave of St Anthony

Zaafarana
(38km)

Monastery of St Paul

N 0 ———— 5 km
    0 ———— 2.5 miles

Top left Monastery of St Paul
Bottom left Monastery of St Anthony

Simplicity-plus Nestled away in the Eastern Desert's northern mountains is a tiny **cave** where St Anthony, who renounced worldly goods at a young age, spent most of his life. Inside, the walls are polished smooth by the hands of countless pilgrims, with a tiny chapel and an icon just visible in the darkness. Outside, the desert fills the view. The cave can only be reached by a stiff climb. If your legs start to feel the effort, think of the monks who still make the ascent each night from the **Monastery of St Anthony** below for midnight Mass. 'You get used to it', says one of the fathers. 'You focus on prayer and the walking just happens.'

Water from a rock The **Monastery of St Paul**, Christianity's first hermit, was built around the saint's tomb and is rather less strenuous to reach. It's also less crowded than St Anthony's Monastery, and the sense of isolation here is absolute, with high walls looming above the desert floor. Several areas, including the chapel with its beautiful wall paintings, are open to visitors. Yet, it is the miracle of water that has made life here possible: see where it springs in unchanging volume from a rock. Some of it is diverted into a garden, showing that 'hope springs eternal' even in harsh environments – a fitting metaphor, explains one of the guiding fathers, of a life dedicated to prayer.

Who Was St Paul the Anchorite?

History suggests that Christianity's first hermit was a wealthy 3rd-century Alexandrian who fled at a young age to the Eastern Desert to escape Roman persecution. Living alone in a mountain cave, sustained only by spring water and dates, he was joined in solitude by a raven who, according to tradition, brought him half a loaf of bread daily until he died well over the age of 100. Buried, according to legend, by his only other visitor, St Anthony, and with the help of two lions, St Paul is often represented by a palm tree, raven and lions – symbols that remain important in the iconography of his final resting place.

Old-Fashioned Hospitality in
AL QUSEIR

CITADEL | WALKING | OFFBEAT

Egypt's affectionately termed 'Deep South' – from Marsa Alam to Berenice – is seldom visited, except by determined travellers seeking out the excellent diving around Wadi Lahami or en route to Wadi El Gemal. If you find yourself here with some extra time, it's worth setting aside a few hours to explore the offbeat charms of the old town of Al Quseir.

PAUL VINTEN/ALAMY

🗺️ **How To**

Getting here Al Quseir is about 150km south of Hurghada. Go Bus stops here on its Cairo–Hurghada–Marsa Alam route. From the station, take a taxi to the waterfront and explore on foot.

When to go Year-round, but temperatures are best from October to April.

Planning tip From Al Quseir, it's only 1½ hours further south by bus or taxi to Marsa Shagra Village (p215) for diving, snorkelling and getting acquainted with the local Bedouin.

RED SEA DIVING SAFARI

The dusty, windswept city of Al Quseir played a major regional role as a trading hub in the annals of the ancients, but slid into obscurity over subsequent centuries. Today, the town attracts only a small stream of intrepid tour groups venturing out from nearby resorts, and the occasional independent traveller. But it is this that makes Al Quseir interesting: with its firmly out-of-the-way status, it offers a chance to explore a typical Egyptian town going about its ordinary business without any special attempt to be something else.

Spending an afternoon strolling around is like stepping into a rather derelict time warp. Seek out Al Quseir's 16th-century **Ottoman fortress**, which has been restored and is especially evocative, with its fortified walls, watchtower and clutch of exhibits. Nearby is the port, backed the old **granary**, which dates to the early 19th century when it was used to store wheat that was going to be shipped to Mecca. Also near the port is the attractive **Faran mosque**, the town's oldest, with its early 18th-century minaret. In the evening, shop in Al Quseir's small **bazaar** before enjoying a supper of fresh fish. While making your way around, you'll invariably be rewarded with the town's old-fashioned hospitality – a herbal infusion from a shop owner, Arabic blessings bestowed by an elderly grandmother or a nod from a shisha-smoking *haji* (one who has made the hajj to Mecca), sitting under the decaying *mashrabiyya* (wooden lattice window shutters) of merchant houses that speak of the town's long-forgotten wealth.

Top left Ottoman fortress
Bottom left Marsa Shagra Village

◎ Al Quseir in its Heyday

In ancient times, Al Quseir was a major port with, according to one Greek historian, a fleet of 120 ships delivering pottery, slaves and wine to the African kingdom of Punt in exchange for spices, silk and stone. In later years, the port played a role in the Ottoman Empire and the British trade route with India.

A final flourish in the early 20th century brought wealth through the phosphate industry but, with the Suez Canal established as the main artery of the region, the town slipped into decline. Even Al Quseir's long history as a point of departure for pilgrims bound for Mecca has been eclipsed by Port Safaga, further up the Red Sea coast.

45 DESERT LIFE
at Wadi El Gemal

DESERT | BEDOUIN CULTURE | WILDLIFE

One of the best places to experience the interconnection of desert and sea is at Wadi El Gemal National Park. Set aside a day to explore inland, visiting Roman ruins, checking out the remains of an old emerald mine and learning about local ecosystems before making your way – via mangroves and marshland – to the Red Sea's clear waters.

MANJA REUSER/SHUTTERSTOCK

🗺 How To

Getting here The main park entrance is 45km south of Marsa Alam. Organise a day visit through a Marsa Alam hotel or Marsa Shagra Village.

When to go September to October and April to May are best. Inland areas get very hot during the summer.

Planning tip Itineraries vary considerably depending on the tour operator, so check what is included before you sign up.

PAUL VINTEN/SHUTTERSTOCK

Top left Wadi El Gemal
Bottom left Mons Claudianus

There's nowhere quite like it in Egypt. A day exploring around **Wadi El Gemal** brings everything together: Roman ruins, the remains of old caravan routes, gazelles, ibex and even the park's namesake wild camels, plus a stretch of truly stunning, undeveloped coastline with crystal waters and a wealth of fish and coral species that draws divers from around the world. But what makes Wadi El Gemal really special is the chance to spend time in the company of the local Bedouin and learn about their life.

At meal time, watch how your guide-cook dips his hands into a bag of flour, scoops it onto a rock and, with a bit of water, kneads it into dough. After expertly building an oven on the desert floor, he covers the loaf in ash and leaves it to bake. The result is possibly the best bread you've ever tasted and a realisation that this land has been inhabited for centuries – far longer than the relatively recent construction of resorts along the coast.

Most visits start in the desert and finish at the coast. Itineraries vary, with some stopping at **Mons Claudianus** (an old Roman granite quarry), and most visiting the ruins of the old emerald mines at **Nugrus**. Some include an excursion to one of the park's small offshore islands and snorkelling, finishing with a Bedouin-style meal. Still not sure whether to give up a day's diving? Consider that a visit to Wadl El Gemal directly supports local Bedouin communities, whose way of life and the park's existence are threatened by encroaching development.

🖐 Guardians of the Desert

For millennia, the Eastern Desert has been home to the nomadic Ababda community, and until the 20th century, the extent of their territory remained as described by their historical foes, the Romans. Today a small number of these expert camel herders continue to live in their ancestral territory between Marsa Alam and Wadi El Gemal. Living in huts decorated with handwoven rugs, the Ababda have traditionally reared camels and livestock, but many now work alongside the tourist industry, typically as camp guards and guides. While sensitivity is required to avoid exploitative encounters, camel or 4WD safaris into their desert heartland offer a valuable chance to learn about Ababda culture, listen to their rhythmical music and sample *jibena*, sweetened coffee prepared from fresh-roasted beans.

MARINE LIFE
in the Red Sea

01 Green turtle
One of four sea-turtle species found in Egypt's Red Sea waters. Look for them at Abu Dabbab, near Marsa Alam.

02 Hawksbill turtle
Smaller than its green-turtle cousin and named for its beak-like mouth. Spot them around the Giftun Islands near Hurghada.

03 Spinner dolphin
These small, sociable mammals are the spinning, leaping acrobats of the Red Sea. Watch for them around Sataya Reef, near Wadi Lahami Village.

04 Lionfish
This impressive-looking, brightly coloured fish has venomous spines which it uses as a defense mechanism. It's found hiding around coral reefs, rocks and jetties.

05 Bottlenose dolphin
Large, graceful creatures, generally found in smaller pods than spinner dolphins. They are frequently spotted around Sha'ab El Erg, northeast of Hurghada.

06 Dugong (sea cow)
These large, primarily herbivorous mammals can eat around 40kg of aquatic vegetation a day and favour the seagrass beds around Abu Dabbab.

07 Red Sea clownfish
Colourful, banded fish that protects itself by living near the venomous tentacles of sea anemone, where it's safe from predators.

08 Sea anemone
The anemone's venomous tentacles provide shelter for clownfish, while clownfish provide anemones with food and chase away nuisances.

09 Blue spotted ray
You're likely to encounter these common rays while diving. Although their sting is painful, they generally only attack when threatened.

10 Hammerhead shark
Hammerheads are generally not considered to be aggressive towards humans unless provoked. You may spot them around Elphinstone Reef (north of Marsa Alam).

Listings

Seafood & Sundowners

El Dar Darak $$

This family-friendly Hurghada restaurant plays songs of the Nubian artist Mohammed Mounir, and its menu continues the theme with photos of the artist. Try local dishes such as stuffed pigeon or *mahshi* (vegetables or vine leaves stuffed with rice and sometimes meat). Portions are large; order a few to share.

Abu Khadijah $

At this local-style place in Hurghada, mains – featuring meat and chicken grills and stuffed pigeon, among other delicacies – come with side salad, vegetables, soup and bread.

El Halaka Fish Restaurant $$

Located in front of Hurghada's fish market, this is a good family-friendly option. The seafood is cooked to order and served with sides, including a delicious seafood soup and shrimp with rice. You won't walk away hungry.

Che Guevara $$$

At the Hurghada Marina, with beautiful views of the water from its outdoor seating area. The menu features steaks (including camel steak) and sandwiches.

Koshary Rezo $

This local-style Hurghada establishment is known for its tasty *kushari* (mix of noodles, rice, black lentils, fried onions and tomato sauce). Choose the dish size and toppings, and they'll give you extra hot sauce to mix in as you like. Service is super-fast.

El Fardous $$

Choose between the cosy interior or shoreside tables at this local favourite, which prepares delicious lobster and shellfish. It's on the waterfront in Al Quseir.

Sweets & Coffee

B Laban $

This popular Egypt-wide franchise is known for its milk-based sweets like *ruz bi laban* (rice pudding) and other puddings and ice cream. It only has takeaway service and lines are long. Located in central Hurghada on Sharia Sherry.

Suez Dairy $

A local franchise in Hurghada for ready-made, milk-based sweets including *ruz bi laban* and *umm Ali* (Egypt's version of bread pudding). There's also a small seating area.

El Mashrabiya Coffee Shop $$

This family-friendly place in Hurghada features traditional decor and a nice outdoor seating area. It's a perfect spot to hang out and drink mint tea, Middle Eastern coffee or fresh lemon-and-mint juice.

JOHANN VIFIAN/SUBEX THE ART OF DIVING

Subex

World of the Sweet $$

A family-oriented place in Hurghada featuring Syrian sweets. The most popular is its *kunafa* (vermicelli-like pastry over a vanilla base soaked in syrup), which comes on a silver platter and is enough for two people. Seating is inside or out.

Tito's $$

This seafront, open-air cafe and restaurant in Hurghada is a great place for sundowners and views. There's traditional Middle Eastern floor seating in addition to standard tables and chairs, and some childrens' swings outside.

 ## Underwater Adventures

Marsa Shagra Village

Well-organised, safety-conscious and sustainable, Marsa Shagra is a top choice for organising both underwater and desert encounters. It's run by the sustainability-focused Red Sea Diving Safari and is about 25km north of Marsa Alam.

Wadi Lahami Village

About 120km south of Marsa Alam, this sustainability-oriented place run by Red Sea Diving Safari offers kitesurfing and diving, including dives at the lovely Sataya Reef famed for its spinner dolphins.

Jasmin Diving Centre

A founding member of the Hurghada Environmental Protection & Conservation Association (HEPCA) and a perennial Hurghada favourite.

Aquanaut Diving Club

This longstanding Hurghada dive centre, located off Sharia Sheraton, offers a wide array of courses, excursions and activities.

Marsa Shagra Village

Subex

The friendly and professional Subex dive centre in Hurghada only caters to small groups, making it an ideal choice for independent travellers. It also has a branch in Sharm El Sheikh.

 ## DJs & Dancing

Little Buddha $$

A not-so-little Buddha-themed place in Hurghada with DJ parties that pull in local and international crowds. While entry is free, there are bar cover and table charges.

Elements Club & Lounge $$

Located at Hurghada's Steigenberger Aqua Magic, with a bit of everything – DJ, live music and karaoke nights. Couples and mixed groups only. A minimum charge applies.

Caribbean Bar $$$

This beachfront bar is located in Hurghada's Bella Vista Resort, but is also open to non-guests. ID is required. There's an extensive food menu.

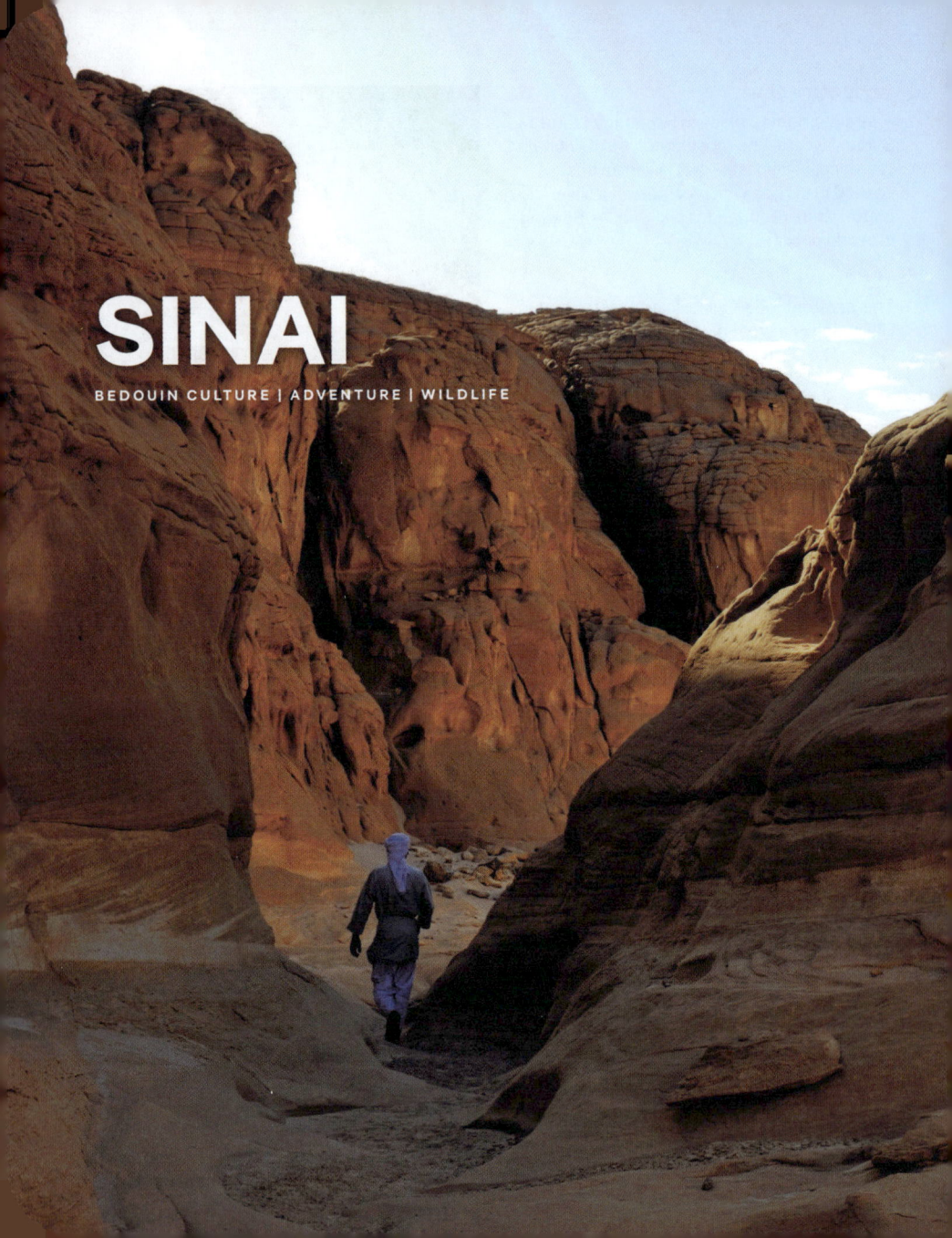

SINAI

BEDOUIN CULTURE | ADVENTURE | WILDLIFE

SINAI
Trip Builder

Swim among a rainbow maze of marine life beneath aquamarine waters at one of the world's best diving spots. Then be moved by mountains inland as you climb Sinai's jagged-tooth sierra before heading back down to lounge on white-sand beaches.

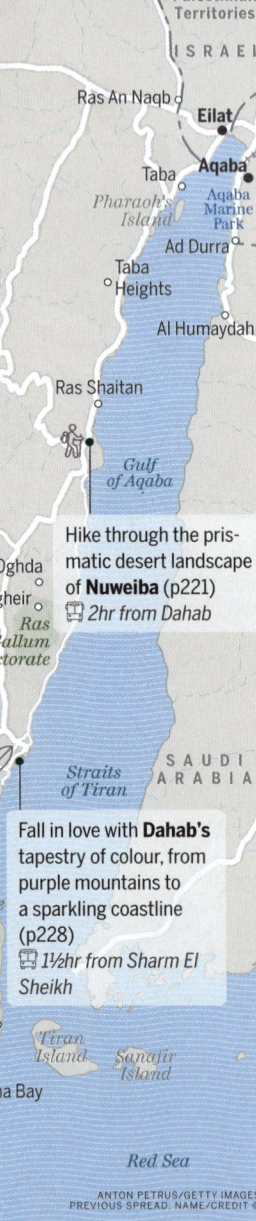

Gaze at some of the world's most ancient manuscripts at **St Katherine's Monastery** (pictured left; p230)
🚗 1½hr from Dahab

Hike through the prismatic desert landscape of **Nuweiba** (p221)
🚌 2hr from Dahab

Let yourself be mesmerized by the towering fortress of **St Katherine's** dusty red peaks(p226)
🚗 1½hr from Dahab

Fall in love with **Dahab's** tapestry of colour, from purple mountains to a sparkling coastline (p228)
🚌 1½hr from Sharm El Sheikh

Swim with sea turtles and sharks through anemone forests in **Ras Mohammed National Park** (p223)
⛴ 1hr from Sharm El Sheikh

Palestinian Territories
I S R A E L
Ras An Naqb
Eilat
Taba
Aqaba
Pharaoh's Island
Aqaba Marine Park
Ad Durra
Taba Heights
Al Humaydah
Ras Shaitan
Gulf of Aqaba
Abu Rudeis
Sinai
Bir El Oghda
Bir Sugheir
Ras Abu Gallum Protectorate
Al Milga
Mt Sinai (Gebel Musa)
Gebel Feiran
S A U D I A R A B I A
Abu Durba
Gebel Katarina
E G Y P T
Straits of Tiran
St Katherine Protectorate
Sharira Pass
Al Tor
Gebeil
Gulf of Suez
Nabq Protectorate
Ras Shu Kheir
Nabq
Ras Nasrany
Shark's Bay
Tiran Island
Sanafir Island
Na'ama Bay
Straits of Gubal
Sharm El Sheikh
Red Sea
Ashrafi Island
Qeisum Island
Gubal Island
Tawilah Island
Eastern Desert
Jemsa
Gemsa

ANTON PETRUS/GETTY IMAGES
PREVIOUS SPREAD: NAME/CREDIT ©

0   50 km
0   25 miles

Practicalities

ARRIVING

Sharm El Sheikh International Airport
Main gateway to South Sinai. Most hotels offer airport shuttle included with accommodation price but you can also take a taxi from the airport.

MONEY
You can pay by card in cities like Dahab and Sharm El Sheikh; cash is required for taxis and in more remote areas.

CONNECT
Wi-fi access is unreliable and often slow, even at your accommodation. Consider purchasing a data plan you can easily top up, like Airalo.

WHERE TO STAY

Town	Pro/Con
Sharm El Sheikh	Primary location for diving. Populated with resorts.
Dahab	Hub for digital nomads. Vibrant, youthful culture.
St Katherine	Best for mountain trekking and historical sites. Lacking in restaurants and nightlife.
Nuweiba	Lazy beach-holiday vibes. Limited restaurants and nightlife.

EATING

Dahab and Sharm El Sheikh have loads of restaurants serving breakfast, lunch and dinner. *Kushari* (pictured left) is Egypt's national dish mixing noodles, rice and black lentils, often topped with crispy fried onions and tomato sauce. Originating in the Levant, *maqluba* (pictured below left) is a pilaf dish prepared in one pot that's turned upside down when serving.

Best Indian food with a sea view Rangoli (p235)

Must-try vegan cuisine Vegan Lab (p234)

GETTING AROUND

Bus Use Go Bus for travelling between cities. You can book tickets online or at a station in advance. Microbuses are available in Sharm El Sheikh but difficult to navigate if you don't speak Arabic.

Taxi Best for getting around but watch price gouging. In more remote areas, your accommodation can book for you.

TOP: HUSSEIN FARAR/SHUTTERSTOCK
BOTTOM: MUSTAPHA BRANDS/SHUTTERSTOCK

SINAI FIND YOUR FEET

JAN–FEB	**MAR–MAY**	**JUN–AUG**	**SEP–DEC**
Coastal temperatures are mild, inland is cold with a chance of snow	Best time for hiking; warmer temperatures and less rainfall	Scorching daytime temperatures reaching above 38°C	Sunny days with cooler temperatures

46 Canyon Hiking
IN SINAI

HIKING | CLIMBING | PHOTOGRAPHY

▬▬ Trade the sea for a daytime safari exploring the awe-inspiring canyons of Sinai. Scale cavernous walls the colour of carnelian and take a dip in a mystical green pool. Yet this trip isn't suited for those fearing tight spaces and heights, as you'll be climbing, crawling and even jumping over rocks and slipping in between the shadows of boulders.

NASTYA SMIRNOVA RF/SHUTTERSTOCK

🗺 How To

Getting here The tour operator will provide transport to/from your accommodation. Note: the ride may be a bit bumpy on the rough, mountainous terrain.

When to go March to May or September to November, when temperatures are mild and rainfall is minimal, are ideal for canyon adventures.

Warning The Egyptian government closed the route to the infamous **Coloured Canyon**, but some Bedouin guides will offer to take you via a much longer route at a more expensive rate. Note, though, this route is illegal.

A. PUSHKIN/SHUTTERSTOCK

Top left White Canyon
Bottom left Closed Canyon

White sands and white walls A hike through **White Canyon** features smooth, cream-coloured sands and narrowing limestone walls just an hour's drive from Dahab. Depending on where your guide has you start, you'll either begin or end at **Ain Khudra** oasis, where a Bedouin camp sits among the lush ravine. The stroll through the canyon is relatively easy, but the entry and exit points are a bit of an obstacle course. Be prepared for shoddy ladders and a steep climb. Yet within the canyon – sheltered from movement and noise – you'll find a sense of peace and stillness.

In between Ain Khudra and Wadi Ghazala is **Closed Canyon**, which gets its name from its narrow path that's often difficult to pass through. At the hike's end, you're rewarded with an open space of land where you can sit and bask in the canyon's glory.

Hidden treasure A well-kept secret is the **Abu Hamata Canyon**, located below Hadabat El Tih, a mountainous plateau running across Sinai. This remote canyon is nearly untouched by visitors so rubbish, graffiti and other traces of tourists are rare. It's considered Sinai's longest canyon. You'll wind through tight passageways lined with layers of jagged red rock until eventually arriving at a panoramic view of Hadabat El Tih.

Note: As of April 2025, the Egyptian government have stopped issuing overnight permits, and only one day passes are available.

⟡ Best Hiking Spots in Nuweiba

One of the most famous short hikes on everyone's checklist is **Wishwashi Valley**. This 2km hike ends with three mountain pools.

If you choose to continue further and hike an additional 4km, you'll reach the end of **Wadi Malha**, a beautiful oasis in the middle of the desert. Here, water flows from a small underground spring, surrounded by date palms and acacia trees – a true hidden gem.

Salama Canyon is another small hike with moderate elevation, but its unmatched colours make it truly special. This sandstone valley has been carved over time by floods and wind, creating breathtaking scenery.

■ By **Gihan Zakaria** and **Khaled Kamel**, founders of Dar Jan Farm & Art Space, Nuweiba @darjan_nuweibaa

Plunge into the Waters of
SHARM EL SHEIKH

DIVING | MARINE LIFE | BOATING

The Red Sea is considered one of the best diving sites in the world, and Sharm El Sheikh is a prime spot for underwater exploration. Swim with schools of colourful fish, be awed by impressive shipwrecks, and let the waves' currents push you through beds of gangly anemone and past intricately laced sea fans.

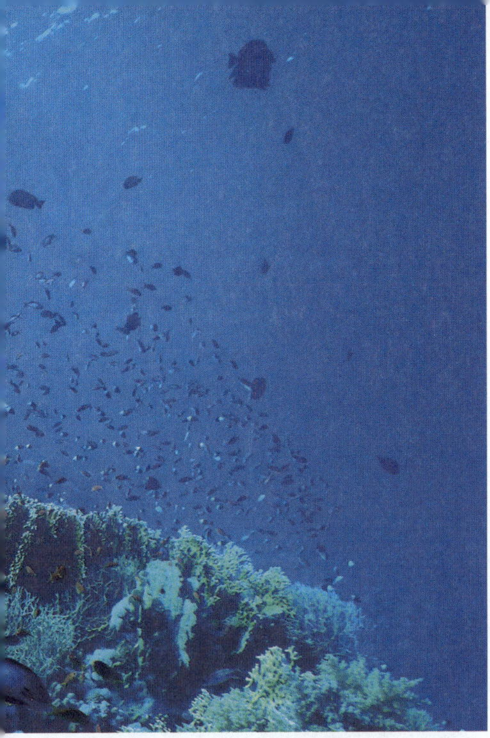

PASCAL VOSICKI/SHUTTERSTOCK

How To

Getting here Most diving tourists arrive at Sharm El Sheikh International Airport, but you can also take the bus from major Egyptian cities using the popular Go Bus service.

When to go While you can dive around Sharm El Sheikh any time of the year, it's best to go from May to October, when water temperatures are warmer and more marine life head to the surface – like hammerhead sharks.

Top tip A boat tour is best for diving as most sites aren't accessible from the shore.

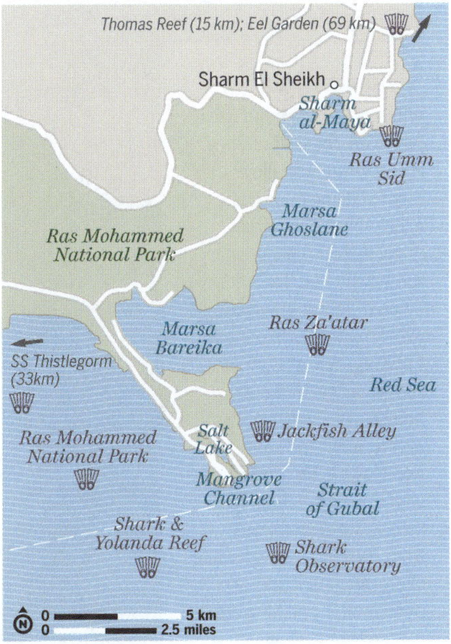
Thomas Reef (15 km); Eel Garden (69 km)
Sharm El Sheikh
Sharm al-Maya
Ras Umm Sid
Marsa Ghoslane
Ras Mohammed National Park
Ras Za'atar
Marsa Bareika
SS Thistlegorm (33km)
Red Sea
Ras Mohammed National Park
Salt Lake
Jackfish Alley
Mangrove Channel
Strait of Gubal
Shark & Yolanda Reef
Shark Observatory
0 5 km
0 2.5 miles

An Underwater Rainforest

Ras Mohammed National Park and Tiran Island are the area's must-see diving sites, where nearly all of the Red Sea's more than 1200 species of fish circle the park's waters.

Shark and Yolanda Reefs at Ras Mohammed is the Red Sea's most famous dive. You'll descend down a massive wall of lavender coral at Shark Reef as schools of goldfish swirl around you before drifting toward Yolanda Reef, where broken pieces of porcelain now litter the sea floor after the reef's namesake, a Cypriot merchant ship sunk in 1980 while carrying British-made toilets and bathtubs.

While Shark and Yolanda Reefs are, by far, the most popular diving destination at Ras Mohammed, the park does have a plethora of other sites to explore including **Anemone**

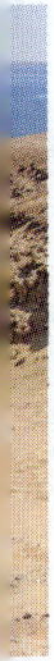

BENNY MARTY/SHUTTERSTOCK

Top left Shark Reef
Left Ras Mohammed National Park

City, where hundreds of clownfish guard a jelly-like jungle of anemone from predatory fish. At the northern end of Marsa Bareika Bay is **Ras Ghozlani**, which is as beautiful as it is versatile. Beginner divers can feel at ease with the site's slow current allowing you to float over a sandy plateau of golden brain coral. At the bay's southern tip lies **Ras Za'atar** (Head of Thyme), known for its stunning sunbeams streaming through the reef's caverns – a sublime photo stop.

Further south is **Jackfish Alley**, nicknamed for its sandy bottom where jackfish often congregate. Larger marine life like white-tip reef sharks can also be found sleeping in the sand. **Eel Garden**, which is accessible by boat or land, is filled with endemic eels growing up to 80cm often seen slithering through the sandy slope to catch plankton. At **Shark Observatory**, you can drift along a coral wall and gaze into the blue to find hawksbill turtles. Named after its towering cliff used to

♜ Sunken Ship

With an average depth of just 80m, the Gulf of Suez is surprisingly shallow, often spelling doom for cargo ships. The fate of many historic carriers has turned the Red Sea's floor into a freighter graveyard with shipwrecks like the **SS Thistlegorm**, a 126m-long British vessel that was bombed by German aircraft during WWII and sank. **Million Hope** is the Red Sea's largest shipwreck, which sank in 1996 on its way from Jordan to Taiwan while carrying phosphates and potash after crashing into a reef near Nabq Bay.

■ **By Fady Shawky**, *diving instructor at Camel Dive Club, Sharm El Sheikh*
@fadi_shawki

♨ The Local Coast

For diving the local coast of Sharm El Sheikh, you have **Ras Ghamila**. You can also go to Ras Mohammed from the land and camp there. El Fanar at **Ras Umm Sid** is a magnificent dive site where you can dive from the shore. On the cliff, beside **El Fanar** restaurant, you can enjoy a sunset view.

spot sharks below, the area isn't as shark-abundant as it once was.

Reefs Galore

Tiran Island is a Saudi Arabian territory whose waters belongs to Egypt's Ras Mohammed National Park. While you can't visit the island, you can dive Tiran's popular reefs – four of which are named after the 19th-century English cartographers who made the first nautical map of the area. The island's fairly shallow seabed gives the waters a sparkling aquamarine appearance but also causes strong currents, meaning some dive centres don't allow beginners to go without a personal guide – increasing the cost of a visit – so check before you book.

Both **Woodhouse** and **Thomas** reefs are advanced dives with whirling currents only to be crossed under stable conditions. **Gordon Reef's** waters are slightly calmer and often teeming with cornetfish, bannerfish, goatfish and Napoleon wrasse.

Tiran is abundant in marine life, with manta and eagle rays flapping through the waves, coral-lined canyons housing groupers and pufferfish, and turtles, giant morays and various species of shark frequently spotted.

Left *SS Thistlegorm* shipwreck
Top Ras Umm Sid
Above Gordon Reef

48 Climbing Sinai's PEAKS

HIKING | MOUNTAINS | VIEWS

Elevate your body and spirit to some of the tallest mountains in Egypt by hiking the summits of South Sinai. These majestic desert peaks above the Bedouin-majority village of St Katherine will shift your spiritual consciousness (and give your quads a good workout).

ISPARKLINGLIFE/SHUTTERSTOCK

Mountain Treks, Day Hikes & Camel Rides

Most recommendations for Sinai are to Mt Sinai, but we have guides for other mountains and activities like Gebel Katarina, Gebel Abbas Pasha, and one-day walks through the valleys or Bedouin herbal gardens. You can also learn to ride a camel.

📷 Trip Notes

Getting here No buses go to St Katherine Protectorate (unless you're going with a tour group for the day), so it's best to book a taxi to the mountain village.

When to go March to May or September to November to avoid the area's extreme heat and winter rains.

Guides Bedouin guides are required for all hiking routes, except ascending the iconic Mt Sinai. You can make arrangements through your accommodation.

Note As of April 2025, the Egyptian government have stopped issuing overnight permits, and only one day passes are available.

By **Salem El Hinaney,** tour guide with Wilderness Ventures Egypt, St Katherine
@salemelhinaney

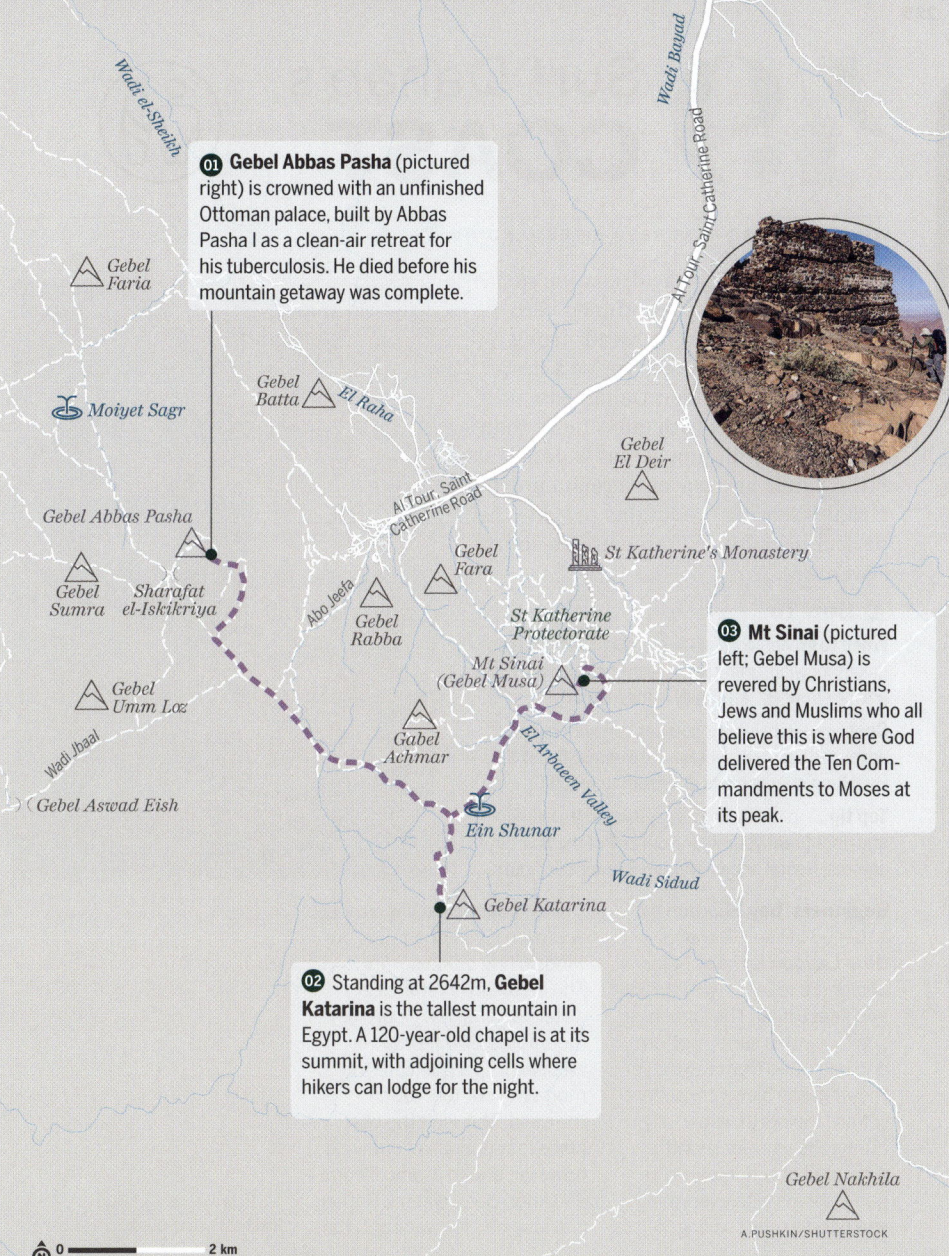

Wadi el-Sheikh

Wadi Bayad

Al Tour, Saint Catherine Road

01 **Gebel Abbas Pasha** (pictured right) is crowned with an unfinished Ottoman palace, built by Abbas Pasha I as a clean-air retreat for his tuberculosis. He died before his mountain getaway was complete.

△ *Gebel Faria*

Gebel Batta △ *El Raha*

Moiyet Sagr

Gebel El Deir △

Gebel Abbas Pasha

Al Tour, Saint Catherine Road

🏛 *St Katherine's Monastery*

△ *Gebel Sumra*   *Sharafat el-Iskikriya* △

Gebel Fara △

△ *Gebel Umm Loz*

Abo Jeefa

△ *Gebel Rabba*

St Katherine Protectorate

Mt Sinai (Gebel Musa) △

03 **Mt Sinai** (pictured left; Gebel Musa) is revered by Christians, Jews and Muslims who all believe this is where God delivered the Ten Commandments to Moses at its peak.

Wadi Jbaal

Gebel Aswad Eish

△ *Gabel Achmar*

El Arbaeen Valley

Ein Shunar

Wadi Sidud

△ *Gebel Katarina*

02 Standing at 2642m, **Gebel Katarina** is the tallest mountain in Egypt. A 120-year-old chapel is at its summit, with adjoining cells where hikers can lodge for the night.

Gebel Nakhila △

A.PUSHKIN/SHUTTERSTOCK

Ⓝ 0 ——— 2 km
   0 ——— 1 mile

49 Surf Dahab's COAST

WINDSURFING | BEACHES | KITEBOARDING

Looking for an adrenaline rush? Dahab's swift breeze combined with calm waters is ideal for windsurfing or kitesurfing. Whether you're a first-timer or an avid rider, Dahab has A-plus weather – with gusts more than 26km/h – for gliding across water. And if the winds and waves weren't enough, Dahab's seaside mountains provide the perfect backdrop for an extreme-sport adventure.

How To

When to go April through September has prime conditions for windsurfing and kitesurfing when the winds are the strongest, especially in the morning.

Cost One- to two-hour courses (beginners and advanced) cost on average between $80 and $90. A weeklong course costs approximately $350.

Top tip Skip the bulky baggage when travelling and opt to rent your gear from any of the nearby centres. Rental prices average $35 for two hours.

Beginners' bay Guarded by a tongue of sand, Dahab's **Blue Lagoon** is the spot for beginners to learn windsurfing and kitesurfing. The lagoon is shallow with a sandy bottom and sheltered from waves, yet the wind still blows consistently from the north, especially during the warmer months. A handful of schools line Dahab's shores with everything you need to start sailing.

Blue Lagoon itself is a must-see, even if you don't plan on windsurfing or kitesurfing. The cerulean crystal-clear waters against hazy purple mountains feel like you've stepped into a postcard the moment your feet touch the sand. This isn't the best place for snorkelling or diving, however, due to a lack of coral and knee-deep waters. Rather, it's designed for wading in the

Top right Windsurfing, Dahab
Right Kitesurfing, Dahab

HOWARD ASHTON-JONES/GETTY IMAGES

☼ Why So Windy?

Dahab's location in the Gulf of Aqaba, between the mountains of Sinai and Saudi Arabia, makes it a superb spot for windy weather. As the wind blows from the north, it pushes its way through the narrowing gulf (only about 15km to 20km wide) and then picks up speed around Dahab as it funnels between the two mountain ranges. Winds are then bolstered further by Dahab's heat. The city's geography makes summertime a particularly windy season, with nearly 90% of the days having 31km/h breezes and the rest of the year having high winds half of that time.

waves while watching kite-boarders practice their tricks.

For the thrill-seeker The area outside the lagoon, known as the 'speedy' zone, is best suited for more advanced wind enthusiasts and freestylers. This 2km-long section is still shallow, but consistently strong winds interspersed with a few choppy waves equal a speedier ride. This section has a floating platform for safety or simply a nice break.

For the real experts, the waves just past **Napoleon Reef** in the open sea reach up to 4m high yet hardly break, nicknaming this area the 'wave' zone. Here, you'll find kite-boarders and windsurfers alike jumping in between the surf.

YOUSSEF MAMDOUH/SHUTTERSTOCK

50 Visiting an Ancient MONASTERY

CHURCHES | HISTORY | ARCHITECTURE

▬▬▬ Step inside the walled compound of the world's oldest continually functioning monastery, home to some of early Christianity's most ancient manuscripts and more than half of the world's surviving Byzantine icons. For centuries, pilgrims have flocked to St Katherine's Monastery, built beside what's believed to be the burning bush where God spoke to Moses at the foot of Mt Sinai.

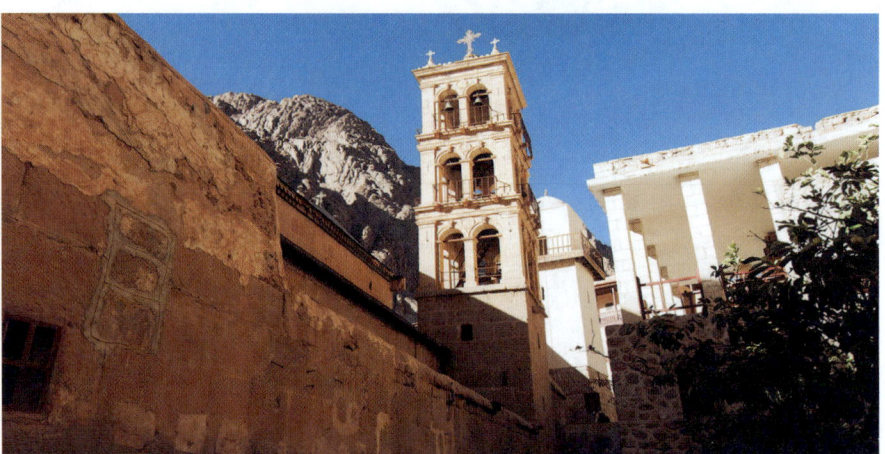

FELIX LIPOV/SHUTTERSTOCK

📍 How To

Getting here Most travellers opt to go on a tour bus from Sharm El Sheikh or Dahab (departing at 10pm) in tandem with a sunrise hike to Mt Sinai before climbing down to visit the monastery.

Cost Entrance to the monastery is free but the museum costs US$2 and a ticket for St Katherine Protectorate is US$5.

What to wear While summers are hot, winter temperatures can reach below 0°C at night, so don't forget warm clothing. The monastery is a religiously observant site; modest dress (no shorts, covered shoulders) is required.

ZORICARK/SHUTTERSTOCK

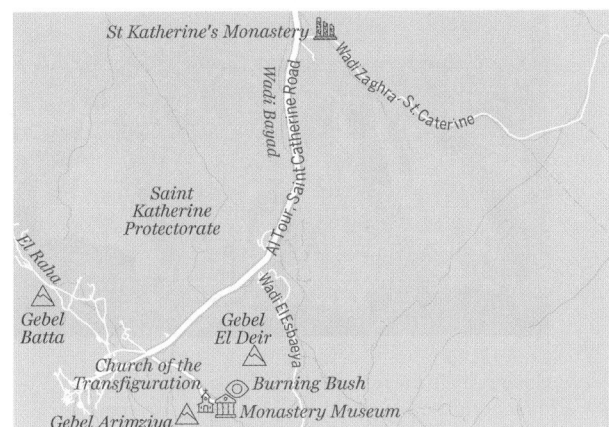

St Katherine's Monastery

Wadi Bayad

Wadi Zaghra–St Caterine

At Tour, Saint Catherine Road

Saint Katherine Protectorate

El Raha

Gebel Batta

Gebel El Deir

Wadi El Esbaeya

Church of the Transfiguration

Burning Bush

Gebel Arimziya

Monastery Museum

Top left Church of the Transfiguration
Bottom left Monastery Museum

Founded around 330 CE by Byzantine empress Helena, the Greek Orthodox **St Katherine's monastery** is named after a saint believed to have been persecuted for her Christian faith and sentenced to death by Emperor Maxentiu in Alexandria. The religious site and its surroundings are now a declared UNESCO World Heritage Site.

Within the monastery's walls, the ornately decorated 6th-century **Church of the Transfiguration** has a nave flanked by massive marble columns and walls covered in richly gilded icons and velvet tapestries. Giant golden chandeliers and censers suspended from chains line the church's ceiling. At the church's eastern end, a gilded 17th-century iconostasis separates the nave from the sanctuary and the apse, where St Katherine's remains are interred (off-limits for visitors). High in the apse above the altar is one of the monastery's most stunning artistic treasures, the 6th-century mosaic of the Transfiguration, although it can be difficult to see it past the chandeliers and the iconostasis. To the left of the altar and below it is the monastery's holiest area, the **Chapel of the Burning Bush**, which is not accessible to the public.

Growing around the back of the church is thought to be a descendant of the original **burning bush** in the monastery compound. Up the stairs on the southern side of the walled area, the **Monastery Museum** displays precious chalices, gold and silver crosses, and ancient manuscripts.

Responsible Tourism?

A luxury eco-hotel, mountainside resort and urban square are nearing completion in the heart of St Katherine. Dubbed the Great Transfiguration Project, the government-sponsored mega tourism endeavour promises closer links between the coast and the mountains. Yet despite being billed as boosting the local economy, the project has been met with backlash from the area's Bedouins. Residents say the upgrade is defacing the ancient village and will push them out of the tourism market. Some fear the centuries-old Jabaliyya tribe, known as the guardians of St Katherine, will be expelled after homes and a cemetery were razed during development.

Bedouin Tourism in Sinai

AN INDIGENOUS PEOPLE SERVING AS STEWARDS TO THE LAND

Having been here for centuries, Sinai's 12 Bedouin tribes are using their knowledge of the land to transform the peninsula's tourism sector from one of mass consumption to ecologically sound pilgrimages prioritising Bedouins' traditional roots and resourceful mindset. After years of marginalisation, the local community is feeling empowered.

Hospitality is the hallmark of Bedouin culture. Even in their nomadic way of life, they always have a space to welcome guests – with floor cushions, a cup of tea and a lit fire waiting. This kind of courtesy is central to Bedouin tourism in Sinai. Yet Sinai's travel industry hasn't always been as welcoming to Bedouins as the Bedouins are to visitors.

Almost all of Sinai's Bedouin tribes originate from Arabia except for the Jabaliyya, who arrived as Romanian soldiers in the 6th century to protect the Sinai monastery nestled in St Katherine's majestic red mountains. This tradition extends to modern times, where the Jabaliyya still serve as protectors of the monastery and its surroundings – often working as one-day tour guides for the religious site.

Deeply connected to the land, the Jabaliyya are also farmers and shepherds, cultivating more than 400 orchards within St Katherine's valleys and leading their livestock to graze where the few patches of green exist between sand and stone.

Despite maintaining a simple way of life, Sinai's Bedouins haven't had it easy. Israel's occupation of the peninsula from 1967 to 1982 caused a rift between the larger Egyptian public and Sinai's Bedouins, with the former suspecting Bedouins' insistence to remain on their land despite Israeli rule meant they were collaborators. In reality, many Bedouins worked as guides assisting Egyptian soldiers to cross through Sinai's mountains without being detected by Israel.

When Egypt regained control of Sinai, the government boosted tourism development of the region yet Bedouins were mostly forbidden from working in the booming industry, with resorts and tour operators preferring to hire Egyptians from the Nile Valley instead. The rapid growth of Sinai's tourism sector led to the displacement of many Bedouins from their ancestral lands to accommodate this expansion.

In recent decades, the rise of armed groups like ISIS in North Sinai deepened the Egyptian state's security concerns of the region. President Abdel Fattah El-Sisi's campaign to crack down on terrorism included the creation of a 79km buffer zone in North Sinai, leading to the demolition of more than a thousand buildings and, again, the displacement of thousands of Bedouins.

> Hospitality is the hallmark of Bedouin culture

After the Bedouins' long exclusion from mass-market tourism, newer initiatives have been established to help put them front and centre in trekking, camel-riding and even diving throughout Sinai. Travel companies like Wilderness Ventures Egypt and Desert Divers prioritise Bedouins as hiking guides and climbing and diving instructors, attracting adventure tourists who look for a more local connection when travelling. They are also taking on the role of an environmental guardian, so Bedouin-led trips have become a key example of ecotourism that benefits the local community.

ⓘ Bedouin Trails Closed

The creation of the **Sinai Trail** in 2015, Egypt's first long-distance hiking route, helped spur the movement for Bedouin-led, grassroots tourism prioritising heritage and slow living over mass consumption. The project is part of the **Bedouin Trail**, a 1200km passage traversing between Africa and Asia, led and managed by a collective of Bedouin tribes. Despite its success – awarded the best new tourism initiative in 2016 – the trail shut down in October 2024. Its sister project, the **Red Sea Mountain Trail** closed the following month. Given increasing government-imposed restrictions over wilderness access along the walking path, the trail was forced to close for the foreseeable future.

Listings

BEST OF THE REST

Outdoor Adventures

Camel Dive Club

Offering accommodation, drinking, eating and diving options, Camel is a one-stop shop for your diving holiday. Located in the heart of Na'ama Bay, the centre offers daily diving trips.

Wilderness Ventures Egypt

Custom-made adventures including star-gazing, camel-riding courses and mountain trekking in St Katherine. Working with the local community, they offer a taste of Bedouin culture – staying in remote villages and sampling herbs from mountain gardens.

Red Sea Relax Dive Centre

Just metres from the Lighthouse Reef in Dahab, this longstanding five-star PADI centre with an excellent reputation offers courses of all levels taught by caring and careful instructors.

Desert Divers Dahab

Desert Divers has it all – offering diving courses and trips (including freediving), diving safaris combined with camel riding, treks in the Sinai mountains with local Bedouins, and rock-climbing excursions.

Charming Cafes

Vegan Lab $$$

Organic, superfood dishes and drinks (ashwagandha, matcha and spirulina) served in a trendy Dahab space that vegans and non-vegans alike will adore. Cards accepted but you'll have to pay an additional 2%.

Bayside Eatery $$

This cafe serves soul-nourishing breakfast dishes and soothing cups of coffee all day in a cosy, lime-green-walled space. Enjoy your signature beverage on the rooftop terrace overlooking Dahab's bay.

Ralph's German Bakery $$

Come here for the best pastries in Dahab (and maybe all of Sinai). Swift service and European-style coffee with a Middle Eastern vibe and hospitality.

Unique Stays

Umbi Sharks Bay Diving Village

Bedouin-owned diving centre with rustic accommodation options and a beachside bar. Friendly vibes and a laid-back locale makes this a charming retreat that's reminiscent of Sharm El Sheikh's earlier days.

Basata Ecolodge

One of Egypt's eco-pioneers with a strict sustainability ethos, in Ras Burgaa area. Travellers gather around communal tables to meet fellow guests and tuck into meals heavy with organic produce and ethically sourced fish.

Umbi Sharks Bay Diving Village

Dar Jan

A 3.5-hectare organic farm and art space offering accommodation, mosaic and pottery workshops, desert hikes and much more in Nuweiba. A perfect dose of entrepreneurship and creativity to counteract the big-box resort experiences elsewhere on the coast.

 Local Favourites

Fairuz $$$

A huge menu of delicious Lebanese mezze and Middle Eastern dishes served on an alfresco terrace overlooking the lights of Na'ama Bay and the glistening Red Sea.

El Fanar $$

Give yourself a break after snorkelling in Ras Umm Sid's tranquil waters with a delicious array of pizza and pasta plus a superb seaside view.

Pomodoro $$

Beloved by locals and tourists alike, this Italian-inspired eatery serves generous portions of wood-fired pizza and homemade pasta dishes. Outdoor seating along Na'ama Bay's promenade.

Fares Seafood $$

A Sharm institution for good-value, fresh seafood, with branches across the city. Dishes are custom-made; take your pick from the selection on ice out front and decide how you want it cooked.

Rangoli $$$

Head here for a romantic night out in Sharm El Sheikh's Mövenpick Resort and excellent Indian food. Snag a balcony table for sublime sunset views.

Castle Zaman $$$

The only slow-food restaurant in the region, north of Basata, dishes up roasted meats

Farsha Mountain Lodge

with sides of *molokhiyya* (garlicky leaf soup) and stunning Red Sea views from its elevated perch.

Farsha Mountain Lounge $$

This cafe at Ras Um Sid has a jumble of knickknacks surrounding low seating at precariously perched intervals. At night, lanterns glow orange, and the air is filled with shisha smoke.

Camel Bar & Rooftop $$

Low-key place frequented by locals and tourists in the heart of Na'ama Bay. Start your evening off here and swap stories with other divers about your underwater adventures.

The View Bar & Terrace $$

A bustling cliffside bar overlooking Na'ama Bay with Latin dancing every Thursday, a DJ and live music playing on Fridays, and karaoke singing every Monday.

Viva Beach & Restaurant $$

Friendly service and chill vibes in Sharm El Sheikh. Relax in a lounge chair after a long day of diving or enjoy your meal on the beachside patio.

Practicalities

ARRIVING

238

GETTING AROUND

240

SAFE TRAVEL

242

MONEY

243

ACCOMMODATION

244

RESPONSIBLE TRAVEL

246

ESSENTIALS

248

LANGUAGE

250

Right 4WD tour, Siwa Oasis (p160)

EASY STEPS FROM THE AIRPORT TO THE CITY CENTRE

Cairo International Airport (pictured below), about 20km northeast of central Cairo, is the main entry point. Useful terminals include Terminal 3 (for international Star Alliance flights and most international and domestic Egyptair flights), Terminal 2 (for other international flights and many regional airlines) and Terminal 1 (smaller domestic airlines and some regional carriers).

AT THE AIRPORT

Local SIM cards The cheapest way to connect, they're sold from kiosks near the luggage belts (bring your passport; expect queues). Carriers include Vodafone, Orange, Etisalat and We. There's no savings by waiting to purchase in town. Prices are inexpensive (about 30GB to 50GB for LE500 or less).

Currency exchange The kiosks are inside the arrivals area before immigration. US dollars, euros and British pounds are the most readily exchanged, and are necessary for purchasing a visa on arrival. Foreign exchange rates are government-controlled, and won't vary much between the airport and town.

Wi-fi Don't count on free airport wi-fi. If you manage to connect, it generally only works inside terminal buildings, not near ride pickup points.

ATMs Found at all the international terminals; most accept Visa and Mastercard only. Rates are similar, although some banks charge transaction fees.

Charging stations There are wall sockets (plug type C) in some, but not all, departure halls for free phone charging.

VISAS

Many nationalities can purchase visas in advance from visa2egypt.gov.eg, or on arrival at approved airport bank kiosks (expect long queues). It's currently US$25 (US dollars, euros or British pounds; cash only) for 30 days, single entry.

For Sinai-only visits (Sharm El Sheikh, Dahab, Nuweiba, Taba and St Katherine, but not Ras Mohammed National Park), get a 14-day Sinai-only visa at Sharm airport or the Egypt–Israel border at Taba.

GETTING TO THE CITY CENTRE

Taxi and Uber (Egyptian pounds; cash only) Cars wait in front of the terminals. While the best have meters, not all do, so you may need to negotiate the fare before getting in. It's about US$20 to the city centre. Uber also services Cairo International. Most vehicle registration plates are numbered in Arabic only.

Hotel shuttle Shuttles are offered by many hotels, and are especially worth considering for middle-of-the-night arrivals or for smaller hotels that may be harder for the taxi to locate. Advance booking is required. Some shuttles are free, while others charge a fee; clarify if it's per person or per vehicle.

HOW MUCH FOR A...

From US$100
1hr

From US$8
10hr

US$90
10hr

Transport fares Taxis accept Egyptian pounds; cash only. While Uber takes credit cards, it's often quicker to get rides with your payment method set to cash.

Airport transfers Don't want a taxi or hotel shuttle? Sixt Car Rental (sixt.com/ride/cairo/airport-transfer) also offers airport transfers.

Cairo layovers With at least eight hours on the ground, it's feasible to consider a quick visit to the Pyramids of Giza or the Grand Egyptian Museum. Allow 1½ to two hours transport time each way, plus two to three hours on-site, and another two-plus hours for the minimum required check-in time back at the airport.

OTHER POINTS OF ENTRY

Airports Cairo's Sphinx International Airport, about 45km west of the city centre, is used by many European budget airlines. Taxis wait outside (US$20 to US$25 to Giza, from US$25 to the city centre). Uber only works here in theory – it's much better to arrange a pickup through your accommodation. There are also direct flights from Europe to Hurghada, Luxor and Sharm El Sheikh airports. ATMs are available at all international airports and there are SIM card kiosks at Hurghada and Sharm El Sheikh.

Land borders The only entry/exit point between Egypt and Israel and the Palestinian Territories is the busy Taba border crossing in Sinai (24hr). You can get a Sinai-only visa here, but full Egyptian visas must be arranged in advance online or through an embassy. There are unreliable ATMs on both sides. The main crossing points between Egypt and Sudan are at Argeen (west bank) and Qustul (on the east bank and accessed by ferry from Abu Simbel). Hours vary for both; there are no ATMs.

Ferries Ferries link Duba (Saudi Arabia) with Safaga, south of Hurghada (kcfmt.com), and Aqaba (Jordan) with Nuweiba and Taba Heights in southern Sinai (abmaritime.com.jo).

TRANSPORT TIPS TO HELP YOU GET AROUND

Transport in Egypt is fairly efficient and very reasonably priced. Flying is quickest – and sometimes among the cheapest options – over long distances, but trains, buses and private car hire with a driver can get you to more places, often with plenty of local flavour. The most romantic travel choice: sailing along the Nile on a dahabiya or felucca.

PLANE EgyptAir (egyptair.com) is the main domestic carrier. There are also several smaller carriers linking Cairo with major centres, including Nile Air and Air Cairo. When booking online, switch your home country to Egypt to get the cheapest fares.

TRAIN This is an option between Cairo and Alexandria, Luxor and Aswan. Express trains have air-con, assigned seats and meal service. For schedules and tickets, consult the Egyptian National Railways (enr.gov.eg) website and the foreigners' window at major stations. Cairo's main stations are Ramses and, for upper Egypt, Bashtil.

CAR RENTAL PRICES

From LE1040

Petrol approx LE19/litre

Diesel approx LE16/litre

BUS Bus is the cheapest option. Go Bus (go-bus.com) has a wide network; it's worth splurging for Elite or Aero class. West & Mid Delta has buses from Torgoman Bus Station (Cairo Gateway) to the Western Desert. Upper Egypt Bus Company goes from Torgoman to Fayoum.

CAR HIRE Hiring your own car isn't common, especially in Cairo, where traffic is chaotic. A popular alternative is hiring a private car with a driver; ask your hotel for recommendations. Rates average from LE1000 and up per half-day, depending on your itinerary, plus 10% or more tip.

DRIVING ESSENTIALS

Drive on the right.

In rural areas, be prepared for frequent slowdowns due to livestock wandering into the road.

Have your passport or a copy handy on road journeys as it's sometimes requested at checkpoints.

Arrange longer excursions at least half a day in advance to allow the driver time to get the required permits.

Afternoon road trips aren't recommended during Ramadan, when drivers are likely to be tired from fasting.

In certain areas, especially in the Northern Nile Valley and sections of the Western Desert, tourists must have police escorts. Minimise hassles by booking excursions through an established local tour company.

Travel to some destinations, including parts of the Western Desert, requires police permits. These are best arranged in advance by your driver or tour company.

When travelling by bus or train back to Cairo, allow extra time before international flight connections to account for delays.

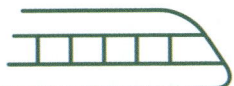

DELUXE SLEEPING TRAINS Abela (abelatrains.com) runs sleeper services from Cairo's Bashtil station to Luxor and Aswan. Ideally, book several days in advance, online or at the special windows at Cairo, Luxor and Aswan stations. Compartments comprise two-bed sleepers with clean linen, pillows and blankets and shared toilets (generally clean, sometimes with toilet paper). Airline-style meals (dinner and breakfast) are served in the compartments.

BOAT Many cruise boats ply the Nile, especially between Luxor and Aswan; see p127. The main place to organise overnight felucca trips is Aswan. Short sails can be arranged in Aswan, Luxor and Cairo. Cruise boats also run on Lake Nasser between Aswan and Abu Simbel.

TAXI AND RIDE-HAILING SERVICES

Regular taxis can be found everywhere and are inexpensive and efficient. If there's no meter, confirm the price before getting in. Uber operates in Cairo, Alexandria, Suez, Ismailia and Port Said. Note that most license plates are in Arabic only.

KNOW YOUR CARBON FOOTPRINT A one-way flight from Cairo to Luxor would emit about 156kg of carbon dioxide per passenger, versus about 86kg for the same journey by bus and 30kg by train. **Climate Stewards** (climatestewards.org) has a handy carbon calculator. The **Egyptian Carbon Center** (egyptiancarboncenter.com) is a useful contact if you'll be in Egypt long-term.

ROAD DISTANCE CHART (KM)

	Cairo	Luxor	Aswan	Abu Simbel	Siwa Oasis	Marsa Matruh	Alexandria	Hurghada	Sharm el Sheikh	Suez
Luxor	665									
Aswan	894	241								
Abu Simbel	1153	500	283							
Siwa Oasis	738	820	667	1527						
Marsa Matruh	439	1172	979	1603	310					
Alexandria	218	668	1128	1382	594	296				
Hurghada	465	280	399	817	1030	899	670			
Sharm El Sheikh	506	335	511	1625	1237	948	727	765		
Suez	123	475	653	853	875	529	341	374	386	
Minya	268	460	650	960	663	686	465	410	731	271

DANGERS, ANNOYANCES & SAFETY

Egypt depends heavily on tourism, and the government goes to great lengths to ensure that nothing will happen to deter visitors. There's a heavy police presence at major sites and the country is generally very safe. Still, take normal street-smart precautions.

LIVEABOARD SAFETY There have been several recent tragedies on the Red Sea. If considering a liveaboard dive safari, thoroughly research the companies you are considering. Also check out the recommendations of the UK government's **Marine Accident Investigation Branch** (gov.uk/government/organisations/marine-accident-investigation-branch).

MEDICAL FACILITIES Major destinations have excellent private clinics. Upfront payment is required. Pharmacies are generally well stocked and helpful.

WOMEN TRAVELLERS Many women travel solo in Egypt, and most have a great time. Unfortunately, however, some do encounter sexual harassment, which generally presents as cat-calling or leering. Dressing conservatively, including covering shoulders and knees, helps.

POLLUTION Problematic in Cairo and Alexandria, especially around November during the annual rice straw burning. Those with respiratory problems should keep inhalers handy.

CRIS BOURONCLE/GETTY IMAGES

BY ERAINBOW/SHUTTERSTOCK

TRAVEL INSURANCE Travel insurance is highly recommended, particularly covering adventure activities and emergency evacuation.

TERRORISM
North Sinai has long been off-limits to travellers because of the increased terrorism risk. While attacks are often aimed at Egyptian security forces, tourists have also been targeted. Check your government travel website for updates and advice.

SAFE WATERS
Avoid swimming in slow-moving parts of the Nile. Bottled drinking water is cheap and readily available. Schistosomiasis (bilharzia) is a bowel and bladder infection contracted through the skin from a freshwater fluke.

QUICK TIPS TO HELP YOU MANAGE YOUR MONEY

CASH VS CREDIT CARD Cash is king in Egypt, although major cards – mainly Visa and Mastercard – are accepted in many midrange and all high-end restaurants and hotels and in most larger shops and tourist-oriented places. In local markets and in remote areas they remain useless. If using a card, always choose to be charged in local currency to avoid mark-ups.

TIPPING Keep small change handy, as baksheesh is expected every-where. If in doubt, tip. Many Egyptians depend on tips for their livelihoods; generosity is always appreciated.

ATMs Widespread in main cities but unreliable in the oases. Many have a withdrawal limit of LE6000; some charge usage fees.

WAYS TO SAVE

Egypt travel can be very reasonable. Look for budget airfares from Europe. Once in the country, travel by bus, eat local-style and stay at budget guesthouses; there are many in tourist areas, usually of good quality. By avoiding more expensive package tours, you'll also help ensure that more of your money goes directly to Egyptians.

CURRENCY

Egyptian pound (LE or EGP)

HOW MUCH FOR A...

Abu Simbel temples entry **LE75**

One-hour camel ride at the Giza Pyramids **LE500**

Bowl of *kushari* **LE20–50**

THE ART OF BARGAINING

Except at fixed-price shops, bargaining is expected. Before starting, check fixed-price stores first to get an idea, decide a budget and then express a casual inter-est. You're never under any obligation to buy, but you shouldn't initiate bargaining on something you don't want and you shouldn't back out of an agreed-upon price. The 'best' price isn't necessarily the cheapest – it's one that you and the seller are happy with.

STUDENT DISCOUNTS Available on museum and site entry fees (generally 50%) with a valid stu-dent ID card plus your passport, or an International Student Identity Card (ISIC; isic. org) arranged in advance online.

SMALL CHANGE It's worth keeping small change handy for taxi fares, public toilets and for purchases at markets or from street vendors. Shop owners are sometimes willing to break larger bills.

HOW MUCH TO TIP?

Cafes and bathroom attendants From LE10

Tourist site guards and mosque attendants From LE10

Restaurants 10% to 15%, more for standout service

Taxis Round up the fare or add 5% extra (from 10% for long hires)

ACCOMMODATION

From rustic beach camps to vintage boat cabins, luxurious resorts and international-class hotels, Egypt has accommodation options to suit every taste and budget. Make things special and get to know more of Egypt by mixing things up, with some nights spent enjoying the country's many good-value hotels and resorts and others staying in community-run places, at local-style budget guest-houses or camping under the stars.

HOW MUCH FOR A...

Cairo budget hostel
US$30 or less

Night on a *dahabiya*
US$250–900

Room in a Red Sea resort
From US$70

HOA PHAM 3587/SHUTTERSTOCK

RESORT STYLE Egypt knows how to do resorts. Some of the best are along the Red Sea coast, where you may have lovely views over the water and several huge swimming pools at your disposal, plus a choice of restaurants. Many resorts offer all-inclusive rates. Booking well in advance can yield major discounts, as can booking off-season (September to November and February to May). If you prefer independent resorts, head to Marsa Alam, Marsa Shagra, Al Quseir, El Gouna, Dahab (pictured above) or Nuweiba.

FLOATING ROOMS Whether you're cruising on a dahabiya, sailing on a felucca, enjoying the perks of a large cruise boat or staying on a houseboat in Cairo, sleeping on the water is special. Amenities range from basic or nonexistent on a felucca to top-class comforts on some dahabiyas and cruise ships.

MULTISHOOTER/SHUTTERSTOCK

CRUISE-SHIP CONSIDERATIONS

While cruise ships offer many perks, it's worth thinking twice before booking one for the bulk of your holiday. If your room is towards the back, you may have to contend with engine vibrations and exhaust fumes. Also consider the journey from an environmental perspective; enquire about the company's policies on things like sewage and generator use.

GETTING INTO NATURE

Especially around the oases, in Sinai and along the Red Sea coast, you'll find the perfect conditions for a chilled holiday focused on rustic lodges, beach camps and desert landscapes. All these destinations offer unique perspectives on Egypt's varied topography and ecosystems and a complete change of pace from Cairo's urban bustle. Marsa Alam, Marsa Nakari and Marsa Shagra on the Red Sea coast, the Nuwei-ba–Taba highway – where you'll find Basata ecolodge – and Dahab in Sinai are especially notable for their beach camps (pictured left) and laid-back vibe. Around Siwa and the oases, Badry Sahara Camp and Eden Garden Camp stand out for their simplicity and welcoming ambience. For an unforgettable Egypt outdoor high-light, visit White Desert National Park by day and then spend sever-al nights camping nearby to enjoy the dark, star-filled night skies. Al-ternatively, stay somewhere more established, perhaps at Shahrazad Desert Camp. Overnight felucca journeys (p139) offer a variation on this theme. Nights are spent moored up at a quiet spot along the riverbank in the Southern Nile Valley, with evenings spent sitting around a bonfire before drifting off to sleep on the boat's deck against a backdrop of the gently flowing river.

FINDING THE BEST VALUE

Good-value budget hotels are readily available in tourist centres, often with air-con. However, midrange options are surprisingly limited, particularly in Cairo and Alexandria, where investment is channelled into Egypt's many top-end international chains. Even if you typically travel in this price bracket, consider budget operations as well – some can be much nicer for half the price, offering very good value for money.

If you're considering home-sharing options, there are some real finds, especially in Cairo and Alexandria; check out brassbell.net. However, it's also worth remembering that Egypt's home-sharing sector is unregulated and traveller complaints are rife. Illegal hotels are also an issue, especially in Giza and among some of the cheaper hotels in Aswan and Luxor, and a lack of insurance and basic safety standards may leave you at risk. Before booking, take time to thoroughly inform yourself. Try to avoid paying for rooms upfront and seek out reliable recommendations from other travellers.

Scan this QR code to search for home-sharing options

SEASONAL VARIATIONS

For upmarket hotels and resorts in particular, rates can vary markedly depending on the season and even the day of the week. It's worth staying flexible while planning your itinerary to take advantage of discounts.

RESPONSIBLE TRAVEL

ON THE ROAD

Go local Tourism is vital to the Egyptian economy. Tips for responsible travel include: supporting locally owned guesthouses, restaurants and shops; using local tour operators; and, where possible, avoiding all-inclusive deals where very little money is spent in the country.

Transport For getting around, consider taking the train, bus or sleeper train to lower your carbon footprint. On the Nile, try a felucca rather than one of the larger, less ecofriendly cruise ships.

Reduce plastic waste Bringing a refillable water bottle such as LifeStraw and purifying as you go can greatly reduce plastic-bottle waste.

Slow down the pace Seek out opportunities, such as those offered by Discover Esna (facebook.com/discover.esna) or the Fayoum Pottery School to engage directly with local culture and communities. These experiences will likely wind up being among the highlights of your Egypt journey.

RICH CAREY/SHUTTERSTOCK

Green Fins (greenfins.net) lists dive operators who follow environmentally sound diving practices. **Red Sea Diving Safari** (redsea-divingsafari.com) runs a PADI cleanup program called Dive Against Debris.

The Red Sea Project (redsea-project.com) carries out extensive educational activities and offers certified divers the opportunity to participate in projects such as sea turtle surveys.

Hurghada Environmental Protection and Conservation Association (preview.hepca.org) is dedicated to conserving the Red Sea's reefs through public awareness and community action.

Animal Care in Egypt *(ace-egypt.org.uk)* is a Luxor-based charity providing free veterinary care and education; get involved by volunteering or donating. Other groups working to help Egypt's suffering animals include **Brooke** (thebrooke.org) and the **Society for the Protection of Animal Rights in Egypt** (facebook.com/spareegypt).

LEAVE A SMALL FOOTPRINT

Consider picking just one or two regions to explore, finding a good base and taking excursions from there. At monuments, stay for an overnight or several, rather than making a quick in-and-out visit.

When booking tours, seek out local operators and support them whenever possible. Consider the carbon footprint of boating or hiking compared to tours using motorised vehicles.

DOS & DON'TS

Do remove your footwear when entering a mosque.

Don't show the soles of your feet; it's considered disrespectful.

Don't use flash photography in tombs, clamber over pillars and statues or touch painted reliefs, all of which threatens ancient monuments.

RICHARD T NOWITZ/GETTY IMAGES

SUPPORT LOCAL

Support local businesses in small towns by booking accommodation and eating in restaurants run by locals, and buying products and handicrafts from the area. See the list of shops selling 100% Egyptian-made crafts on p136.

Book tours run by locals. Egypt has many excellent, trained and highly knowledgeable local guides who can help you get the most out of your visit, for example, those listed on p165 and p173.

EGYPT RESPONSIBLE TRAVEL

CLIMATE CHANGE & TRAVEL

Lonely Planet urges all travellers to engage with their travel carbon footprint, which will mainly come from air travel. While there often isn't an alternative, travellers can look to minimise the number of flights they take, opt for newer aircrafts and use cleaner ground transport, such as trains.

One proposed solution – purchasing carbon offsets – unfortunately does not cancel out the impact of individual flights. While most destinations will depend on air travel for the foreseeable future, for now, pursuing ground-based travel where possible is the best course of action.

The UN Carbon Offset Calculator shows how flying impacts a household's emissions:

The ICAO's carbon emissions calculator allows visitors to analyse the CO_2 generated by point-to-point journeys:

RESOURCES

redsea-project.com
ace-egypt.org.uk
facebook.com/discoveresna
roundtripfoundation.org.au

ESSENTIAL NUTS & BOLTS

WEEKEND The official weekend is Friday and Saturday. During Ramadan, opening hours are often shortened at offices, museums and tourist sites.

PUBLIC TOILETS There are few public toilets, but you can generally use the facilities in restaurants and hotels. An attendant sometimes provides toilet paper for a tip (LE5).

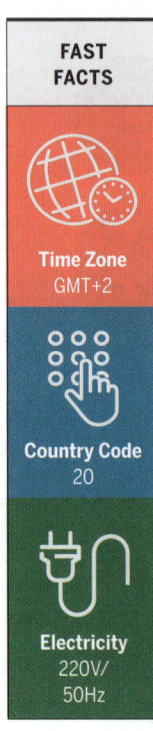

FAST FACTS

Time Zone
GMT+2

Country Code
20

Electricity
220V/
50Hz

GOOD TO KNOW

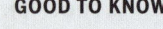

Eat and pass things with your right hand; the left hand is used for ablutions.

During the fasting month of Ramadan, don't eat or drink in public during daytime.

The legal drinking age is 21. Drinking in public spaces is prohibited.

Smoking is common in restaurants and bars; there are few nonsmoking facilities.

One hour of shisha smoking is roughly equivalent to smoking 10 cigarettes.

ACCESSIBLE TRAVEL

Away from tourist areas, there are few or no concessions for travellers with a disability. However, a number of tour operators offer accessible itineraries and Egyptians are generally very willing to assist. The Grand Egyptian Museum, the Egyptian Museum, the National Museum of Egyptian Civilization and Alexandria's Graeco-Roman Museum are all accessible, as are the main museums in Luxor and Hurghada and Aswan's Nubia Museum. Sites with at least partial access include the Pyramids of Giza and the temples of Karnak, Hatshepsut, Horus and Abu Simbel.

Many Red Sea resorts cater for travellers with mobility issues with ramps and handrails, wheelchair-friendly beaches and facilities for divers with disabilities. Camel Dive Club & Hotel in Sharm El Sheikh is a standout.

For wheelchair-accessible Nile cruises, contact Responsible Travel (responsibletravel.com) or Memphis Tours (memphistours.com), both of which also offer land-based, accessible itineraries taking in Cairo, Luxor, Aswan and Abu Simbel. The Egypt Travel Gate (privatetoursinegypt.com) portal is also useful.

Londoncabegypt.com has a fleet of wheelchair-accessible cabs fitted with access ramps, and English-speaking drivers.

FAIR TRADE

Egypt's first certified fair-trade shop (fairtrade egypt.org) showcases hundreds of local crafts and products.

RELIGION About

90% of Egyptians are Sunni Muslim. Most of the remaining 10% are Coptic Christians.

BIODIVERSITY

Egypt's 30 protected areas preserve the country's impressive biodiversity. Check out eco egyptexperiences. com for listings.

FAMILY TRAVEL

Egypt is a thrilling destination for children, full of ancient monuments, exciting experiences such as camel rides, felucca trips and tomb exploration, and many swimming pools.

Egyptians' warm manner towards children helps smooth over the small practical hassles you may encounter. In cities and resort areas, formula and disposable nappies are available and hotels are generally willing to add a cot to your room with advance notice. However, don't expect car seats (or seatbelts) in taxis or private cars.

TRIP PREPARATION Child and student discounts are widely available, as are well-priced family packages. Egypt suits kids old enough to engage with its epic history and adventurous activities. Before departing, get imaginations fired up with activities such as those at britishmuseum.org/learn/schools/ ages-7-11/ancient-egypt or watching films like *Death on the Nile*.

TOTS & TEENS Egyptians' generally doting attitude to small children is one of the great pleasures of travelling in the country. In most restaurants, waiters will be delighted to see kids and happy to accommodate their needs. Teens should abide by grown-up etiquette when meeting similarly aged Egyptians.

LGBTIQ+ TRAVELLERS

Homosexuality is technically not a crime in Egypt. However, homosexual acts in public are, and gay men have been prosecuted under morality laws.

An underground social scene exists, including in Cairo and Alexandria, but accessing it as a foreigner can be risky. Be discreet when (or refrain from) using LGBTIQ+ dating apps. Displays of affection are best kept private.

International hotel chains and most upmarket accommodation will have no problem with a same-sex couple sharing a room. At smaller hotels, it's better to request separate beds.

LANGUAGE

As in other Arab countries, the written and spoken word may differ in Egypt. Roughly speaking, written Arabic is usually in the form of Modern Standard Arabic, or MSA. This is a standardized form of the language, used throughout the region and largely derived from the Arabic used in the Quran (Quranic Arabic), though with some modern words thrown in.

Colloquial Arabic, or 'Amiyya, is the variety people speak, and it changes based on region. Although 'Amiyya is not, strictly speaking, a written language, a written version of Egyptian 'Amiyya has evolved, based on Modern Standard Arabic, but with sentence structure and spelling adjusted to reflect the spoken word.

Don't forget that Arabic is, of course, read and written from right to left.

BASICS

Hello.	أهلا	ah·lan
Goodbye.	مع السلامة	ma' sa·la·ma
Yes.	أيوة	ai·wa
No.	لا	la'
Please.	لو سمحت	law sa·maht (m)
	لو سمحتي	law sa·mah·tee (f)
Thank you.	شكراً	shu·kran
Excuse me.	عن إزنك	'an 'iz·nak (m)
	عن إزنك	'an 'iz·nik (f)
Sorry.	متأسف	mu·ta·'as·if (m)
	متأسفة	mu·ta·'a·si·fa (f)

What's your name?

إسمَك أيه؟	is·mak ay (m)
إسمِك أيه؟	is·mik ay (f)

My name is ...

... إسمي	is·mee ...

Do you speak English?

بتتكلم/بتتكلمي	bi·tit·ka·lim/
	bi·tit·ka·lim·ee
إنجليزي؟	in·gi·lee·zee (m/f)

I don't understand.

مش فاهم	mish fa·him (m)
مش فهمة	mish fah·ma (f)

TIME & NUMBERS

What time is it?	الساعة كم؟	is·sa·'a kam
It's (2) o'clock.	الساعة (إثنين)	is·sa·'a (it·nayn)
Half past (2).	الساعة (إثنين) و نص	
	is·sa·'a (it·nayn) wi nus	
morning	الصبح	is·subh
afternoon	بعد الظهر	ba'd·duhr
evening/night	بالليل	bi·layl
yesterday	إمبارح	im·ba·rih
tomorrow	بكرة	buk·ra

1	واحد	wa·hid	6	ستة	si·ta
2	إثنين	it·nayn	7	سبعة	sa·ba·a
3	ثلاثة	ta·la·ta	8	ثمانية	ta·man·ya
4	أربعة	ar·ba'	9	تسعة	ti·sa·a
5	خمسة	kham·sa	10	عشرة	'a·sha·ra

EMERGENCIES

Help!	إلحقني!	il·haq·nee
Go away!	إمشي!	im·shee
Call a ...!	إتصل ب...	i·tas·al bi ...
the police	البوليس	il·bu·lees
a doctor	دكتور	duk·toor (m)
I'm lost.	أنا تايه	a·na ta·yeh (m)
	أنا تاية	a·na tay·ha (f)

Index

000 Map pages

'When the man at the Egyptian Museum in Cairo saw me trying to cross the street, he gave me some tongue-in-cheek advice: "Close your eyes and open your heart to God."'

LAUREN KEITH

'"Want to see a mummy?" It was an "alas poor Yorick" moment as we realised we were surrounded by the wrapped and unwrapped limbs of Egypt's ancient dead.'

DR JENNY WALKER

'It was an unforgettable Egypt memory – waking before sunrise and seeing the magnificent Abu Simbel temples, almost deserted, at dawn.'

MARY FITZPATRICK

'That time I was waved up to the top of a pigeon tower for a spectacular Cairo sunset.'

ANTHON JACKSON

'For tranquillity and timelessness, nothing beats a sunset felucca sail, with the water lapping against the hull and the sun slowly disappearing behind Aswan's Tombs of the Nobles.'

MARY FITZPATRICK

THIS BOOK

Destination Editor
Zara Sekhavati

Production Editor
Joel Cotterell, Alison Killilea

Cartographer
Bohumil Ptáček

Image Editor
Dominic Allen

Coordinating Editors
Kellie Langdon, Brana Vladisavljevic

Assisting Editors
Melanie Dankel, Natalie Howard, Gabbi Stefanos

Cover Researcher
Kat Marsh

Thanks
Ronan Abayawickrema, James Appleton, Karen Henderson, Lucy Jones